FINDING YOUR WAY
WITH AN MBA

FINDING YOUR WAY WITH AN MBA

INSIGHTS FROM THOSE LANDING THEIR IDEAL JOBS

Susan Cohn

Don Hudson

John Wiley & Sons, Inc.

New York ▪ Chichester ▪ Weinheim ▪ Brisbane ▪ Singapore ▪ Toronto

Copyright © 2000 by Susan Cohn and Don Hudson. All rights reserved.

Published by John Wiley & Sons, Inc.
Published simultaneously in Canada.

This publication is designed to provide accurate and authoritative information in regard to the subject matter covered. It is sold with the understanding that the publisher is not engaged in rendering professional services. If professional advice or other expert assistance is required, the services of a competent professional person should be sought.

Library of Congress Cataloging-in-Publication Data:
Cohn, Susan, 1959–
    Finding your way with an MBA : insights from those landing their
  ideal jobs / Susan Cohn, Don Hudson.
      p.   cm.
    ISBN 0-471-38378-3 (pbk. : alk. paper)
      1. Vocational guidance.   2. Career development.   3. Professions—Vocational
  guidance.   4. Master of business administration degree.   I. Hudson, Don, 1927–
  II. Title.
  HF5381.C6824   2000
  650.14—dc21   99-089690

Printed in the United States of America.

10   9   8   7   6   5   4   3   2   1

Preface

This book is the result of more than 15 years of counseling graduates of MBA programs at New York University Stern School of Business and at the Yale School of Organization and Management. After working together for two years at the Stern School, we decided to write the book we always wished we had for our MBA students. We have compiled the insights, strategies, and tools that help graduates of MBA programs conduct successful job searches. We have found that people learn best from other peoples' stories and therefore we have provided profiles of MBAs in a variety of careers, people who tell it like it is and will give you insight into finding the career that gives you satisfaction.

Today, MBA holders seek fulfilling careers in a highly competitive market; success requires understanding one's true calling and constructing an aggressive self-marketing program—anything less will not do justice to your potential and your investment in an MBA program.

We have divided the book into five chapters as follows:

1. Seek a True Calling.
2. Launch an Aggressive Self-Marketing Campaign.
3. Insights from the Field.
4. Doers' Profiles—Passion in Action.
5. Resources to Assist Your Search.

The career development portion of this book is short because of the plethora of materials out there. We have distilled what we think are the *key* elements to consider and build into your career development plan. We have supplied references for more resources in Chapter 5.

Please contact us when you have found your job and let us know your thoughts. We will update this book based on your suggestions, insights, and career stories.

SUSAN COHN
DON HUDSON

v

Acknowledgments

Thanks to Karen Serieka, Jane Ratcliffe, and Elizabeth Botero for all preproduction editing, administrative, and design work and to all those who dedicated their time to being profiled. Thanks to Mike Hamilton, our Senior Editor, who believed in the book; our production team at Publications Development Company; and to our colleagues at the New York University Stern School of Management and the Yale School of Management who worked with us in our years of counseling at these schools.

And finally, a special thanks to our respective spouses, Bob Schulz and Sue Hudson, who endured our periodic preoccupations and frustrations in seeing this book through from an idea to publication.

S.C.
D.H.

Contents

FINDING YOUR WAY
WITH AN MBA

1

Seek a True Calling

The students and graduates and job seekers we work with hope to find a career that allows them to direct their energies and passions toward their individual skills and talents. Denial of this desire can lead to frustration. Many people experience the Monday morning blues, that is, the feeling that "I can't believe I have to spend my time doing this, there has to be more to life." People we counsel consistently express the wish to find their *true calling*, or an ideal job that matches their skills and values.

What is an ideal job to you? What job would you find exciting? What moves you and gets you going in the morning? This is a job that resonates with your drives, values, and skills. An ideal job can also offer you the flexibility to have balance and security: your desired trade-offs between making a living and having time to pursue other dreams/loves (i.e., gardening, writing, sports). This book focuses on a wide range of jobs for people who want to use their special capabilities and have a rewarding time doing so.

Your challenge is to identify the most meaningful match of career options to your talents and interests. This task is not as easy as it sounds. It is complicated by factors such as an obscure sense of self, a wide range of potential career opportunities, and a vague notion of what success means to you and to society as a whole. What can you do about this? How can you identify and understand the different elements that make you tick? How do you fit the "real" you to the "right" job? Doing so requires a range of actions, including *reflection, assessment, exploration,* and *networking.*

REFLECTION: THINK ABOUT YOUR EXPERIENCES

Reflect on your experiences. Think back to significant jobs, projects, and activities in which you participated. Cover the full range of your experiences: occupational, community, academic, professional, and recreational. Pick out those experiences that really excited and energized you. Then try to identify the features of those experiences that gave you a sense of joy, vigor, and satisfaction. By reviewing these experiences for a sense of where your passions lie and what gives you drive, you can begin to integrate your feelings about these past experiences into your future career goals.

Build on this reflection. Think about an ideal work day. Ask yourself what kinds of activities would be most invigorating to you. Examples include going to meetings, talking on the telephone, researching information, analyzing data, selling a service or product, making presentations, leading teams, developing plans, strategizing on new products, organizing events, and so on. Also, think about the flip side. What kinds of activities would you find most boring and disagreeable?

There are many books and publications that delve more deeply into reflecting on your experiences and offer exercises to help you to identify your favorite skills and activities. Chapter 5, Resources to Assist Your Search, lists some of the best publications that we have found.

The key is to unlock your mind and allow yourself to visualize and feel the best of your experiences as a solid and meaningful base for making your career choices. During the course of your career, reflection can help you track your career interests and progress—and pro-actively define the nature of work and kinds of positions you desire.

ASSESSMENT: ANALYZE YOUR INTERESTS

Most business schools and career development offices offer career assessment tests—*instruments*—that can help you to identify the skills you enjoy using and are good at, thereby helping you to clarify your vocational interests. Make use of them. These instruments are valuable tools for giving you a language to express your skills, interests, and work preferences. Examples of such instruments include the Strong Campbell Vocational Interest Inventory and the Myers Briggs Type Indicator. These tests can give you some very useful insights about yourself; they can affirm your strengths and interests, and your preferences for work style and career choices. They are best used with the guidance of a qualified counselor who can administer and interpret them properly, and help you to recognize their limitations.

If your placement office offers these instruments, take advantage of this opportunity. Outside career consultants may charge $150 or more for these assessments, while career development offices usually administer them at cost. They have served our students very well and we recommend them highly.

EXPLORATION: SURVEY YOUR OPTIONS

Next, shift your attention from finding those things that move you to using that information to identify what career options best suit your skills, talents, and personality. Survey your options by reading the career profiles provided for you in this book. You can also read the books we have listed in Chapter 5 on resources, which provide more information on the specifics of particular areas. This step can help you to further eliminate from consideration obvious job or career mismatches and to narrow your range of choices.

By utilizing your reflection and assessment steps, you can better study and evaluate the career profiles to get a sense of which might be a good fit for you. This process provides you with a more realistic list of top career priorities based on real peoples' experiences in the field and on what those people believe contributed to their success. This particular step in the career process is crucial because it grounds your ideas about what you want to do in the reality of day-to-day experiences of people in the field. You will want to survey your leading options (i.e., go to corporate presentations, read the profiles provided in this book, and talk to students a year ahead of you who may have interned at a company of interest) before you *network*. You don't show up for a test without studying. The same holds true for surveying your options. You study the industry and then talk to people to be prepared to ask intelligent questions when networking.

NETWORKING: TEST YOUR PRIORITIES

The best way to test your career priorities is to talk to as many people in the field as you can about what they do. Find out what they like and don't like. Also, find out how each person chose a career and how that person developed or created that opportunity. What were their processes? Speak with people at different stages within their careers: newcomers, veterans, and those in between.

All too often we encounter students and job seekers who are well-read on their career priorities, but who have not talked with people employed in these fields. Remember that the map can be different from the territory. Networking provides an opportunity for you to find out about *reality* from people in the field. You can build confidence during your job search when you fully understand the day-to-day responsibilities of people already working in your desired career area.

When you have defined what you see as your best work options, you can then consider which associated quality of life factors you are seeking, for example, job security, financial rewards, free time, and family life. Finding one's true calling requires a balanced perspective. Some careers offer great financial rewards but limited job security. Some careers offer terrific professional satisfaction, but limited financial rewards. The key is to define success for yourself in broad terms, including both work and quality of life considerations.

Fortune magazine found that 75 percent of MBA candidates prioritized developing a career, 71 percent building a family, 51 percent their own personal development and growth, 23 percent spending time with close friends and relatives, 22 percent starting their own business, 19 percent exercise and fitness, 17 percent travel and leisure activities, 5 percent contributing to nonprofit organizations, 3 percent developing artistic and creative talents, and 2 percent to other (*Fortune*, April 4, 1997). This survey suggests that most MBAs are striving to balance their work and personal lives. To balance these considerations, you need to have a sense of what makes you tick and what makes you uniquely you—your skills, interests, and work preferences and how they fit in with the culture of and skill sets required by a particular organization and job.

For you to get a reality check on how you fit into an organization, once again we stress the importance of networking. If you aren't networking, chances are you won't be working. The two go hand-in-hand.

By talking to people in your field of interest, you will be better able to obtain the information you need to make the best balanced decision. The path to your true calling and the search for your ideal job may include some risks, sacrifices, and unexpected turns, but with real world input from your contacts, you can construct a practical, long-range plan for reaching your goal.

This chapter has focused on your defining a true calling, a career described in terms of function (what to do) and sector (where to do it). A thoughtful, thorough process of *reflection, assessment, exploration,* and *networking* can provide the drive and direction for the aggressive self-marketing campaign recommended in the next chapter.

2

Launch an Aggressive Self-Marketing Campaign

Attack the employment market with a well defined, sharply focused strategy that features an aggressive self-marketing program. Success requires a market-centered approach. Think of yourself as a *service* to be offered to an employment market. Remember your marketing courses. Take those principles of marketing and apply them to yourself.

The major steps in self-marketing are *define yourself, research your market, promote yourself,* and *sell yourself.* These steps are aimed at maximizing your success in a highly competitive employment arena.

DEFINE YOURSELF

With a clear sense of your interests, options, and priorities (discussed in Chapter 1), you can paint a self-portrait to meet the demands of the employer market for your ideal career.

Marketing yourself is closer to marketing a service than to marketing a product. You are offering a package of intangibles, a background to produce results in an organization. They are revealed in the composition of your resume, the focus of your cover letter, and the way in which you present yourself in interviews. There is not a perfectly standardized set of demands for employment in your ideal job. There will be differences from organization to organization, depending on variations in culture, size, structure, and the specific job. This myriad of variations will require that you tailor your presentation of yourself to each prospective employer.

❥ Think competitively about yourself—how to position yourself, differentiate yourself, sell yourself, and so on. Some sources of information on employer market demands and job leads include organization brochures and annual reports, announcements of on-campus interviews, job postings received by your placement office, recruiting advertisements in the public press, your own function/sector/organization network, your school placement staff, various career reference books, and Internet career sites.

Produce a profile of yourself that meets the needs of the typical employer for your ideal job. Your profile of yourself as a service needs to cover depth and breadth of education (What in your educational history matches the range and focus sought by your target employer market?), length and level of work experiences (What in your roles, responsibilities, and results demonstrates that you could be a significant contributor in your target employer organizations?), and personal attributes (How have you shown the interpersonal, communication, and related skills needed to work with and through others?).

So far, you will have defined yourself in relation to the market for your employment, but not against the competition for your employment. One way to assess the competition is to talk with as many people as you can in your desired field to find out how they see you in relation to newly hired employees. Find out what other candidates have to offer and what the differences have been between those candidates hired and those not hired for entry-level jobs. Talk to graduates from your school, talk to second-year students who have had internships with your target organization, and review resumes of candidates with employment objectives similar to yours. Find what works and what doesn't work—what it takes to win.

Once you can describe the competition for your target employment market, think of ways to distinguish yourself from this competition. Identify your areas of strength in depth and breadth of education, length and level of experiences, and relevant personal attributes. Some examples include:

- Academic awards and other forms of recognition for achievement and excellence; leadership roles in school, community, athletics, or related activities;
- Relevant job experiences, internships, or special projects;
- Understanding of foreign cultures through living overseas or extensive travel and language proficiencies;
- High level or major leadership responsibilities for departments or projects;
- Outstanding results on significant internal assignments or consulting engagements;
- Mastery of cutting-edge technology in relevant software, hardware, engineering, or related areas;
- Participation in a range of activities and hobbies, indicating a person with well-rounded interests;
- Participation in MBA-related activities that may be relevant.

Finally, highlight current management *hot buttons*, because your employment market might have particular demand for your skills in areas such as e-Commerce, hi-tech start-ups, venture capital, and emerging economies.

RESEARCH YOUR MARKET

Having defined yourself as a candidate, you need to identify target organizations within your target sector. To start, you need to outline the qualities that define your target organizations, such as size, growth, competition, finances (profit performance and financial stability), reputation, location, culture (informal vs. formal structure, team vs. individual emphasis, limited vs. close control, and the prevailing value system), turnover, compensation, and advancement.

In conducting research on target organizations, an understanding of the concept of *channels of opportunity* can be useful. Most employment opportunities come through three channels:

- *On-campus recruiting* by organizations who conduct interviews on your campus,

- *Position posting* by organizations who list staff needs with your school placement departments, and

- *Hidden market* leads identified through your own researching and networking.

Access to each of the first two sources is usually well publicized and well understood. Working the hidden market requires comprehensive identification and exhaustive use of your unique networks (e.g., check out your family, friends, undergraduate school alumni, former employers/colleagues, professional association contacts, and community acquaintances).

Unfortunately, this approach can string out the search process beyond the typically late spring hiring deadlines. The hidden market generally requires the longest lead-time of the three channels because of the number of contacts needed. Therefore, a word of caution: Do not use a sequential approach to employment opportunities. You need to use all three paths *concurrently* to maximize your opportunities.

So, how should you start building a list of contacts? Print and online references are an excellent starting point for developing your list of employment targets. There are general industry (e.g., *Standard & Poor's Industry Outlook*) and general occupational (e.g., *Occupational Outlook Quarterly*) publications that provide an overview along with business directories (e.g., *Ward's Business Directory*) and CD-ROM sources (e.g., *General Business File*). You can also do online job searches by reviewing national employment databases and related systems. In addition, you can conduct literature searches of specialized trade magazines, business journals, sector publications, and newspapers. Usually, your placement department and library can provide considerable guidance on where to obtain information once they know the focus and scope of your search for target employers. Also see the resources in the back of this book.

Complement your print and online research with informational contacts. Some organizations make on-campus group presentations. These occasions are chances not only to obtain answers to your questions, but also to add people to your follow-up network. Other organizations set up information desks at regional job fairs or schools, affording the same opportunities to obtain information and gain contacts. Finally, your own network of function and sector contacts can be extremely helpful in filling in information on potential targets for employment. This network is especially important because it is uniquely yours and less likely to be tapped by others.

Additional suggestions on market research include:

- Finding out what your school is doing to cultivate organizations' interest in its graduates.

- Extending your research to the international arena to be sure to tap the growing global opportunities.

- Concentrating not only on your high-priority employment targets, but also on alternatives that *stretch* you a bit (i.e., look at secondary career options that might be a good fit for you).

- Taking a long view in scanning employment targets—think about where immediate opportunities become useful steps to reaching your ultimate career goals.

In summary, breadth can be as important as depth in your market research on target organizations. Be sure to conduct a search that uses a wide range of contacts and leads to maximize your success rate in the job hunt.

PROMOTE YOURSELF

Once you have created your personal profile and your target list, you are ready to promote yourself. For this step, you need a *commercial*, a short, snappy answer to the question, "Why should I hire you?" Your personal profile is the basis of your commercial. You need to draw out the four to six features in your background that your potential employer will be most interested in. How long should the message be and how should it sound? Imagine that a recruiter has interviewed you and recommended that you be invited for another round of interviews. The hiring manager says, "I have 30 seconds before I have to go to a meeting, so tell me quickly why we should bring this candidate back for more interviews." What would you want the recruiter to say?

This exercise forces you to focus on the best you have to offer to meet the needs of a prospective employer. Your commercial will be a useful guide in writing cover letters and handling interviews. The message will usually require a little tailoring for each of your target employers. Highlight those features in your background that are most important to each employer, especially any features that give you a competitive edge.

Testing your commercial is a good idea. Try it out on others to assess its clarity and impact. Ask your audience to feed back to you what they remember and how they would react as prospective employers. Would they want to interview you and if so, why?

The right audience is as important as the right commercial. A strong message to a weak audience can fail. The challenge is to develop the best *employment* contact at each of your target organizations.

Good *informational* contacts are the key to the best employment contacts. One script for such a contact, in this example a graduate of your school working at your target employer, might be:

> Hello. I am graduating from [name of school] this June. I was given your name by [person's name] (or obtained your name from the alumni directory, etc.). I am hoping you can take just a few minutes to answer a few questions I have about your organization.
>
> • Where might someone with my background best fit in your organization?
>
> • Who are the best leads to contact for these opportunities? (ideally function managers or department heads, instead of recruiting department contacts)
>
> • May I use your name in my cover letter, not as a reference, but just to note that you suggested that I write to these people?

You might also have some more direct informational contacts who can help and with whom you could be less formal.

The objective is to get beyond the gatekeepers and reach the decision makers or employment contacts who have the authority to hire you. Sometimes several informational contacts are required to identify these decision makers. If additional communications are adding to the quality of your eventual employment contact, they are worth the extra effort. Four or five informational contacts may be needed to produce one really strong employment contact.

At this point, you have your basic commercial and your target employment contacts and can move on to formally applying for job interviews. The first step is to promote yourself for the position. The cover letter is the key promotional document. The cover letter acts as an *executive summary* to one particular person in one specific organization whereas the resume is a *reference document* for many people in many organizations in a major sector. Look at the cover letter from the perspective of the reader, your employment contact. Often, this person has to review many applications for employment. Each communication usually includes a cover letter and a resume. The initial screening of applications for candidates to interview is often based on the short cover letter rather than the long resume. A winning cover letter can be what puts you on the *short list.*

A cover letter is a dialogue between you and a specific person, the addressee. Tailor your cover letter to your specific reader and target organization. Fortunately, the variations in cover letters usually require just a few creative adds and drops to a basic document.

One of the best ways to draft a cover letter is to think in terms of the reader's probable questions and your answers.

Why Should I Read This Letter?

One of the more compelling ways to answer this question is to open a cover letter with a personal reference such as "I appreciated this opportunity to meet (or talk) to you last week," or " I am writing to you at the suggestion of [name of your informational contact] of your company." If you have no direct contact, you might open with a one-liner about yourself as a professional, such as, "I thought my background, a combination of chemical engineering and management in both education and experience, might be of special interest to your company." Using both a *personal* hook and a *professional* hook can produce a very strong opening paragraph.

Why Should I Consider You as a Candidate?

A strong answer to this question is to state your commercial. The letter might read: "The highlights in my background that I think might be of most value to your organization are:

- A combination of a chemical engineering degree and an MBA with a marketing concentration.
- Four years experience with Company A in sales and engineering, the last year as a supervisor.
- Significant experience in project management and presentations to senior executives.
- Summer internship in the Strategic Planning Department at Company B.

These points should be short statements (i.e., preferably one-liners) in a logical order (i.e., strongest first). Think of constructing a good *memory aid* for your reader, something that simplifies his or her remembering your key points.

Why Are You Interested in This Position and Organization?

This section of the cover letter is probably not as important as the first two sections. If you have some truly unique reasons for your interests, be sure to include them (e.g., you have talked to graduates who work there, you were impressed with some specifics about the organization's future, you have found this type of work appealing in past jobs, or you have discovered a special interest in this career through your coursework). Use a few words to indicate that your decision to contact the reader's organization about the position was an enlightened choice, not just part of a mass mailing.

What Next?

What do you want to happen next. One way to close the letter is to say, "I would like to follow up on this employment inquiry by telephone on [day and date]." This closing suggests to the reader a time frame within which you will make contact. Also, it gives you an opening to make a telephone call (i.e., "I am calling you as I indicated I would in my letter of three weeks ago"). Finally, it places a commitment on you to make the call.

The test of the final draft of your cover letter is how well it answers these four questions for its reader. As with your commercial, trying out your cover letter with others can be useful.

Most employment candidates have written their resumes before they've done cover letters. Unlike cover letters, one resume can cover a major function/sector combination (e.g., brand management in consumer products, strategy in management consulting, or investing in financial services). There are many books that address preparation of resumes and that offer sound counseling. Therefore, we provide very limited coverage of resumes. As with the cover letter, some tests can be useful in composing and finalizing a resume:

- Do you have the proper resume format if one is specified or expected (e.g., what is required with regard to content, order of information, use of headlines, type selection, or length of text)?

- Are the level and scope of your responsibilities clearly outlined (e.g., section leader reporting to department head, responsible for marketing research for Food Division, or internal clients included company officers)?

- Are the details of your background quantified where possible (e.g., length of assignment, number of people supervised, or dollar value of operating budget)?

- Are your major accomplishments noted, both quantitative and qualitative (e.g., successfully installed new management information system for $100 million Industrial Products Division, developed cash management system that saved $40 million, or delivered new salesforce training program, or graduated with top honors in finance)?

- Does your resume clearly present your progression in level, scope, and diversity of responsibilities (e.g., how you advanced within each organization or how you advanced from organization to organization)?

- Do you differentiate yourself as much as possible from your probable competitors for employment (i.e., are your best features clearly documented)?

- Can a reader easily pick up the highlights of your education and experience along with your capabilities and achievements by skimming your resume (i.e., is your resume easy to read)?

- Does your resume present a positive and honest picture of your background (i.e., is your resume both compelling and credible)?

- How would you rate your resume against those of others (i.e., what are the strengths and weaknesses of your resume relative to resumes produced by your peers)?
- Is the text of your resume a good, clean copy (i.e., is it on attractive paper and free of grammatical and spelling errors)?

As with the cover letter, trying your resume out on others can be very useful. The final test is to make sure that the cover letter and resume in each application package coordinate properly. The highlights in your cover letter should stand out in your resume. Your resume should be consistent with your cover letter, providing more detailed references on the highlights in the cover letter.

In summary, the resume and cover letter are crucial marketing documents designed to sell your *unique* background to a targeted employer. They should highlight major points that relate to your employment goals. Remember to target your resume and cover letter to those accomplishments, experiences, and skills that relate to the specific position you seek. Do not put all you have done into a cover letter and resume. Instead, keep them relevant to the job applied for. Be clear on your audience and what they are looking for in new employees.

SELL YOURSELF

Once you have obtained employment interviews, the challenge is to make the most of them with effective selling tactics. The interview is one of the most crucial activities in your job search. It is where all the cover letters, phone calls, and resumes are finally connected with a real person.

We will start with a quick synopsis of the general interviewing/ hiring process at an employment target. Usually, there is a sequence of interviews, each interview having a specific purpose, such as to:

- *Screen:* The interviewer's objective is to reduce a large number of promising candidates to a more manageable number of excellent candidates.
- *Test:* There can be several variations of this type of interview. Sometimes the interview is with a senior "specialist" to verify an area of expertise. Other times the interview is with a person

who is assessing whether the candidate will fit the corporate culture, focusing on personal chemistry and attributes.

- *Inform:* In the more sophisticated interviewing processes, there might be a session with one of the newer people in the organization to afford the candidate an opportunity to gain first-hand knowledge of life at the entry level.

- *Sell:* As the interview process progresses, there might be contacts with people whose objective is to sell the candidate on the advantages of joining the organization.

- *Hire:* Ultimately, someone makes the hiring decision and the offer of employment. This step might be a two-part process, wherein the hiring decision is made in one interview and the offer in a following session.

Some interviews might combine several of these purposes. The key is to learn as much as you can about the interviewing/hiring process and the roles and backgrounds of the players in the process. Possible sources of information include your school's placement department, contacts who have interviewed at your target employer, alumni or acquaintances who work or have worked there, and even the first screen recruiter.

Much anguish can go into preparing for an employment interview. To alleviate some of the anxiety, take time to think first about what makes a good day for the typical interviewer. Feedback from recruiters indicates that if they can come up with some excellent candidates and if they have some compelling reasons to recommend each candidate, they have a good day. Simple and straight forward, right? So the candidate's job is to make the interviewer's job of *selection* and *documentation* as easy as possible.

Start by making sure you know as specifically as possible the responsibilities of the target position. With this information, you can prepare an excellent answer to the question "Why hire me?" This response is your basic commercial tailored to the needs of the target position and the organization.

Also, you need to have an answer to the question "Why this?" referring to why this position and this organization interest you. In addition to your knowledge of a position's responsibilities, your knowledge of the organization should include your initial market research and newsworthy items on subjects such as major products/services, key executives, and industry trends and developments. All too often, candidates do not know why they are interviewing with the company and appear to just be going through the motions. Remember, you aren't just competing with the people on the recruiter's list at your school. A company may be interviewing candidates from many other schools as well. You need to project knowledge, expertise, energy, and enthusiasm.

The answers to why me and why this questions are the substance of a session that provides the interviewer with hard information, specifics on your capabilities and interests. The interviewer also has to feedback soft information, the style aspects of the interview, including:

- *Physical:* The entire personal package that defines your appearance and presence, including your body language, voice level, and eye contact. Typically, the candidates with enthusiasm for themselves and their opportunities (i.e., strong answers to the why me and why this questions) do very well on these style factors.

- *Intellectual:* How you think on your feet, your practical intelligence (some refer to this attribute as basic street smarts with the tools of the MBA trade). The interviewer might present a case or a problem for analysis or ask you to discuss step by step some key decision in your experience or education. Typically, the interviewer is not looking for a perfect answer, but rather a reasonable thinking process. One tip for handling these tests is to imagine that you are responding to a close friend's questions or requests for help and not that you are trying to dazzle the interviewer.

- *Interpersonal:* How well you relate to others. One major clue is the ability to listen, as demonstrated in a candidate's physical attentiveness and the ability to ask smart questions. Another major clue is the degree to which a candidate can demonstrate empathy for the interviewer, or in other words, the candidate's capacity to understand another's feelings.

To the degree that you make it easy for the interviewer to understand what you have to offer and why you want to offer it and to the degree that you open up your real self to the interviewer, you will make the interviewer's job easier and enhance your chances for moving ahead in the job interview process.

Success in interviewing also requires understanding the purpose of the questions you might be asked. For example, if the interviewer opens by asking about a recent trip you took, the purpose is probably no more than to break the ice with some casual conversation. Soon after, the interviewer might ask you to tell about yourself. This lead is usually an opportunity to deliver your commercial rather than a request to regurgitate your resume in a long narrative. If the interviewer asks you why you switched college majors or why you chose to change jobs or why you chose to go to graduate school, the intent is not to challenge your decisions, but to learn about your thinking process. When the interviewer asks you to tell about the most difficult situation you were in with a manager, client, or subordinate, the intent is to gain some insight into your approach to interpersonal relationships. If an interviewer asks you to summarize your strengths and weaknesses, the purpose is to test your ability for self-evaluation and initiative in self-improvement. In this context, weaknesses are areas for further development not barriers to hiring. In short, when asked a question, consider why it is being posed so that you are able to provide the most useful response.

Implicit in interviewing success is your providing the interviewer with a clear picture of why to hire you. Ideally, the interviewer should be able to recite your commercial almost verbatim. Therefore, throughout the interview you need to monitor how well your commercial is covered, understood, and valued. For example, if you are near the end of the interview and you have not stated your commercial, you might say something like, "Based on what you (the interviewer) have covered so far, I think that the highlights in my background that would be of most value to your organization are. . . ." Or if one or two highlights have not been covered or reinforced, you might say something like, "Some features in my background that might be of further interest to your organization are. . . ." The tactic is to track the interview against your commercial, filling in where necessary for completeness. Interviewers really appreciate and value candidates' summaries of what they have to offer. After all, an interviewer sometimes listens to as many as 10 prospects in one day. So your memory aid can be very helpful to them.

A final point, the impression you leave can be enhanced by a prompt, brief thank you note to your interviewer. Don't forget to write one!

The end of the selling cycle is handling compensation and related matters. The dominant issue is salary, and possibly bonus. Some sources of information on this subject are the ranges that many prospective employers post with job opening specifications, the counseling staff in your school placement department, previous graduates, and special contacts you might know who know the market or the prospective employer. Some related areas to consider are sign-on bonuses and coverage of moving expenses or education costs. The important point is to know as well as you can what is typical and fair.

If you follow the steps outlined for you in these two chapters, you will be able to chart a course and navigate the career terrain with a sense of confidence and energy necessary to reach the job you desire. The last chapter in this book provides a sampling of additional resources. We believe that if you use the information provided here and talk to as many people as you can about your career interests, you will be well on your way to finding the job that is right for you.

3

Insights from the Field

This chapter provides a structure to aid you in reading and reflecting on the Doers' Profiles presented in the next chapter. Many of the people interviewed found jobs through a network of contacts, or displayed such enthusiasm about and knowledge of an organization that they impressed the recruiter. Many of the Doers positioned themselves to meet people who supported their career goals, whether at parties, in conferences, or through associations. They usually had their share of good luck as well. Think of these common themes as messages from the real world of career search and as living examples of people who have followed their dreams and have come up with something that works for them.

Here is a collection of some of the most useful insights from the profiles:

1. *Pursue your vision:* Don't be afraid to live out your vision. Know and seek what you like. Remember that the working environment you desire should be included in your vision. See what resources and what people show up to assist you along the way. A supportive mentor or two can help you stay on course.

2. *Do your homework:* When approaching any job search, study your opportunities. You learn about an industry by reading its trade publications and talking to people in the field. You

learn about jobs by consulting career books, library resources, online services, alumni, counselors, and advisors.

3. *Research your targets:* Be sure to do your homework on the organizations you have targeted for employment. Be curious. Ask a lot of smart, informed questions. Read up on the field, and know the players.

4. *Consider smaller organizations:* Don't fret the on-campus feeding frenzy. Look for positions away from the crowd where your particular background will be more distinctive. Go directly to organizations that may not have a formal recruitment process or a human resource department.

5. *Obtain sector experience:* Through an internship or part-time work in the sector that interests you, you can show credibility and the ability to go the extra mile to get into the field of your choice. Without it, you are competing with people who show their eagerness for the opportunity by doing what it takes to open doors.

6. *Seek functional experience:* Take the time to volunteer, do an internship, and make yourself stand out from the others competing in your functional area. By direct experience, you will be one step ahead of the competition. Also, many organizations hire those people who have interned with them to increase the odds of a good match for full-time employment.

7. *Network aggressively:* Pursue networking actively, but don't abuse your network. Approximately 85 percent of the jobs in the market are found through informal networks. Keep yours active and vibrant. Include a group of continuing support contacts. Help those who have helped you, not only because you may need them again, but because this practice establishes your reputation. Never stint on thanking those who help you. Graciousness is a form of personal capital. Remember to maintain contacts.

8. *Perfect your story:* Develop a clear and persuasive story that tells people why you want to enter a particular field. Be able to talk about your unique skills and attributes. Feature the linkages between your background and the needs of a prospective employer. Practice is key to perfecting your story.

9. *Focus your writing:* Tailor your cover letters to specific readers while keeping the content brief and easily readable. Indicate clearly how your skills and experience fit a prospective employee's needs and requirements. Be clear about what you have to offer. Seek out good examples of cover letters and resumes, including career books as a resource.

10. *Practice persuasive interviewing:* Figure out what each interviewer wants to know. Compose a short message to meet these needs. Make it easy for the interviewer to construct a case for hiring you. Be honest about who you are, what you want, and why you deserve it. Try to check out your approach in advance with people your own age at the prospective employer or at similar firms. Practice interviewing with your counselors and colleagues.

11. *Utilize group discussions:* Working in groups and in teams can foster creativity and confidence. Rarely do people succeed on their own. Find ways to engage in group presentations and discussions of career opportunities, searches, and strategies.

12. *Learn from colleagues:* Seek mentors from organizations and positions where you would like to be. However, just as there is no lifetime employment, there are usually no lifetime mentors. Even if you don't have the luxury of constantly working with brilliant people, you can always learn something from those around you. There is great value in remembering this point.

13. *Remain flexible:* There is no one way to get a job and make it to the top. Top executives have come from sales, marketing, finance, strategic planning, and other functional areas. There is no predestined path to an ideal job. Keep developing alternative routes to your objective to keep moving on your career path if your first choices don't work out.

14. *Persevere and follow up:* Stay the course and remember to never take no for an answer. It may not be now, but that doesn't mean not ever. Stay in touch with your contacts and continue to check in with those people with whom you have interviewed and otherwise met along the way. Always follow up, especially with human resource departments. For bigger

organizations, you might call the human resources department every week. When you write your cover letters state that you will follow up because most people will not call you.

Some short, but still provocative, thoughts from the profiles follow:

- *Follow your dreams:* You only have one life so make the most of it. Don't be afraid to reach for your dreams.

- *Think out of the box:* Think outside of your proscribed vision; always try and consider new possibilities or avenues for career opportunity.

- *Keep adding to your career tool box:* It's never too late to take another course, learn another skill, and so on.

- *Remember that you are unique:* You have something unique to bring to the table; never forget this as you look to create your competitive advantage.

- *Look the part:* Even the best of brains have trouble landing the job unless they have some style and look like they fit into the culture of the company.

- *Be polite:* Kindness and consideration can get you farther than you can possibly imagine.

- *Be technology adept:* The Internet is here to stay, learn it and the lingo . . . and use it!

- *Be your own best manager:* Learn to manage yourself, because you may not get a good "manager" who knows how to coach and develop you.

- *Focus on your goal and force yourself to do something every day toward that goal:* Write a letter, go to a lecture, join an association, read a book, take a class, network, and so on.

- *Home is where the heart is:* Inspiration comes from those closest to you; almost all the profiles mentioned family as a source of inspiration for their understanding of integrity, dedication, and thoughtfulness.

So far, we have coupled the key success factors in a career search with a summary of insights and thoughts from the real Doers. These ideas are enriched and covered in more detail in the profiles in Chapter 4.

4

Doers' Profiles—
Passion in Action

This chapter, the largest section of this book, contains profiles of people who discuss their jobs and offer observations and advice about how to find your ideal job. Each profile can be viewed as an initial information interview where we, the authors, asked the questions and you, the readers, can read the responses of people who have found their desired jobs in a wide range of sectors and functions. These are people with diverse backgrounds, abilities, and interests who have varied work/life paths and goals. The profiles include students and alumni from Columbia Business School, Harvard Business School, New York University Stern School of Business, University of Washington Graduate School of Business, and Yale School of Management. We chose people who made changes or who pursued difficult careers—to provide insights for you as you embark on your own unique career path. These profiles provide information and inspiration as you seek the career you want. Regardless of your undergraduate or graduate degrees, these profiles ground you in real-life stories and situations.

Chapters 1 through 3 have been structured to highlight the key success factors in career searches drawn from our experiences and student contacts. This chapter is not highly structured, more free-form, to preserve the actual thoughts and feelings of the students in our survey—to give you a real-world perspective. Therefore, we have not followed exactly the same question-and-answer format for each profile.

Also, the careers and experiences do not necessarily represent patterns for particular schools—or, for that matter, the pattern for MBA graduates in general.

Finally, recognizing the unstructured nature of this chapter, we have some aids and suggestions for you to use while exploring these profiles:

- The list that follows breaks down the profiles by sector (i.e., management consulting, financial services, consumer products, entertainment/media, other business fields, and not-for-profit world) and functional areas.
- Begin by focusing on those sector/function combinations that are of most interest to you. The list presents the page numbers for each sector and profile.
- Then scan the remaining profiles because there can be interesting ideas in past job histories and in career areas that might be of alternative or secondary interest to you.

There is a brief introduction to each of the six sectors to draw you into the profiles.*

Management Consulting (page 29)

Financial Services (page 59)

---

* These profiles are "snapshots" of career information taken mainly in late 1997; thus, a few references to specific jobs, titles, employers, and the like are no longer current.

Investing: Janet Cochoff (page 59), Kate Cornish (page 66), Eric Gelb (page 70), Curtis Jensen (page 74), Matt Koob (page 75), Diana Propper (page 80), David Skrilloff (page 85)

Brand/Product Management: Susan McSharry (page 78)

Product Development: Susan McSharry (page 78)

Sales: Matt Koob (page 75)

Finance: Eric Gelb (page 70)

Consumer Products (page 91)

General Management: Timothy Crew (page 93)

Strategy: Timothy Crew (page 93)

Brand/Product Management: Alison Bard (page 91), Timothy Crew (page 93), Robbie Kahn (page 96), Margie Wong Kuo (page 101), Tracy McNamera (page 114), Robyn Rothke (page 122), Robert Scheckman (page 127), Virginia Stults (page 133)

Market Research: Erina Du Bois (page 95)

Product Development: Alison Bard (page 91), Robbie Kahn (page 96), Scott Nadison (page 120), Scott Tucker (page 140)

Advertising: Mary Maricucci (page 110)

Sales: Scott Nadison (page 120)

Operations: Scott Tucker (page 140)

Entertainment and Media (page 145)

General Management: Paul Jelinek (page 161), Doug MacKay (page 172), J.B. Miller (page 181), Caroline Turner (page 190)

Strategy: Paul Jelinek (page 161)

Brand/Product Management: Lisa Fink (page 145), Susan Lopusniak (page 168), Doug MacKay (page 172), Philip Sidel (page 183)

Market Research: Jeffrey James (page 152)

Product Development: Lisa Fink (page 145), Susan Lopusniak (page 168), Philip Sidel (page 183)

Advertising: Jeffrey James (page 152)

Sales: Doug MacKay (page 172), J.B. Miller (page 181)

Finance: Caroline Turner (page 190), Michael Whalen (page 196)

FINDING YOUR WAY IN
MANAGEMENT CONSULTING

Many MBA students are interested in management consulting because of the range of this work—the variety of organizations, functions, and assignments. They are also attracted by the emphasis on problem solving, the level of client contacts, and the potential for impact. Other positives include the opportunity to associate with highly intelligent, high-energy professionals and to work in team structures. There are trade-offs in the form of travel and time demands. The profiles that follow touch on both the positives and negatives. There are pointers for those who want to enter the field. In addition to profiles from consulting firms, we have included profiles from internal consulting (i.e., Andrew Zorn) and contract services (i.e., Andrew Feerst).

▶ Jean Cusick is a Senior Associate with Coopers & Lybrand L.L.P. She received a BA from the University of Michigan in Economics in 1987 and an MBA in Management from New York University Stern School of Business in 1992.

What do you do on the job? Describe a typical day.

I am a consultant in the Integrated Healthcare Consulting Services (IHCCS) Practice at Coopers & Lybrand L.L.P. in the New York office. IHCCS provides strategic, operational, and clinical consulting to hospitals, physician groups, pharmaceutical and biotech companies, and other suppliers to the health care industry.

Specifically, I work on projects involving strategic planning and operations improvement for hospitals and physicians. In the course of these projects, I conduct analysis to assist senior management in developing strategic and operational improvement plans. Areas of analysis include models to predict future utilization of health care services (i.e., how many hospital beds will be needed in a particular market); interviewing potential partners, competitors, and insurers to gauge how they perceive the market and our client; developing documents to help the client understand his current environment; analyzing hospital operations to evaluate operational efficiency; and making recommendations as to strategic and/or operational action plans.

What part of your day is spent doing what?

On a typical day, I:

- Spend about 40 percent of my time on the computer—creating spreadsheets, writing presentations, writing letters, corresponding via e-mail.
- Spend about 15 percent of my time on the phone—scheduling meetings, conducting interviews, networking with other consultants around the firm.
- Spend about 35 percent of my time interacting with my colleagues, and/or clients.
- Spend about 10 percent working with support staff, answering questions, helping colleagues.

What do you like best and least about your present job, including pitfalls, challenges, and rewards?

What I don't like about my job:

- *Lifestyle:* In consulting you are always at the mercy of someone else. While this is true in any client industry, people seem to expect more from consultants. Clients and partners will make very difficult demands with many time constraints and you (the grunt) are the one to execute. The flip side of this is that I have flexible schedule. As long as I manage my clients, deliverables and other commitments, I can schedule my day as I want; I still have to be in by 9 A.M., but there is more flexibility than in other industries. Travel is also an issue. When I work on strategic planning projects, I tend to travel 10 percent to 20 percent of my time—primarily for client meetings. For operations restructuring/redesign projects, however, I am on the road four days a week—about 80 percent of the time. You need to ask very specific questions and get the real story about the travel.
- *Mission:* As a consultant there is not a strong sense of having a corporate mission. We have billable hours and monthly profit targets that must be met. We do all we can to help our clients, but there is little sense of working for something else—something a little bigger—except vicariously through our clients.

This did not bother me at first, but after five years, it seems a little limiting.

What I do like about my job:

- *Varied tasks:* Every project is different. About the time I get a little tired or bored working on one thing, I'm assigned to something else.

- *The opportunity to learn:* There is no better way to learn about an industry. The people I work with are among the brightest I have ever met. Each person brings their own brand of expertise and experience to the table so we can give our clients the best team for their money. It's really exciting to see how people's different backgrounds can lend unique perspectives to different situations.

How were you able to obtain this position? What steps led you to this? What is your career history or prior work experience?

My path to this position was somewhat unusual. Before I attended Stern, I worked for three years as a commercial underwriter for a large, commercial insurance company, which had nothing to do with health care or the health care industry. I went to Stern thinking I wanted to get into management consulting, but had no particular interest in health care.

After my first year at NYU, I obtained a position at Coopers & Lybrand as a researcher in the Market Analysis Department, an internal research group. During that summer, I worked on an insurance project, focused on life/health insurance. The summer experience was invaluable, and I was invited back for a full-time position in the Market Analysis Department. The director of market analysis talked a great deal about the health care consulting practice and the potential opportunities there. At that time, people usually stayed in Market Analysis for about two years then transferred to other client service groups within the firm.

At the director's recommendation, I started focusing on the health care industry—providing research, proposal and engagement support, and helping with marketing and other internal projects. I began to learn a lot about the health care delivery industry. During my first summer there (1992), I wrote a monograph on the industry forces that were acting on hospitals and other health care providers. The monograph was meant as a "get smart quick" document for our audit staff and it was very well-received.

During the winter of 1993, the health care consulting lead partner in New York asked me to assist them on a project on which they were short-handed. I began to learn more about what exactly was involved in consulting and to establish a network of contacts in the firm, not just among the partners but among other people working at my level. Their support proved to be invaluable when I eventually transferred over from the Marketing Analysis Department to IHCCS in April 1994.

After President Clinton announced that he would propose a comprehensive health care reform bill to Congress "within the first 100 days," my daily responsibilities in the internal research group changed. Coopers & Lybrand created a task force on health care reform and decided that they would produce a comprehensive monograph on how health care reform would affect the entire industry. I was asked to write the section on providers. The experience was very worthwhile and I learned a great deal. I worked with people from all over the firm, which again, was key to further building an internal support network.

While I was working on this project, I also continued to assist the health care partner in New York and do research on trends or new competitors, and so on. During the summer of 1993, I worked on another client engagement, spending a lot of time on-site with a team of consultants from all over the country. My work was well-received and I felt that I was now in a position to request that I be transferred to the health care consulting group.

You may wonder why it was so important to be in a consulting group instead of in a research group doing occasional consulting projects. The answer is money—not salary, but the way the firm makes money. You get more respect, have more opportunities for advancement and are better received outside the firm (in terms of future career opportunities) if you are on the "money side." The money side is the client side of the business. The support side is just that—nonclient work. While some people do well there, you need to have real client experience if you really want to move ahead. The majority of partners and managers have had direct client experience.

I first requested a transfer in the fall of 1993. It was delayed until April of 1994 while I finished a major project for the director of market analysis. I have been in the health care consulting group since.

What skills do you use most in your career?

To be a consultant, regardless of the industry, you need to:

- Have good analytical skills; by that I mean you have to be able to take vast amounts of data and make it tell a story.

- Be a good listener—your clients are constantly communicating with you and you have to know what they are saying and what they are not saying.

- Be an effective communicator—turnaround times are very short and you have to be able to communicate quickly and con- cisely through written and oral presentations.

- Have good writing skills.

- Be astute about political situations—clients often ask you to come in and make unpopular recommendations or to support a given position that may not make sense and consultants need to be aware of these pitfalls.

- Specifically in not-for-profits, be aware that they are doing more than taking in money, be sensitive to their mission.

What do people need to know to get into this field? What are the most important skills to have?

Three key things helped me get into the consulting group:

1. *Industry knowledge*—I had a golden opportunity in the Market Analysis Department to learn about the health care industry and I used it.

2. *Network*—I kept my name in front of people and delivered for them. I became known as someone people could rely on to get things done.

3. *Patience*—I had not been hired into the health care consulting group, therefore I had to put in my time and be patient about transferring, being aware of politics, and other needs. The po- litical situation in the firm was not bad—I just had to recognize

that there was more at stake than my desire to transfer to a different group.

Do you feel your work makes a difference to you, your family, society?

One of the things I really like about working for health care providers industry is the societal aspect of health care. I work with not-for-profit institutions to help them deliver better health care per dollar. It's not just lining CEOs' or stockholders' pockets; it's about helping the hospital become a better community citizen. Not that all my clients are such altruistic beings—many are trying to preserve income and power—but overall we are helping a department or unit or person better achieve the hospital's mission, which is to provide quality health care to the members of its community.

Where do you see yourself in 5 to 10 years?

I would like to take my skills to a health care organization and work in the strategic planning area—this is basically what I have been doing and I think that with my experience I could enter as a vice president or director.

Alternatively, I could continue in consulting and eventually (after about seven years) make partner. Successful partners make tremendous personal sacrifices to attain their position—long hours, lots of travel, considerable time away from their families, and so on. I'm not sure that this route is for me.

What are the misconceptions people hold about this kind of work?

One misconception is that consultants spend all their time hobnobbing with CEOs. You are more likely to work with division/department managers than with the CEO or senior vice presidents of client companies.

Another misconception is that consultants cause change in client companies. Managers and employees change companies; consultants advise, recommend, facilitate, and assist with implementation of that change.

A third misconception is that your rate per hour is tied to your salary. Unless you work for yourself, the rate charged to your clients is nowhere near your salary on an hourly basis. I do believe that I am well paid, but I am not paid in accordance with my billable hours.

Last, there is the misconception that consultants, by their nature, have instant credibility with a client. You have to prove yourself constantly to your clients. Not even partners have "instant credibility."

▶ Adam Feerst is a Contract Financial Analyst. He received his BA in Economics from California State University in 1985 and his MPPM from Yale School of Management in 1993.

What is your employment history since graduation?

My dates and places are as follows:

- 1/94–4/95   Kalfact Plastics (Greenville, Michigan) as training director, safety manager, assistant quality director, and production supervisor.
- 6/95–5/96   Accountemps in various accounting and financial analysis assignments.
- 1/96–5/96   Self-employed as quality trainer and other special projects.
- 6/96–Present Contract financial analyst (Denver, Colorado).

How would you define your desired career path at the time of your graduation?

I wanted to work in operations/quality management in manufacturing for a few years and then switch to the financial side of management, possibly in venture capital. The next step would be to be doing business/manufacturing development in developing countries, probably through nongovernment organizations.

What led you to your career objectives?

Pursuing my own dream was key! I grew up in a politically/socially active family where my parents encouraged realistic pursuits. As an undergraduate, courses in economics shifted my focus from mathematics/computers to business/policy. Service in the Peace Corps strengthened my desire to work in needy areas. Classes and projects in graduate school shifted my focus from finance to manufacturing and management. Also, I think my experience coaching high school and other youth sports sparked my desire to begin focusing more on people instead of just numbers.

How are you identifying the key qualities needed to pursue your ideal career?

I am still working on it. Alumni and other contacts through alumni in manufacturing, specifically people who have also taken more of a nontraditional career path, have encouraged me and given me tips. Conventional wisdom would tell me not to pursue this career so I try to avoid traditional sources of advice.

How did you identify the target organizations for your career path?

I referred to Wards, Standard & Poor, Dunn & Bradstreet, and regional manufacturing directories selecting by industry (i.e., SIC code), size, and location. Also, stories in the *Wall Street Journal,* business section of local paper, local business journal, Bloomberg, and other electronic data sources.

What is your advice on composing cover letters?

I am still trying to figure it out. I try to make a few brief points/references to my resume. I do not like to just repeat the resume. In addition, I like to include anecdotal experiences of success that are difficult to cover on a resume. Also, I explain my motivation in choosing manufacturing and why someone with my background is needed. If you are changing careers and/or going into something without a strong background, you need to be different.

How do you recommend preparing for employment interviews?

Practice! Anticipate and prepare responses to standard questions. Think through explanations of weaknesses or areas in your resume that are likely to raise questions, especially if you are changing careers or have followed a nontraditional path. Even if you like to improvise (I hate to sound like I am reading from a script), it is easier to do so if you have already prepared a strategy.

What do you like best and least about your work?

My current work as a financial analyst is only temporary to pay the bills while I am looking to continue on my ideal career path. As to what is best about the current work, I am good at it and can do it fairly easily without diverting much energy away from my job search, which gives me a chance to explore new industries. As to least, I have done a lot of quantitative work so more does not add to my resume, does not add the type of knowledge and experience I want. This work does not give me the kind of challenges I want.

Looking at your varied career search experiences, what advice would you pass along to a graduating MBA?

It is easy to get sucked into the on-campus interview frenzy. If your goals are different (e.g., not for Wall Street or management consulting), you can still use the on-campus interviews as practice, but do not let them distract you from your primary goal. Seek out alumni who have followed similar paths and build a support network of friends. Decide what your goals are—whether that's money, functional, geographical, or industry. Keep your goals fairly narrow. You can be open and change your goals, but you will be more effective if you "focus" your search.

▶ Guy Fish is Founder/President of Ivy Enterprises (Ivy Consulting and Ivy Ventures). He received his AB in Biochemistry from Harvard in 1981, MD from Yale Medical School in 1985, and MPPM from Yale School of Management in 1994.

As background, what is your employment outline since graduation?

1994–1998, Consultant	Boston Consulting Group, Boston, MA
1998–1999, Sell-Side Equities Analyst	Sanford C. Bernstein & Company, NY
1999, Founder/President	Ivy Consulting and Ivy Ventures, Cambridge, MA

How would you define your career target at the time you were completing your MBA? What were the sector, group within sector, functional area, and any other key criteria?

Sector: Public

Groups: Health care/management consulting

Functional area: Organization and systems design

How did you identify your ideal career?

A large variety of influences helped:

- Interviews with industry firms were helpful in thinking through what I didn't want.

- Policy courses and seminars illustrated the low probability of being taken seriously in public policy circles straight post-MBA.

- Courses on consulting helped form a positive opinion of being a change agent from a vantage external to the organization.

How did you decide what key qualities and competitive edges you needed to offer to employers for your ideal career?

I spoke with others pursuing consulting as a career. I think the Yale environment was uniquely suited for that in allowing classmates to discern that my specialist background made me not a direct competitor for the slots they were likely to want in consulting. As a result, we fairly freely shared information about what various companies were like, looked for, and how to beat their interview cases. The Consulting Student Interest Group was especially helpful in sponsoring the interview workshops.

How did you identify target organizations for your ideal career?

Identifying the big five or six consulting firms was all too easy. They were selected because of the desire to leverage the credibility garnered by having been there. A more difficult task awaited colleagues who sought smaller boutique consulting opportunities in environmental and telecom. Here it was largely networking that produced the leads.

What special tips do you have for writing cover letters and resumes, including the tips of substance and style that you found most useful?

Cover letters: Keep them to three paragraphs. In the first paragraph, state briefly who you are and what you want: an informational interview or a specific posted position. In the second, state why they should bother considering you. Point out your relevant resume details that uniquely prove the job was made for you. Include snippets of any advanced thinking you have done in your target company's field. Third, set concrete steps on next steps (who will call whom, when, and where).

Resumes: One page only. Emphasize actions and results. Every single line must read as to how you contributed by cutting costs or increasing revenues by X% or $$. All else is "fluff." Estimates are fine. And yes, no one miraculously does this single handedly, but if you were part of a team, take credit for the results.

What special tips do you have for preparing for employment interviews? What were the three or four major questions from your prospective employers?

If it is a consulting firm using the case study method, remember that it is the process of your thinking which is being tested as much or more than your answer. The mindset is to approach the case like a conversation between two colleagues discussing an interesting problem. You will naturally fall into an iterative process of developing hypotheses (ideas) about the situation described and testing them (showing your "friend" how to solve or analyze the situation) with direct questions, simple math, or a proposed process. This approach usually opens up a different part of the case that you approach in the same way.

Besides these ideas, the one best piece of advice I got was from a classmate who said, "In the case, behave as if you are the manager. Give answers well suited to the structure of the firm so that they see you fitting in and being promoted." For example instead of saying "I think I would do X . . . ," say "I would assign one person the task of doing X, and if they find out the answer is a, then I would have them look into Y. Meanwhile I would have some other team or person do Z and if they find . . ." The idea is that from day one you can be left on your own and help the firm do the work rather than needing a lot of guidance.

In non-consulting interviews, the minimum of knowing a lot about the company, its goods or services, and competitors is no longer enough. You must spend some time understanding the key issues facing the firm and its industry. You must then walk in prepared to offer some of your best ideas on how to solve some of these problems. There is a small risk that the company will take your ideas and run with them. But the potential gain is that it will see you as bright, insightful, and a team player. The company's assumption should be yours: Anyone who could come up with one such good idea and give it away is likely to come up with many more.

What do you like best and least about your current work?

When people say "there is nothing like starting your own company," or "working for yourself," there are two aspects to which they are referring. One is the daily rush of being at risk. For the risk seeking, this is a manna from heaven. It gets you up everyday wondering if it will work or bust, or if you can make it bigger and better.

The other aspect is not having to put up with the games inherent in any industry. You can opt out of the hierarchical and nonmeritorious, competitive structures and find yourself quite able to survive as a professional. To pursue this kind of career usually requires reaching two points: understanding the game in an industry and understanding whether playing the game is worth it to you.

Reflecting on all your work experience to date, what additional tips might you have on career selection and search for graduating MBAs?

"KNOW THYSELF" as the Oracle would say. Figure out your risk tolerance and timeframes for results.

On the latter front, remember, remember, remember. In Internet time, life is very fast, but also it is a multi-period game. Few of you will have the same job three years after graduation. Most of you will be on your third job five to six years after graduation. So factor in what are the skills and tools you need, and go figure out the jobs as if they were stepping stones to get you there.

As lucrative and desirable as it may be, if the career doesn't get you out of bed with a passion for it each morning, it's the wrong career. There is a saying, "Life is too short to drink bad wine." The same can be said for bad career choices.

When you are feeling a bit unsure, there is a very cool site which provides you an assessment of your skills and strengths for minimal investment. International Assessment Network is the organization and its test is the Motivational Appraisal of Personal Potential (MAPP) found at http://www.assessment.com.

▶ Richard Hu is President of Planning and Logic, Inc. He received his BSEE in 1983 and MSEE in 1985 from the University of Minnesota. He received his MBA from Columbia Business School in 1993.

What was your employment history after graduation?

My career sequence since graduation was as follows:

- 1993   Product Manager, Coherent Communications Systems
- 1994   Vice President, Sales and Marketing, Sinper Corporation

- 1995   President, Sinper Corporation
- 1997   President, Planning and Logic, Inc.

What was your career target at the time of your graduation?

I was looking for a product management position in small, high-growth, and high-tech companies.

What was your process for identifying your ideal career?

I established long-term career and achievement objectives using career books (e.g., *How to Turn Your MBA into a CEO* by Bob Lear) and related resources.

How did you identify the key success factors for your ideal career?

I identified the steps needed to reach these objectives by talking to counselors and advisors, in addition to library research.

What do you recommend for identifying and contacting target organizations?

I would establish the characteristics for my target organizations (e.g., industry, size, and growth). I would use online information systems (e.g., Lexis/Nexis and ABINFO) and related research resources to identify specific firms. For writing cover letters and resumes to your target organizations, I would check out the various career books. They usually have some good examples.

What has been your experience in preparing for employment interviews?

I found it useful to ask the question, "If I were the employer, what would I want to know from the candidate?" Then answer all the questions this inquiry generates. Some of the questions I recall were, "What relevant experiences and successes do you have?" and "If you got the job, what would you do (including plans, directions, and strategies to 'excel' in the job)?" Finally, I studied annual reports, industry magazines, competitor information, and general industry information.

What do you like best and least about your job?

I like the responsibilities, authorities, and the sense of accomplishment. I dislike some necessary, but uninteresting tasks.

Reflecting on your experience, what other comments would you pass along to the graduating MBA?

Take "initiatives" on every aspect of the process. Identify targets. Set objectives. Contact the prospective employers. Present what you plan to do for the company.

▶ Dorothy Sadd is a Manager with Kurt Salmon Associates. She received her BS from Purdue University in 1988 and her MBA from Columbia Business School in 1990.

What has been your career path since graduation?

From 1990 into 1994, I was a management associate with Springs Industries. Over the course of four years, I held strategic planning, merchandising, and sales and marketing positions within various divisions of Springs. In 1994, I joined Kurt Salmon Associates, a management consulting firm, to focus on product development and merchandising issues from a broader industry perspective.

What was your career objective when you were completing your MBA and how did you identify your goal?

My initial interest was in merchandising in retail, apparel, or textile organizations. I spoke one-on-one with alumni from Columbia in these industries as well as consulting, investment banking, and packaged foods. I really did not know which of these was "ideal" and used our conversations to clarify my goals.

How did you decide what key qualities and competitive edges you needed to offer to employers in your fields of interest?

I drew on previous experiences with colleagues and clients. I also referred to various career books and conversations with alums.

How did you identify target organizations to meet your career objectives?

Research, research, research. First, to find the organizations in one's chosen industry and then, to find meaningful contacts within those organizations. The latter is the most difficult as it takes some creativity to succeed.

What advice do you have on cover letters and resumes?

Be specific! Take the time to learn about the organization to which you are writing. Weave the information you gather, including what you perceive to be the organization's needs, into your letter and resume.

What suggestions do you have on preparing for an employment interview?

Be clear about where you are in your search. Are you exploring (i.e., still learning about what you want) or do you know exactly where you want to be and if so, how well are you prepared to succeed there? The key interview questions appear to be: (1) Who are you—what do you want in a career? (2) Will that (i.e., your goal) fit with my organization? (3) Have you prepared to succeed—will you be a successful addition?

What do you like best and least about your present work?

I like the variety of people and the range of issues I work with. However, with that comes travel, which is time consuming and disruptive to my personal life.

Looking at your work experience, what additional ideas would you like to offer on career search?

Follow your dreams and prepare yourself to achieve those dreams. Be open to change and willing to work hard.

▶ Maja Sholler is a Senior Business Analyst in the Health Care Group with Marketing Corporation of America. She received her BA from Harvard in 1985, completed Circle in the Square Drama School in 1988 and received her MBA from New York University Stern School of Business in 1996.

What I do:

Work in a consulting group at a small company that engages in marketing and consulting for other companies:

- 200 in company.
- 50 in consulting group.
- 14 in our practice (health care consulting).

The health care consulting group does primarily strategic consulting with some implementation strategy. I have worked on the following cases for major health care and pharmaceutical companies:

- Integrated business plan to maximize the value of a $500+ million product across three market segments, including entry into one new segment.
- Worldwide R&D operating strategy to align R&D strategy with commercial needs in order to effectively implement a global strategic plan.
- Strategic execution plan to manage a portfolio of 12 products (5 new products) within 4 business franchises.

My work ranges from the menial to the sophisticated: from faxing to global market analysis. There is a fair dose of each of the following:

- Sensitive/confidential information.
- Client contact.
- Trust.
- Understanding of client needs.

Consulting is very changeable and not for people who like steady routines. It can change instantaneously and there is an uneven work flow.

You learn to write/speak/think in bullet points because everything must be boiled down to the essential in a strategy case. For instance, we may be doing a new product launch strategy. We need to understand a lot of things about the market to decide on the appropriate launch strategy. But for the client, we must be able to communicate the essentials which support the recommendation without digressing or explaining every bit of data that led us to that conclusion. I was an English major in college, used to writing well-crafted papers, and an actress for many years—the ability to write/speak concisely and clearly is absolutely essential and my background has stood me in good stead.

My background:

I went to college as a biology major, but had been studying drama as an actress since I was a child. After the first year of college, I decided to make a go of it in acting because I felt I would kick myself for the rest of my life if I didn't try. I switched to an English major because it had very few requirements, allowing me to take a broad range of courses. While many of them were in fact literature courses (Chaucer, Shakespeare, etc.), they also allowed me to take things I had no experience with such as Chinese culture, European history, Italian, and political science. I felt that the breadth would be beneficial as an actress.

I spent a year performing in shows and working, but decided if I really was going to succeed, I needed more formal training and went to Circle in the Square Drama School. In the next seven years, I continued to hone my craft and learn the skills that anyone running his or her own business must.

However, as the seventh year came around, I was disillusioned with the theater and felt that I had reached a dead end, that there was little I could do to change. Thus began a painful and disorienting period of reevaluation. If I changed careers, would I be throwing away all that hard work and betraying my vision? Would that be quitting? And what would I do instead?

I began to think about the skills that I had learned as an actress and "business owner" to see where I might fit in. I went to work at a fairly informal company to see how I would feel about the more structured work environment. I began to think about business school because I felt that I would need legitimization—who would hire me into a business position from an acting career? I also felt that there were a number of tools and skills that would prepare me better for a business career and make me more marketable. Finally, I had no idea what kind of business/job I wanted—I would find out through exposure.

Within a year I was at the Stern School of Business. Unlike many of my classmates, I had no difficulty adjusting to life back at school because I had been taking classes all through my acting career. I found that my skills were readily transferable. As an actress, I had to put myself in different people's shoes and analyze the many external and internal factors that caused them to behave a certain way at a certain time under certain circumstances. This is precisely (or so it seemed to me) what we did in our casework—although I found that numbers and "facts" are in a way much easier to work with than the psychological and environmental intangibles I had dealt with as an actress. Once I learned the tools, it was not too difficult. I also learned that just as in acting, one is always trying to make decisions based on incomplete or inadequate information—there are no right answers—there are better and worse choices, but not wrong ones.

The most important skill, I have found, is the ability to communicate effectively. But many other "acting" skills gave me an advantage. My ability and training in working on teams as well as individually was a big plus. My ability to take on different roles depending on the dynamics of a group meant that I could fill whatever role was unfilled, be it leader, facilitator, mediator, and so on. Because I was used to working under difficult conditions, pressure and deadlines did not overly deter me.

While at Stern, it became clearer to me that a job in marketing would be my goal. It was about people—how they use things, why they decide to purchase things, how you can influence them—as much as it was about sales, profits, and product objectives. I thought about market research, but decided that the big, visible jobs were in product marketing.

My job search:

I interviewed with something like 50 firms for close to 9 months. They would almost always call me in when they got my resume because they thought I was so "interesting." I had a Harvard degree, I had been an actress, and I had a business degree. I developed a well-crafted story that would help them understand that the skills and experience I had were transferable to their business environment. I think everyone needs to have a well-thought-out story to help the interviewer bridge what they may see as a possible gap or lack of fit, but it's especially important for a career changer. Don't get me wrong; this should not sound canned, but the interviewer must see how your experience relates to what the company does (or wants to do). I always did research to make sure I had an understanding of the issues the company might be facing. I would have intelligent questions to ask. Never leave an interview without asking a question. This shows interest or understanding.

But despite their assertions that they wanted diversity, these companies never hired me. I think that when it came down to me and a few other candidates they got cold feet about my lack of business experience. Who can blame them? Needless to say, it was very frustrating. But from having auditioned so many times and lost the part so many times, I was able to deal with rejection fairly well. There is only a certain percentage of the hiring/interviewing process that you can control. A rejection is not a rejection of you personally—in acting it could be your hair color or your height—in business it could be what school you went to or something that got mentioned in someone else's interview. You need to separate yourself from what you perceive as "rejection." You can't let rejection letters keep you from sending out the next letter or looking confident for the next interview. I was always able to do this because I understood that companies hire confident, capable people. *Lesson:* Always play the part.

How I got my job:

I wasn't even looking for a consulting job, but it was geographically right and because I was having difficulty finding a straight marketing job, I began to spread my net a little wider. *Lesson:* Don't limit yourself to job titles or industries—look also at the skill set required. Since consulting looks for a broad set of skills and generally requires the ability to think on your feet and be flexible, this seemed like a possible match. I already had a story and a set of skills/experience that I would bring up during an interview for a product management job, but you need to tailor each interview based on the culture of company and the kind of skills they are looking for. Yes, it's a lot of work. Yes, you have to do it.

While I didn't completely abandon the story I generally told to bridge what might be an experience gap in the interviewer's mind, I did something drastically different for the consulting interview. I presented them with a "case"—a project I had done at a previous company (with names changed to protect the innocent). I set it up as a problem to be solved, showed them the process I went through to solve it, and finally told them the conclusions I had drawn based on the information I had gotten. This enabled me to show them a problem-solving process that could be applied to any problem. *Lesson:* Don't be afraid to take risks. Interviewing is something you get better at—try different things. And always have a debriefing with yourself afterwards. What did I do well? What could I have done better? Did I talk about the kinds of things that would be meaningful to the interviewer? Don't dwell on the negative—everyone makes mistakes, but not everyone can learn from them.

One final note on interviewing. Don't try to be someone or something you are not simply because you think that is what they are looking for. Even if they tell you they are looking for XYZ, it may not be true—they may not know what they're looking for. The best policy is to bring out the parts of your past/experience that are relevant. Trying to be something you aren't will ring false and snag you up in the long run.

Now that I'm here . . .

A small consulting firm is nice in some ways:

- Informality.
- Opportunity to make yourself valuable quickly.
- High visibility.

And it's difficult in other ways:

- Lack of role definition, processes, and responsibilities.
- Lack of formal training, wheel spinning.
- Small structure can make elevation within company take too long.
- No one to pick up slack.
- Business practice very personality dependent.

Lessons:

Treat each job as a learning experience whether or not you intend to stay there long, build skills, industry knowledge, and confidence and learn from everything and everyone. Also:

- Get contacts/make allies.
- Ask more/better questions to get clarity if it is lacking.
- Record key learnings, how it could be done better next time.
- Keep other people in the loop/keep yourself in the loop.
- Stay flexible.
- Manage your managers.

▶ Matthew Siegel is an Associate with Booz Allen & Hamilton. He received his BS in Chemistry from Ursinus College in 1985 and his MPPM from Yale School of Management in 1994.

What is your current employment?

I joined Booz Allen & Hamilton in the Energy and Chemicals Group (ECG) in New York City as an Associate.

What was your career target upon graduation?

I was focused on the private sector, specifically management consulting to the energy industry. My key criteria for a target consulting firm were the opportunities to work on top-level strategy assignments, build transferable skills, participate in novel projects, and work with talented colleagues. The top priorities were the type of work, talented colleagues, and geographical assignment (i.e., the East).

What helped you determine your career target?

My career has leveraged off my energy background. Also, I interviewed Yale and MIT alumni at Booz Allen & Hamilton about my industry interests. My ultimate test was to ask first-year hires to recount their experiences.

What did you decide were the most important success factors in your career search and how did you identify these qualities?

I needed to have an understanding of a target company and what I could bring to the organization. Also, I needed the ability to problem solve in an unstructured environment. My information resources included publications on the field (e.g., *Harvard Business School Guide to Management Consulting*) to understand company differences. Also, I used personal contacts to expand on written themes, to discuss alternatives, and to help prepare for case interviews. I identified target organizations from my personal networks. I reviewed published references as homework prior to calling my personal network.

What special tips do you have for writing cover letters?

I think that a cover letter should introduce a resume by simplifying what you intend to offer the company, the qualities you expect the company to value and need. Key tests include (1) substance—can my accomplishments be measured (e.g., led three-member team to identify and capture $3 million in cost savings in 6 months) and (2) style—Have I answered the questions, "Why am I writing; what do I have to offer, and when will I contact the reader?"

How do you recommend preparing for an employment interview?

Conduct extensive literature searches and integrate this information with inputs from counselors, professors, and alumni on what target companies seek. Prepare responses to these inquires: (1) Tell me about where you have been and where you see yourself heading; (2) describe how you led change; and (3) take me through an example of how you dealt with failure.

What appeals to you the most and the least about your present work?

I like the "cutting edge" assignments with increasing levels of responsibility. However, I am concerned about the high level of turnover in the profession.

What additional tips on job search would you give a graduating MBA?

Be focused on a few areas and a few companies and be flexible if your top choice does not work out. Be sure to leverage your personal networks. Finally, prepare for case interviews and make contacts with people within your target companies.

▶ Andrew Zorn was the Software Development Manager at Christie's Inc. from 1992 until 1996, when this survey was completed. He is currently at Johnson & Higgins as a Project Manager in software development. He received a BA from Vassar College in 1984 and an MBA from New York University Stern School of Business in 1992.

What do you do on the job? Describe a typical day.

Although currently they call me the software development manager, my previous title as project manager is probably more accurate. Software development managers are usually senior programmers; I do very little programming myself at this job.

I analyze business procedures and recommend changes to increase efficiency. I often recommend information systems to help automate procedures, but sometimes efficiency can be increased just by updating procedures. I support all areas of the auction business, the specialist departments (e.g., Modern and Impressionist Painting, European Furniture), and the administrative departments (e.g., Finance, Customer Service, Saleroom Crew).

On a typical day, I receive calls about PC-based systems that need troubleshooting or an upgrade. Upgrades usually become necessary as staff use their systems and see ways that the systems could be enhanced. I also support several minicomputer-based, multi-user systems: one tracks the property here for auction; one tracks our client base, their address(es) and interests; and one handles our catalogue subscriptions. For the central systems, I analyze users' needs, review them with other users in our offices worldwide, and design systems solutions that are programmed at group headquarters in London. I monitor the progress of programming in London and report back to the staff in New York. When I am doing my job well, I help prioritize programming projects to make sure the most important needs are met first.

I also take time to develop long-term systems growth. I analyze new technologies for possible application here and I design systems that will greatly alter the way we process information. I support the current systems, put out fires, keep users educated about systems changes, and in the long run attempt to re-engineer the systems to develop a more cost-effective organization.

Who is part of your team?

I have one staff member (recently added), who assists in systems analysis, design, and implementation for a few PC-based projects. Most of my other teams are ad hoc and are composed of cross-functional groups pulled together to complete a specific project.

What part of your day is spent doing what?

Writing	15 percent
Analyzing	25 percent
Phone	15 percent
Meetings	25 percent
Problem solving/support	20 percent

What are three things that make a great project manager?

1. Ability to manage a diverse group of people involved in a project, none of whom you have direct authority over. This takes a tremendous amount of listening and negotiation.

2. Ability to work on several projects at once, monitoring their progress and pushing them forward when necessary. This takes time-management skills and the ability to decide between delegating a task or taking the initiative and doing a task yourself. You cannot do all the tasks yourself, but often you have to know that no one else will do them and you have stick to them until they are done.

3. Ability to see the big picture and ensure that all projects are moving toward the ultimate goal. This is why you can't do all the smaller tasks yourself. Of course, you have to define that ultimate goal if it hasn't already been defined.

What do you like best and least about your present job, including pitfalls, challenges, and rewards?

The best part of my job is when the analysis of business problems leads to the design of a computer system and to changes in business and systems procedures that improve the way people do their job. When a staff member says that the enhancement I have worked hard to ensure was designed correctly and implemented, with proper warning and training, was good, there is no better feeling. It is the classic satisfaction that comes from a job well done. There are lots of hurdles to overcome before you get there, but if you do it right, it is all worth it.

What I like least about my job is working with people who cannot or will not specify exactly what improvements they want. It is a common pitfall in information systems to have end-users who know that the "system" should work better but cannot articulate how. I do not mind attempting to draw out from them what improvements they would like (it's my job after all), but when they expect me to be able to discern with any degree of accuracy how a system should better suit their needs without them telling me, it is very frustrating indeed.

Is there growth potential or compensation potential?

The growth potential is somewhat limited because this is a small company and is not really expanding in any new directions. Growth only becomes available when someone leaves. Compensation potential is available, but it is very dependent on the art market.

How does your position affect your after-work life?

People I meet in social situations think it must be an interesting job and often ask detailed questions about the auction business. The fact that I am in computers seems to take some of the mystique out of the job though; most people are more interested in the glamour of the art specialist side.

The deadlines that I work under and the systems I support cause, I am sorry to say, more sleepless nights and anxious weekends than they should for me to properly spend time with my family.

What do you hope to achieve with your work?

A satisfied end-user community, able to either process more work in the same amount of time or add more value to the work they do because of adequately designed, programmed, implemented, and supported computer systems.

How were you able to obtain your current position? What steps led you to it?

My career counselor at Stern sent my resume to Christie's the day Christie's sent a job listing to the Office of Career Development at Stern. I had previously worked in a nonprofit arts organization and have a BA in Art History. It seemed to my counselor that I was a good match for Christie's.

I made it a priority to get to know my Career Counselor at Stern, and my counselor was always available and made every effort to remember me and my interests.

In all honesty, I wanted to get out of the arts and was interested in working in information systems at a larger organization, but Christie's had a place for a liaison between end-users and programmers, and I had defined that as a general goal for what I wanted to do.

What is your career history, or prior work experience?

Before business school, I worked for three years at a nonprofit organization in Washington, DC, the International Sculpture Center. It is a membership organization for sculptors, and I ran a computerized database and referral system (complete with images) to match sculptors with people seeking to purchase or place sculpture. Before that, for about a year, I was an office manager for an organization that offers training in management, communications, and systems for individuals from developing countries who are studying in the United States. During the two years before that, I was a bartender in Chicago, and before that I was in college.

How did your education impact your career?

I have a BA in art history. Though this background is actually unnecessary to do my job, I am sure it helped me get the job, so it has had a profound impact. Also, it does help a little bit to have an appreciation for what the company sells, but it's not like any specialist asks for my opinion on the art.

The MBA I received has had a very profound impact. Not only was it a selling point when I was interviewing, but I use the knowledge I gained in systems, organizational behavior, operations, and statistics every day. The classes I took in Finance also help because I support a variety of financial systems, but I am not actually required to do any accounting. The case studies I read have kept me from repeating some previously documented mistakes (though I have had to learn many for myself). The experience I gained in management communication classes is called on often, mostly for informal presentations, but in more stressful circumstances as well. I often wish there were more MBA-trained people in Systems here; an MBA provides an overview that many technical people don't get to see as they plug away at the latest systems fix.

How did your interest in this field originate?

My interest in this field originated in a computer course in college. I never thought I'd focus my work on computers, but I always wanted to keep my hand in the field. I supported all of the computer applications at the International Sculpture Center and found I had an aptitude for it. Stern's strong information systems department kept my interest high.

Working closely with a variety of people, working with liberally educated people, and having the ability to see a project through from theory to implementation were all factors that attracted me to my present career.

What skills do you use the most in your career?

I mostly use diplomacy and negotiation. I often work with irritated end-users, training them, explaining the time frame for computer enhancements they have requested, and suggesting alternative ways of doing their business.

I use management skills to motivate both the information systems department staff and the staff involved in the projects I oversee. I use management skills to delegate authority, mediate disputes, and listen to and solve problems.

I use technical skills to determine whether systems solutions are possible and/or affordable. For most technical know-how, I rely on staff members who work with me; that leads back to the management skills I have to use.

What pieces of advice you would like to share with someone contemplating this kind of career?

- Learn to work with a team.
- Take criticism as it is meant. Have a thick skin when necessary.

- Always be willing to be fired for doing the right thing.
- Don't let the fact that information is on a computer make you responsible for how people use the computer. Just as people are responsible for keeping their pencils sharpened and their writing skills honed, they are responsible for backing-up PC data, keeping it current, keeping it consistent and using it appropriately. You can't end up doing someone's job for them just because they use a computer system you support.

What do you see as trends in your industry?

The biggest trend is our attempt to get items to auction in a more efficient, less expensive way. The auction business thrives on customer service, but too many times low value lots get the same high service treatment as the very expensive lots.

Other trends include utilizing digital imaging, utilizing bar coding, and employing a greater degree of statistical analysis of the business.

What do people need to know to get into this field? What are the most important skills to have?

The most important skills are still technical skills. To really go places in the information systems field a knowledge of programming languages, database applications, communication technology, networking, and client-server implementation will make you a hot ticket. I am not very technical by comparison, and I see it as very difficult to find a place as a business systems analyst without strong technical skills. In fact, most companies seem to leave the business analysis as a low priority. It takes a very enlightened company to see that you need to do more than just throw technology at a problem.

How can someone get your job?

To get my job, you have to present yourself as technically literate and also experienced in dealing with end-users. You have to be able to communicate to nontechnical people, present solutions to their problems (not always systems solutions), be patient with them, be responsive to them and be available for them.

What motivates you to do what you do?

Good question. I have to admit that money is still a big motivation for me. I am not yet paid so much that salary has become somewhat removed from my motivation (as I imagine could happen).

Aside from that, I am glad to be in a field that is still growing and I find computers fascinating not so much for what they can do but in a way for what they can't. I like working with people to find out how to best use the power in a PC, often much of the power going unused. I like getting a sense of how computing has changed jobs and how it hasn't. I like developing personal theories of technology in the workplace. I don't think the PC has yet changed jobs that much and I wonder if it ever will. The computer industry has promised a lot and not delivered on most of it if you ask me.

A PC user has to bring a fair amount of background and knowledge to be effective with most tools. It is kind of like the contemporary art we sometimes sell. You are expected to bring a lot to the artwork, such as knowledge of art history or experience with the artist, and without that it can appear to be pretty worthless. My motivation comes from trying to get the most from technology we have.

What are similar areas in this field that people might consider?

I have begun to think that what I do might be placed outside of the systems area in other companies. Similar areas in my field might be planning, operations, or even finance. Some places might have a position like mine defined as end-user support, but not on the telephone hot line.

What is your favorite quote?

I don't think I have one. When I read this question I thought of "Luck comes to those who are prepared," but I don't say that a lot, just some advice once given to me during a job search.

Any pearls of wisdom for people with similar aspirations?

Shore up your technical skills. They can get you in the door, then you can move into analysis and project management.

What do you see as the most challenging issues in your industry?

The auction business is going to have to face doing business more efficiently. It can no longer survive running as a country club and a "gentleman's profession." Though who you know will always be very important when it comes to selling important art works, the volume of middle-priced and lower-priced items we bring to sale has to be processed more efficiently.

Where do you derive your inspiration?

From my wife, my two daughters, and my son.

Where do you see job growth in your field?

Networking and telecommunications.

Where do you see yourself in 5 to 10 years?

I don't know; time is going by so fast these days. Perhaps overseeing the operations of a medium-sized organization, perhaps art or artistically related (museum, publishing house, television station).

What are the key points in your answer to the question "Why hire me for my ideal job?"

- I can communicate to both technical and nontechnical people in a way that makes them both comfortable.
- I can get tasks done, I don't get bogged down in analysis and I don't let implementation hurdles (like reluctant staff) kill a project.
- I have leadership and management skills and experience.
- I have experience supporting PC and multi-user systems in financial, operational, and administrative areas.
- I bring a positive attitude to work every day.

Who participated in the employment process for your job and what were their roles?

A recruiter from Christie's human resources department got my resume from my career counselor. She interviewed me for a position in the operations department (business analysis regarding sale scheduling, overseeing the crew that sets-up art viewings and sales, for example) for which she advertised, but I mentioned I was more interested in business analysis in the information systems area.

I was interviewed two subsequent times by the Director of Information Systems and the Director of Operations. After talking to them, I said I was more interested in an information systems job.

I was later interviewed by the head of Information Systems Worldwide, who was in town. He approved my hire, but because it was not the position advertised for, Christie's Group Human Resources had to approve the additional head count.

After the job offer, there was some salary negotiation and then my wife and I decided to accept.

If you wanted people to understand your profession, what would you want them to know?

That computers are neither the cure for all ills nor the cause of all problems. The promise of computer technology is that over time, very redundant, mind-numbing tasks can be reduced or eliminated and done very quickly by a computer. Getting the task done right by a machine takes a lot of time and planning. During that development time, it will certainly appear that a computer is causing all the problems and, no matter how well the development goes, the act of human creative thinking will not be replaced by a machine. Even if they can get one to play chess, active, rational, creative, and multipurpose thinking by a machine is a long, long way off.

What other thoughts would you like to share?

I think real success is defined by being able to have a career that is rewarding enough to you personally, a difficult thing to define (e.g., it gives you pride, it gives you happiness or, it allows you to express yourself) and allows you to live a lifestyle that is comfortable to you, which again, is different for each person.

For example, if an artist is driven to create art every day but cannot sustain a comfortable lifestyle even if his or her definition of comfort does not involve a lot of material goods, then that artist is not successful. If an artist can sell enough art to sustain the level of comfort he or she seeks, that is a successful artist, even if the works are not in a museum.

Money is important, but shouldn't be mistaken for the only measure of success (unless your concept of a comfortable lifestyle consists of many cars and homes). It is important to keep life in perspective, to balance other aspects and to try to be one of the lucky ones who doesn't simply slog through the work week and live for the weekends. If that isn't too heavily sappy, I think it's a pretty good closing comment.

FINDING YOUR WAY IN FINANCIAL SERVICES

There is an amazing variety of jobs in financial services. In investments, there are opportunities in both the buy and sell sides as manager or analyst. There are large "department store" firms and small "boutique" firms. There are specialized transactional services and opportunities to be involved in strategic planning and marketing within the sector. Equally diverse are the backgrounds of the people entering the field of financial services, including many with nonbusiness, nontechnical undergraduate backgrounds. Certain personal attributes are unique to each type of work. Also, persistent, continuing networking is the key element in the job search. The profiles that follow display the diversity of both opportunities and backgrounds in addition to the demands in this sector.

▶ Janet Cochoff is an Assistant Vice President with Coutts & Co. AG. She received her BBA from Kent State University in 1990 and her MBA from New York University Stern School of Business in 1996.

What do you do on the job? Describe a typical day.

A typical day on the job begins with a thorough reading of the *Wall Street Journal* and Bloomberg News Services to discover what is new in the world and what I missed while sleeping last night. My position is heavily dependent on knowing what is happening in the world and determining how events translate into stock market performance. My days are spent talking to brokers, analysts, and company management trying to get an angle on a company that no one else has discovered. I spend time reviewing annual reports and Wall Street research reports learning everything I can about the fundamentals of the companies that we are invested in currently or are considering as a future investment. I do not concentrate on any specific industry, which makes my job both exciting and crazy at times. Every day I sit in front of my Bloomberg terminals and watch my client portfolios trade and try to find points of entry and exit in stocks. I also spend time visiting company management and sitting with analysts either in private meetings or broker-sponsored conferences.

How were you able to obtain this position? What steps led you to this?

I was able to obtain my current position because I had a strong background working at bulge bracket firms doing equity analysis. I thought

I needed an MBA to obtain a position as an analyst on the buy-side, but looking back, I think Coutts would have hired me without one. However, I do believe that the MBA did help me negotiate a higher status and bonus.

What is your career history or prior work experience?

My first "real" job as an undergraduate was at The First Boston Corporation as a Research Associate covering companies in the specialty chemicals industry. The job entailed a lot of grunt work, but I did learn a lot and it was my first exposure to the antics of Wall Street. I remember my first week at First Boston when about five people left the firm for another. I was a little surprised and worried until I realized that this happens quite often. I also learned at First Boston that you really have to get aggressive to get anywhere in this business. Not necessarily pushy aggressive, but you have to be determined to get what you want.

After a little over a year, I moved to Salomon Brothers as a junior analyst covering the same industry. I was still considering this business as a life-long career, and the position at Salomon afforded me more exposure, more money, and someone to answer my phones! I learned at Salomon that things are pretty much the same wherever you go, and you still have to deal with bureaucratic nonsense, but I was much better prepared this time! The most important lesson I learned from my experience at Salomon Brothers was that I did not want to be a research analyst following one industry. I was getting a little bored with specialty chemicals and decided that my personality was better suited for a little more variety.

While at Salomon, I had the good fortune to work for a great manager who supported my decision to begin graduate work at New York University while continuing to work. I admit it was a little stressful at times for both of us, but I was able to acquire an MBA in just over two years while maintaining a respectable salary. I was also able to determine what I wanted to become when I grew up and I was able to chat with our clients and others within the bank about my job search.

What is your favorite aspect of this job? Least favorite?

There is no feeling like the one when you make a call on a stock, commit money to it, and watch it skyrocket! Everyone in this business will have the same answer. On the sell side, analysts make recommendations and convince their clients to buy or sell stocks. They are one step removed from the investment process. But on the buy side, we have to take the plunge on a stock and every day we are put to the test by watching it either go up or down in the market. It can be a very gratifying and—at the same time—a humbling experience.

What do people need to know to get into this field? What are the most important skills to have?

People need to keep in mind that there are many ways to get a job managing money. I work with people who have very diverse backgrounds. Some have liberal arts degrees, some have business degrees, some have MBAs and some do not. It may be a lot easier to get a job as an analyst with a business degree, but it does not necessarily mean that the person with a major in history is shut out of the recruiting process. The most important skills to have are logic, natural curiosity and skepticism, and good judgment as well as a firm grasp of numbers. It also pays to be an abstract thinker. The best way to make money is to go against the tide and make a call no one else was able to see.

What motivates you to do what you do?

The motivation I have is the challenge of the market and money. I enjoy buying a stock for my clients and making money for them. The market is constantly challenging and a day does not go by when I am not second-guessing myself on a recommendation. The challenge is being able to continuously justify owning a stock when its performance is telling you otherwise. And the most rewarding aspect of the job is when the stock you have been buying all the way down is finally turning around and becomes your best performing investment.

What are the three most important things that make a great portfolio manager?

Three things that make a great portfolio manager are good judgment, patience, and confidence. The good judgment enables you to take numerous sources of information (i.e., analyst reports, newspaper articles, and discussions with management) and determine the best course of action. Patience is key when you watch the market and try to time entry and exit points for stocks. Sometimes, you may think a stock is oversold and hastily step in to purchase shares, but it sells off even further as more negative news is distributed. Each stock tends to trade differently and after spending some time watching the trading patterns and looking at charts, you can begin to understand it much better. Confidence is perhaps the most important quality of a good portfolio manager. Confidence will let you pull the trigger on a stock or sell when the tide seems to be going against you. It will also help when you have to explain to your clients why their portfolios are not always out-performing the benchmarks.

How did your interest in this field originate?

I received my BA at Kent State University and my MBA at New York University. Each school was at opposite ends of the spectrum! At Kent State, I had an exceptional investments professor, Dr. Alan Twark, who taught us practical applications of theory in the stock market. Dr. Twark was an extremely successful investment manager and was able to bring a wealth of knowledge to his students. I enjoyed his classes immensely and decided that investment management was the field that I wanted to pursue upon graduation. So, for me, my undergraduate education was the reason that I entered the investment field at all.

How did you choose your graduate program?

When I applied to New York University, I knew that I wanted to stay in the field and that I wanted to take my career from the research side to the portfolio management side. I chose NYU because it was the only top-tier university in New York that offered a part-time MBA program. I wanted to add a more prestigious university to my resume while maintaining full-time employment. Part-time education is not the answer for everyone, but it made the most sense for me. I already had a job that most students were praying to have after graduation and I did not want to give that up for a little extra time on the weekend. The best thing about going to school and working is that you actually can apply what you learn in class to your job and vice versa. It was extremely rewarding and I think I learned by being able to put my just-acquired knowledge to work every day at the office.

What are similar areas in this field that people might consider?

There are so many ways to be involved in the stock market without actually managing investments. I spent several years working at First Boston and Salomon Brothers doing equity research where I was involved in the market, but not in the actual investment decision. In equity research, you have a narrow focus on one industry and you become an expert in the industry and in the companies within it. As a sell-side analyst, you make recommendations to investment managers to buy or sell the stock, but you are not involved in the final decision. Sell-side analysts can do extremely well once they attract a loyal following of clients; however, because of the nature of the business, they burn out quite young and many eventually become portfolio managers. The sell-side analyst is required to know all the nitty-gritty details on each company, whereas the portfolio manager is responsible for companies in many different industries and will have a broader knowledge. Because of this, the portfolio manager is somewhat reliant on the expertise of the sell-side analyst and will seek out the best analysts on the Street for information.

Rather than becoming a portfolio manager, some people opt to remain investment analysts. Buy-side analysts work closely with the sell-side analysts and make recommendations to portfolio managers. The buy-side analyst and portfolio manager are within the same firm. I always thought this was redundant because the buy-side analyst is often receiving the same information from the sell-side analyst that the portfolio manager can receive, so I sometimes fail to see the value added. I look at a buy-side analyst position as a step toward becoming a portfolio manager and would recommend that if you want to be a true analyst and have no interest in managing money, then you should pursue opportunities on the sell-side.

Who is part of your team?

We have a small investment department in the United States. Coutts is a much more well-known entity in Europe, especially in London, and our entire organization in New York is roughly 200 employees. I work closely with four individuals: a senior portfolio manager, two portfolio administrators, and a trader. Between us, we set North American equity policy for all of Coutts worldwide. In other words, we develop and maintain forecasts for the overall market, which are then communicated to the other regions and translated into several different portfolio structures. We also develop and maintain a list of North American equities that we recommend for client portfolios as well as manage our own client portfolios and a mutual fund for offshore clients. All of us have different responsibilities, however. With a group so small and with so much work, these responsibilities often overlap, which makes for an interesting and busy day. That was one of the reasons why I came to Coutts. After working for two large brokerage firms, I was ready to join a small shop that afforded me a lot more responsibility and hands-on experience.

How does your job affect your after-work life?

Fortunately, my position does not cramp my after-work life. My goal for going to business school was to be able to land a position where I did not have to work exhaustive hours and yet could maintain a certain standard of living. I suffered through exams and a full-time job in order to be able to enjoy my life once I graduated. Since the work that I do is so closely tied to the market, the most important hours of the day are from 9:30 A.M. to 4:00 P.M., when the market is open for trading. Therefore, it is extremely important that I am in front of my Bloomberg terminal during those hours. Time spent doing my other work, such as reading reports and talking to analysts and company management, is up to my discretion. I really do not have anyone looking over my shoulder counting the research reports I have read or how many hours I have spent on the telephone.

I believe that one can spend 14 hours of the day working, but more than likely that person is not very productive or not a good manager of time. I am a firm believer in a good mix of both work and play. Some people on Wall Street will tell you that you have to pay your dues by spending night after night working at the office. You may reach the next level sooner, but you will likely burn out faster and have no fun in the meantime!

What resources did you use to identify specific job leads in your industry?

I began my career search during my last year at New York University. I took advantage of the Career Development Office to interview with the large companies that were coming to campus. I signed up for anything that sounded remotely interesting and was very open-minded about my search. I was pretty sure about the type of position I wanted, but I did not want to rule anything out. On my own, I targeted clients with whom I had dealt while at Salomon to get their advice on companies and to seek out opportunities. I looked within Salomon as well to find out about any training programs that were available.

The funny thing is that I eventually found my position through a headhunter! Never believe all those people who tell you not to use a headhunter. A friend of mine put me in touch with this individual after he had called her for an interview. I figured that I had nothing to lose and I was not overwhelmed with any position I had been offered thus far, so I called. I accepted an interview with a company I had never heard of before. I never turned down an interview for any reason because I believe that with each interview you improve your skills and presentation. So, I walked into this interview with very low expectations and ended up finding out about an extremely interesting opportunity. The most important things to keep in mind when looking for a job are to be open-minded and creative and to network. Someone looking for a job in this business should read all the trade journals and look for potential contacts. The *Wall Street Journal* and *Barrons* have articles regularly featuring analysts and portfolio managers discussing their views.

I would stay away from the easily recognizable names and focus on the less well-known. These people will have more time to talk to you and they will be flattered that you noticed their name. *Nelson's* is another directory of brokerage firms and leading analysts at these firms, and *Institutional Investor* publishes frequent surveys that rank analysts.

How would you summarize your reasons for applying for your job at this particular company?

I originally applied for the position because the description sounded ideal. I honestly knew nothing about the company. I learned enough basic facts to have a clue when I went on the interview, but I was hoping to learn a lot more by speaking to others at the firm. The more I learned about the firm, the more I became excited about the opportunity. Coutts is a well-known entity in Europe, especially in London where it is head-quartered. It is the private banking division of National Westminster and its claim to fame is that it is the bank of the Royal Family. Coutts is a private bank providing a slew of services to extremely high net-worth individuals. The company had been in the United States for less than three years and the strategy was to grow the business here.

The investment management department was small and I was able to meet with everyone. I had gone through several interviews with the senior managers and I was asked back to speak with everyone in the department. I highly recommend this for anyone interviewing. It is the best way to get a feel for the group and the organization. I knew that because the group was small, coming from a larger organization might be frustrating, but the energy I got from everyone made me forget the shortcomings. I was sold on the position because of its entrepreneurial nature. I wanted to be part of a growing organization and I had enough big company experience that I was ready for a change.

What other thoughts would you like to share?

I was at a business lunch with a new salesperson and we were starting with the usual "getting to know you" chat. It turned out that this individual was a recent business school graduate and previously an insurance salesman. I asked him why he became an equity salesperson after business school. His response was that he always wanted to be in the business, but didn't get into it sooner because he didn't go to a prestigious undergraduate college and he didn't know anyone. I couldn't help but think that this was such a lame answer. I went to Kent State, which is a wonderful university—but hardly a top-ten college, and I didn't know a soul on Wall Street. And I can bet that there are a lot of successful people in this business with similar backgrounds. Don't think that you are automatically counted out because of your non-ivy league education. Firms aren't looking for people who are just well educated. They want creative, talented, unusual people who can grow. It may be a little more challenging to break into a business where you have no contacts, but if you are creative and persistent enough, it is not impossible.

▶ Kathryn A. Cornish is an Associate at Smith Barney Inc. in the investment banking division. She received her BA in Political Theory from Villanova University in 1992 and her MBA from New York University Stern School of Business in 1996.

As background, what is your employment outline since graduation?

Associate in the Financial Institutions Group at Smith Barney Inc.

How would you define your career target at the time you were completing your MBA? What were the sector groups within sector, functional area, and other key criteria?

I had entered business school looking for a job in investment banking but I was open to different coverage group opportunities. I wanted to be at a bank where I would build a strong foundation of experience on which to build a career. I wanted to work with bankers who were willing to take the time to teach me what I did not know, and who seemed ready to let me use the skills I already had. To me that meant a firm with a large enough banking effort that junior employees would be given both formal and informal mentoring and yet a firm which was still growing so that I would get client experience quickly.

How did you identify your ideal career? What experiences, tips, contacts, and other sources were most helpful?

Prior to my time at Stern and at Smith Barney, I worked for Sullivan Marketing, a start-up venture that marketed, produced, and distributed Free Standing Inserts (FSIs) for over 370 newspapers nationwide. This job was a priceless experience. The job offered endless opportunity to have an impact largely because my job description was _not_ restrictive. Everyone had to pitch in to get even the most basic of tasks accomplished. There was one main phone and everyone answered it. One of my favorite memories was the day we got the A/B switch so we could print from more than one computer. A year and a number of successful distributions later we had put a stake in the ground as the first start-up in the sector to have actually made it to press. The company had grown from 13 people when I started to over 60 people and four offices. Then the real challenge began. Could the firm get past the start-up stage and continue to compete against the established competition? We survived for another year on funds received from a Morgan Stanley merchant banking fund. A year later found the firm bleeding cash and alternative means of funding drying up. Morgan Stanley chose to sell while they could and in 72 hours we went from reading rumors about a sale in the _Wall Street Journal_ to watching an announcement of the sale come over the wire. The Sullivan Marketing dream was over. Most people will never understand how crushing a blow it is to have something you worked so hard to build just sold from under you. That whole experience really taught me a lot about what it is like to be part of a small company with limited resources and a good idea. It takes capital and a strong financial structure for that company to really be able to survive.

How did you decide what key qualities and competitive edges you needed to offer to employers for your ideal career? What published information, special events, and personal contacts were most helpful?

When I was younger all I had to offer an employer was blind ambition. Ambition can get you further than most people give it credit for but at some point you need to be able to offer a real skill set. So I set out to learn which skills most people categorize as part of an investment banker's "tool-kit." I started by talking to people who work with investment bankers (accountants, lawyers) to get an outside view of what an investment banker "looks like." Then I started to talk to investment bankers themselves. During that time I was in business school, so I did a lot of digging into what my fellow classmates knew or had learned from their job searches. Without a doubt, while career resources that describe corporate finance are helpful, these conversations were the best source of information.

How did you identify target organizations for your ideal career? Beyond campus interviews and job postings to the hidden job market, what sources did you use to select target organizations in that market?

My hidden job market search involved developing a personal network of people at all different firms that I could call to ask questions. I did not have a very strong personal network on Wall Street before I started this search but I have a fairly strong one now and I think that is testimony to getting out and just introducing yourself to people while not wasting their time. I received a fairly supportive response from almost everyone I talked to, which was encouraging since only half of them were alumni of Stern who might have felt obligated to give me that response. In addition to talking to people, I have to say that while it sounds cliché, reading pop-fiction stories and biographies about Wall Street gave me some insight into the unwritten rules of interacting with people on Wall Street.

What advice do you have for writing cover letters and resumes, including the tips on substance and style that you found most useful?

Cover letters should say something meaningful. While it is important to highlight some key elements in the attached resume, there is no need to list in a cover letter the accomplishments that are going to be reviewed in the resume itself. I had a nontypical cover letter because I had a unique background. I needed to highlight reasons people should even consider taking the time to talk to me, so I set my letter up to drive home three important points. The key to a good cover letter is to show creativity while staying within the guidelines of appropriate behavior for the sector or industry you are searching for a job in.

What special tips do you have for preparing for employment interviews? What were the three or four major questions from your prospective employers?

The key to interviewing is to have three to four points to make and drive them home. Do not go off on tangents that cannot be pulled back to one of your points. Do everything within reason to close the loop for people so they understand why those selected points make you the best candidate for the job. By exploring what it is that the employer is looking for, you will be able to figure out whether you really fit the desired profile. That will help you choose the skills you have that match best.

What do you like best and least about your current work?

I love the challenge. I am one of those people who strives to excel at everything I do. I am driven crazy when I can be good at what I do without much effort. There is always something to learn at this job. Every transaction seems to have some new twist that requires learning a new subset of detail you have not previously explored. What I like least is the inability to walk away. There is always something to do and you rarely can walk away for the evening without feeling like there are loose ends. Also, I do not like the time commitment that is required. There is no one who does this job, no matter how long they have been doing it or at what point in their career they are, who is not making significant sacrifices in their personal life in order to excel in their professional life.

What spiritual beliefs or principles govern your career thinking and how have these factors affected your choice of career and your approach to professional progression?

Things don't come to those who sit around and wait for them to happen. People who work hard and challenge themselves and those around them make things happen. That is the closest thing to a professional or life mission I have. As for guiding beliefs, I believe no job defines a person. This job takes a lot of dedication and requires personal sacrifice. At the same time I do not believe I have to become the "stereotypical" investment banker in order to keep this job. You just have to learn to carefully balance what is important to you personally and professionally.

Reflecting on all your work experience to date, what additional tips might you have on career selection and search for graduating MBAs?

MBA program graduates should realize that they are being given a unique opportunity to choose what they are going to do with their lives. An MBA not only opens doors but it gives you two years to decide which one to walk through. Most people never get the chance to reflect on who they want to be and what they want to do with their lives. My advice is to take full advantage of the time, ask questions and learn as much as you can. Once you start to work full-time again, you lose the luxury of an objective viewpoint and life takes on a more narrow perspective.

▶ Eric Gelb is a Vice President of Citicorp Securities, Inc. He received his BS in Economics from the University of Pennsylvania in 1984 and his MBA from Columbia Business School in 1989.

What is your employment history since graduation?

After completing my MBA, I joined my present employer as an associate in the leasing and project finance group. Currently, I am a vice president and senior transactor in the group and have worked at this company for the entire eight years since graduation. I worked in the leasing group for seven years in total. During my fourth year, I entered the firm's Institute for Global Finance (five months) and spent the other seven months in the private placement (debt distribution) group.

How would you define your career target at the time you were completing your MBA?

Initially, I was interested in starting my own business. Accordingly, I tailored my resume to reflect an entrepreneurial spirit, and I was seeking an entrepreneurial/functional position instead of a skills-oriented position. This goal is a departure from the traditional corporate employment route that is the thrust of the school. This path was a mistake because it is difficult to find such a position. I interviewed with the small business consulting groups at Deloitte & Touche and Coopers & Lybrand, but did not receive a job offer. As graduation approached, I regrouped and sought a position in corporate finance and was fortunate to land a position with my present employer.

How has your thinking proceeded in seeking an ideal career?

Over time, I have developed a better sense of myself and my skills and interests. In particular, I find I am very good at originating and structuring transactions. In addition, I have written several books on personal finance (i.e., *Personal Budget Planner, Checkbook Management,* and *The Ten Minute Guide to Understanding Annual Reports & Prospectuses*). After these books were published, I became more and more interested in wealth building and managing money. I considered a career switch. I suggest that the best way to find your ideal career is to focus on your interests first and then skills. I find that the most successful people love their jobs. It is worthwhile to read as much as possible (i.e., books, magazines, and newspapers) to see which topics interest you the most. Then, contact people in your network (i.e., alumni, church, club) to learn about their careers, continuing to seek what interests you.

What did you decide were the key success factors in your target career and how did you identify these factors?

In my case, my books and financial planning lectures led me to the realization that I thought I wanted to pursue a career in money management and investments. As I began networking, I realized that there were a number of important qualifications: curiosity, financial statement (accounting) skills, understanding of business, analytical abilities, and drive. I read a tremendous amount of material on companies and investing. Personal contacts, alumni, and peers were most helpful in giving me feedback and insights. These resources helped me to hone my story and to play up my important relevant skills. However, after going on a number of informational interviews, it became clear to me that such a career switch was not feasible. First, such a switch would have meant starting from scratch. And, the common point of entry was as a "sell-side" analyst, which did not interest me.

How did you select your target organization?

In some cases, I have contacted companies who are mentioned in the financial press. Whenever possible, I have contacted companies through personal contacts (e.g., friends of friends). Personal contacts and referrals seem to work best, especially with a career switch. Most important, I suggest that you pursue all sensible leads.

What tips do you have for writing cover letters?

Cover letters should never exceed one page. I prefer four paragraphs. The first paragraph should be the opener. Ideally, if you can open with a referral or name of a person that the recipient knows, you are ahead of the game. Where I could not do this, I have used a relevant reference. The middle paragraph or two should be the substance. Pick a particular position or program and be as specific and directed as possible. Succinctly and clearly describe why you are interested in the position and why you are qualified. Present a story of why you are qualified for the position based on your work experience and educational background. The fourth paragraph should be the close. I usually write that I will follow up—most people will not call you. Finally, make sure your letter is typed neatly and that there are no spelling or grammatical errors. Production errors are sins in today's era of word processors.

What thoughts do you have about routing communications to prospective employers?

I find that many letters do not reach the desired destination. They get lost or routed to the human resources department, and thus a personal call often gets the applicant and the letter personal attention. Sometimes, it can take three or four attempts to contact the right person. I often call a company's main number and ask the operator to connect me with the person's secretary. In this way, I do not interrupt the person I have written the letter to. Also, you may find that you have to fax your materials to the right person.

What advice would you offer on preparing for employment interviews?

I try to prepare as much as possible, just like studying for a final exam. I read as much as possible on the position, company and industry, and think through my story. I try to get a sense of the interviewer's job, role, and status in the company. I try to anticipate potential questions the interviewers might ask. In particular, I try to develop answers to the "holes" in my background with respect to the target position. In other words, if there is a deficiency in the experience or some other question, such as why you are switching careers, you need a clear and confident response.

What questions should be addressed in getting ready for employment interviews?

I find the most popular questions are as follows:

- Why are you interested in this position?
- How can you demonstrate you are qualified for the job?
- Why did you choose your particular career path and what led you to this point?
- What are your career goals and why do you think this position at this organization will help you attain those goals?
- What other positions and organizations are you considering?
- What else would you do if . . . ?

What are your likes and dislikes about your present work?

I like the responsibility and challenges of my position. As a senior transactor, I am responsible for originating, developing, negotiating, and closing complex corporate finance transactions. I dislike the fact that politics consume a tremendous amount of time and energy.

What advice do you have for MBAs who are switching careers?

If you are using the MBA to facilitate a switch in careers, you should switch as definitively and forcefully as possible. And do it as early as possible. You will need to show commitment to the new field, demonstrate success in the relevant coursework, and land a good internship.

What personal characteristic do you think is most important in the career search process?

Be persistent. Most MBAs are highly qualified professionals. Often the deciding factor in landing the position is persistence and demonstrating that you are keenly interested in the position, more so than your peers. Without being a pest, keep calling your target companies. Positions and opportunities open up a different times, and often, the familiar name gets the job.

What other tips do you have on the career search process?

Overall, it is important to focus on a specific career path, function, and industry as early as possible, perhaps prior to entering business school. Then shape your coursework, extracurricular activities and work experience (i.e., internships and special projects) in that direction. This approach will help you to tell a credible story and to better meet your competition. Also, target your position as early as possible and aggressively network, write cover letters, and so on. If you know what position you want when you enter the MBA program, all the better. If not, do your homework and begin networking right away. Otherwise, you run the risk of floundering and conducting a scatter-shot job search. Thereby, you might or might not realize your fullest potential. It is likely that some of your classmates worked in your target companies and industries prior to business school and can therefore provide useful information and contacts.

▶ Curtis Jensen is an Equity Analyst with the Third Avenue Value Fund (New York). He received a BA in Economics from Williams College in 1984 and a MPPM from Yale School of Management in 1995.

What do you do on the job? Describe a typical day.

I work as an equity analyst for a $1 billion mutual fund and co-manage a second smaller fund. I started in August 1995. I spend my day looking for new investment ideas and monitoring existing positions.

What was your initial career target and how did you establish this target?

I wanted to be in a small shop doing buy-side research. I wanted my job to be an information-based job that I could eventually take anywhere (i.e., so that I could locate myself anywhere). I knew from experience that I did not like to manage people, though I was okay at it. Specifically, running my own business, I learned I did not want to manage a large number of people. With technology and information becoming more important in our economy, I wanted my job to take advantage of those trends. Also, I wanted the potential for geographic mobility in my career. I knew I had to start in New York, where my wife was living.

How did you get started on your job research?

I was lucky. I got a job offer from one of my business school professors, who runs various investment partnerships, a mutual fund and a securities broker/dealer operation. I also looked in unusual places. For example, I saw a tombstone ad for a new investment partnership. Therefore, I reasoned that they might be hiring and faxed my resume and cover letter. They called me!

Going beyond on-campus interviews and job postings, how did you find and follow up on additional opportunities?

I used Internet position postings, job reference books in our business library, and my college alumni network and directory. Based on my experience, I recommend that cover letters be personalized (i.e., to the specific reader and organization). Also, the spelling, grammar, job titles, dates, and the like should be triple checked. When I receive cover letters and resumes now, I throw them out immediately if there is a typo. Also, I suggest to people looking for a research analyst position that they try to make their mark, distinguish themselves— for example, enclosing a piece of written research on a security or industry.

What are the most important tips you have for students on preparing for employment interviews?

Really do your homework. And thereby avoid asking questions that are answered in the organization's annual reports, press releases, and other literature. Think creatively, "outside the box," that is. Be honest about who you are, what you want and why you deserve it. As a foundation, try to talk to people your age at your target organizations or similar organizations.

What do you like best and least about your current work?

As to what I like best, I like the autonomy and entrepreneurial environment. Also, that I work for a small firm with a casual dress code (except when with clients on the outside). My so-called "value-added" in the organization is tangible and quantifiable. I have a clear sense of whether or not I am contributing. As to what I like least, since we are small, I often get asked to wear a lot of different hats outside my core job.

▶ Matt Koob is an Institutional Equity Salesman in the Corporate & Institutional Client Group with Merrill Lynch. He received his BA from Claremont McKenna College in 1989 and his MBA from New York University Stern School of Business in 1994.

What do you do on the job? Describe a typical day.

Entering business school, I had no idea what an institutional equity salesman did. Even as a first year MBA candidate, I wasn't clear on the specifics. My job, by its simple definition, is to sell the vast amounts of global equity research generated by Merrill Lynch, as well as the firm's syndicate transactions (IPOs and add-on offerings). I am also expected to provide seamless coverage with regard to international equity and derivative products. Put simply, I am a relationship manager. While the sales process can take many forms, the following is an example of a "normal" day as an institutional equity salesman at Merrill Lynch.

I typically arrive at the office between 6 and 6:15 A.M. The morning research broadcast begins at 6:45 A.M., so up to that time I read the newspaper and get a feel for what stocks and industries we'll be discussing. The morning call consists of approximately 10 speakers, who discuss individual stocks, industry developments, and macroeconomic events. The level of detail is significant. At the conclusion of the call I have 5 to 10 minutes to determine what is relevant (of the 10 reports, perhaps 2 to 3 are worthy of discussion) and which topics are important to my specific client base. For the next two hours, I am on the telephone with my customers, disseminating the information discussed that morning and adding color and perspective when appropriate. During this two-hour period, we have inevitably received at least one "break-in" call, which consists of an opinion change or earnings revision on a particular stock. This information is communicated to clients in a manner similar to that outlined previously. In addition to marketing the written research of the firm, the salesforce is also responsible for marketing the research analysts themselves. My high priority accounts are located in Michigan, so perhaps three times a month I find myself visiting the accounts with an industry analyst. We meet with industry analysts and portfolio managers, discussing stock recommendations and industry perspectives.

Equity syndicate transactions are very profitable to the firm and are an important part of my job. The typical transaction includes a roadshow, where company management, investment bankers, and the equity salesforce visit targeted accounts and discuss the company and the transaction. The meetings and discussions are very time consuming. The next step is for the account to give me an "indication of interest" or an order. Once all the orders have been received and considered, the equity syndicate desk allocates the shares available to the investment public. This is the most difficult part of my job from a sales relationship and political perspective. Any spare time is spent reading and discussing stock ideas with my fellow salespeople.

How were you able to obtain this position?

To secure my current position, I leveraged relationships that I had developed while working as an intern after my first year of business school. Specifically, a Merrill Lynch salesman recommended to an individual in the human resources department that I be given an interview. At that point, I controlled my own destiny. I had no more help. The initial interview went well and soon I was meeting with members of the New York salesforce. After approximately 30 individual interviews, I was referred to a senior human resources contact, who monitored the availability for equity sales positions on my behalf. It was January of my second year in business school.

For the next three months, I spoke to the contact weekly, only to be told that nothing had come along. In early April I informed my contact that I would be going "over her head" and directly contacting the global head of equity sales. With her blessing, I faxed a letter to the global chief, detailing why he should hire me. The letter was direct and persuasive. The next day I was on a plane to Chicago to interview with the head of the regional sales office. The following morning I was offered a sales position in Chicago. How was I able to obtain my position? Persistence, persistence, persistence. All along, however, I was careful not to become a nuisance to those with whom I was negotiating.

What do people need to know to get into this field? What are the most important skills to have?

The skills needed to succeed as an institutional equity salesperson included an articulate nature, confidence, and persistence. A deep knowledge of and love for the stock market is an important ingredient as well. A majority of salespeople in the industry have a finance background, but this is by no means a prerequisite. One must be conversational and inquisitive because account personnel are not always willing (at least initially) to part with information. The most important factor affecting a candidate's ability to secure a position in the industry is a network of contacts. My advice to such candidates is to meet as many people in the industry as possible. Not every opportunity will work out, but one's ability to leverage ongoing relationships will keep one in the flow. As with the industry itself, information is the most valuable commodity during the recruiting process.

How did your education impact your career?

Today, an MBA is a prerequisite in order to be hired as an institutional equity salesman. It wasn't always that way, but given the thousands of candidates who compete for positions each year, the industry needed an accurate screening device. The only reason I mention this is that for the most part this is the only way my graduate education has affected my career. The MBA was a means to a specific end. That is not to say that certain things I learned in my two years at NYU are not applicable to certain business situations—just that most of the learning and skills development is done on the job.

▶ Susan McSharry is a Consumer Segment Manager at First American National Bank. She received her BA from Columbia University School of General Studies in 1993 and her MPPM from Yale School of Management in 1995.

Where have you worked since graduation?

I have been employed at the First American National Bank since completing graduate school. Through most of my first year I was a retail product manager. Currently, I am consumer segment manager.

What was your career target upon graduation?

At the time I was completing my degree, I planned to continue my career in marketing within the private sector. Yet, I was open to changing industry. I had been in the publishing field. In fact, I had a wide set of criteria for my job search.

How would you define your ideal career?

My ideal career would be one in which I have an opportunity to work on innovative marketing projects. I would like to be continually challenged and always broadening my knowledge base. Finally, I would like a career where I have significant decision-making responsibilities. My experience managing long-term projects that affect an entire corporation was the best preparation for my ideal career.

What do you feel are the keys to success in your field and how did you identify these factors?

I think the key qualities and competitive edges for my career are confidence, commitment, public speaking ability, industry-specific and general management knowledge, and project management skills, including the abilities to resolve financial issues and to work as part of a team. I drew on published information, including business journals, internal job newsletters, and the Tennessee Job Bank. I arranged informational interviews in the Nashville market. Also, I established some useful contacts through school projects and followed up with meetings. Referrals from informational interviews on the industry helped me gain several contact names at other organizations.

What is your advice for identifying target organizations?

I read business journals and spoke to local business schools to identify key organizations in the area. Contact potential job sources during your years in business school and try to work with them on projects. Get referrals during informational interviews.

What special tips do you have for writing cover letters and resumes?

Tailor cover letters, yet ensure that they are brief and easily readable. In my experience, a strong resume has to be customized to the reader. Also, if you are looking at a new industry, focus on "global" abilities (e.g., "project manager for a major initiative" instead of "led development of a new newsletter"). Quantify results in previous jobs.

How would you suggest preparing for an employment interview?

Research the company thoroughly, including analyzing the annual reports and conducting a literature search. Also, research the industry thoroughly, including knowing the major competitors, salient issues, and forthcoming trends. Let the organization know what you, personally, can bring to the position. Have an "action plan," if possible.

What do you like best and least about your present work?

Best, I like the strategic element of segment management, the participation in strategic planning, and involvement in major bank initiatives.

Also, I enjoy participating on various teams and in new product development. I would enjoy more creative work at times.

What are your additional thoughts on the search for an ideal career?

Always follow up, especially with human resource departments. For bigger organizations, call every other week. For me, informational interviews were very helpful. Also, be open to new industries. I never expected to be in banking, but now that I am involved in it, I find it very interesting. A final word of advice, negotiate salary.

▶ Diana Propper is a Managing Director with EA Capital. She received her BA from Duke University in 1984 and her MBA from the Harvard Business School in 1990.

What is your employment history?

- Save the Children, program manager of development projects in Africa and South America (prior to MBA).
- Cultural Survival Enterprises, business manager Brazil and product manager U.S., 1990–1992.
- Co-founder and managing director, EA Capital, 1993–present.

What was your career target at time of completion of your MBA?

I was very focused at the time on wanting to work at the intersection of business and environmental conservation. While the whole notion of sustainable development was a nascent concept, from my previous work experience, I knew the two (business and the environment) not to be mutually exclusive. In fact, my whole decision to get an MBA was guided by this belief and interest. I didn't know exactly what job to seek in this emerging area. There were no specific jobs out there that targeted this opportunity. I thought very seriously about trying to find a consulting company that was doing interesting things so that I could learn more about options and opportunities in broad sense before focusing on a particular company/organization.

How did you define an ideal career?

When I worked for Save the Children, I realized that this nonprofit, as well as other environmental and social services organizations, were having limited impact. They controlled few resources and thus seemed to operate at the margins, without being able to effect major change. The key as I saw it was to get the private sector involved in solving these problems. I chose to focus on the environment, which had always been a passion of mine dating back to when I was 12 and my grandmother took me to Africa. Thus, I went to business school to learn the language and skills of business and to develop my thinking on what were the business advantages that companies could gain from solving environmental problems. I sought out professors at the business school as well as the Kennedy School who could guide me and challenge my views. I also read a tremendous amount about companies who were in different sectors (i.e., chemicals, energy) to learn about their strategies when dealing with the environment.

How did you decide on the key qualities and competitive edges you needed?

In many ways, I experienced the process of defining my career as that of building a new path. Most people working on sustainable development projects were doing so within the nonprofit sector. I wanted to work within the business community, and I knew I was going to have to do a lot of convincing and "selling" to companies to which I applied that my background was relevant and that there was a business opportunity in the environment. I knew it would be important to gain the skills and credibility with the private sector, and hence one reason I took the summer job with McKinsey & Co. Otherwise I relied a lot on my MBA and my work experience in which I had proved myself to be a successful manager of projects and people. Much to my surprise, I learned from McKinsey that one reason they hired me was because I had much more actual management experience than my counterparts who came from the consulting and financial services sectors. McKinsey believed this would make me more effective in interacting with the client and in working with teams. I ended up with a full-time job offer from McKinsey, which provided a confidence boost to me to pursue alternatives. I thought that I could always go to McKinsey should my other job search fail.

How did you identify target organizations?

I used published materials, information systems, career books, job fairs, and so on. At least 90 percent of my search was through the "hidden job market" off-campus. I relied primarily on my network of contacts that I had developed through work and business school professors. I also contacted friends and family, told them what I was looking for and asked for leads. Every lead, no matter how small or tangential it seemed, was pursued. At the time of my graduation in 1990, the job postings and career books for the more untraditional jobs targeted undergraduates. And as I mentioned earlier, businesses were not focused on the revenue opportunities to be found in solving the world's environmental problems, and those organizations that were focused on sustainable development were nonprofits. There was very little in the way of jobs at the intersection of business and environment.

So I ended up inventing my job. I researched all the fellowships available to me as an MBA (through Harvard and outside of the university) and put together a proposal that outlined a "theoretical" job that brought together business interests and environmental conservation. At the same time, I sent letters out to about fifteen environmental organizations and told them that I was an MBA student who was self-financed and was looking for a project that related to my interests. The fellowships were specific to jobs in the nonprofit sector. As it turned out, one of my professors at business school told me about a nonprofit, Cultural Survival, which was setting up a nonprofit trading company, Cultural Survival Enterprises (CSE), which would export nontimber forest products to companies in the United States and Europe. CSE would give local businesses and the local communities in South America and Asia an economic incentive not to destroy the rainforests by creating markets for nonwood products. It was a perfect fit. I received fellowship funding and worked in the Brazilian Amazon for two years, working with local businesses and communities to supply nuts, fruits, oils and essences to companies like the Body Shop, Ben & Jerry's, and Knudsen's.

Who did your network include?

My network was a patchwork of different people from various points in my life. I guess the lesson is that you start networking early in life, whether consciously or not, and don't be shy about casting a wide net into it. For every contact one can generate an average of 3 to 5 new leads. My network included Duke University (where I did my BA), Harvard Business School, the other graduate schools at Harvard, friends, family (and their whole contact network), contacts from old jobs and articles I had read about interesting people or companies.

What helpful hints do you have on cover letters, resumes, and interviews?

First, on cover letters and resumes. Be specific in your resume about three things with respect to each of your previous employment experiences, including your accomplishments. I always look at the extracurricular activities a person participated in during graduate school, as well as their personal interests. I find these to be important insights into a person's character, values, and leadership ability. On cover letters I look for focus. Is this a generic letter, or, preferably, has the person learned something about the company to which he or she is applying? I look for the answers to three questions: Why does the person want to work in this sector? What is the attraction to my company in particular? and What skills does the person have which he or she thinks will contribute to his or her work at my company?

With respect to interviews. The key for me is that the person project energy, confidence, and "go" during the interview (without being cocky or arrogant). For a lot of employers, the interview is where the candidate is evaluated on their thinking skills and on their interpersonal skills. I think it is important to be able to demonstrate critical/creative thinking and leadership ability (as opposed to management skills). Many interviews will be with young companies, which are looking for people to not only do the day-to-day work but also to help build the business and bring in clients. Being competent and conscientious on a given assignment is only part of the picture.

What key trends do you see in employment opportunities and hiring requirements?

Our company's work is focused on providing financial and consulting services to natural resource industries (e.g., forestry and energy), companies that solve environmental problems gain business and competitive advantage. The opportunities at the intersection of business and environment are growing. The range of jobs is quite vast. A graduating MBA can work for a eco-efficient technology company in the energy sector, a sustainable forestry company operating in the tropics, or a number of venture capital and investment management firms that are doing private equity placements in the renewable energy, energy efficiency, aqua-culture, ecotourism, and sustainable forestry sectors.

The key hiring requirements are primarily strong business fundamentals. A lot of companies in these emerging sustainable industries suffer from a lack of business skills. Core competencies in finance (from venture capital to equities analysis and debt financing), marketing, and business development are particularly valuable. Of all of these, a finance background, coupled with good interpersonal skills is what my company looks for.

What do you like best/least about your current work?

The best thing about my job, as I imagine with other more nontraditional jobs, is the pioneering nature of the work. We are developing new financial instruments and products for sustainable forestry and renewable energy investment opportunities. If successful, we will transform the way the financial markets relate to sustainable industries worldwide. (I often compare ourselves to the mad scientists on Wall Street, though of course to our clients we appear no different from other investment banks.) There is never a dull moment and the work draws fully on our collective creativity: how to take our financial and other business skills and use them to solve pressing environmental problems.

I like least the uncertainty of the adventure. It takes a long time to develop new ideas and to test them out in the market. To get through the challenges requires two parts faith, three parts perseverance, and five parts a good sense of humor.

What are the spiritual beliefs that govern your career thinking?

Without a doubt my work has been guided by beliefs I have held since I was a young girl—to try to make a difference in the world. To me it is the most normal of pursuits to link one's job with making the world a better place. As an MBA and as a businesswoman I find it incredibly exciting to leverage my skills and resources to pursue my ultimate dreams.

Have you any additional tips for graduating MBAs?

Number one: Follow your dreams. This is the most difficult thing to accomplish in your career (and maybe in life, too). If you don't allow yourself to follow your dreams at some point, you may forget what they are, or never get to know them in the first place, and you will thus be cut off from the most powerful fuel within you.

Number two: Don't be too hard on yourself. If you know what you would love to do but feel you need to take a "mainstream" job upon graduating in order to build up your skills and credibility, then by all means do it. But don't shy away from that dream job because you are scared to jump in. It only gets harder and will feel riskier as you get older to leave that comfortable consulting or marketing or finance job. With an MBA under your belt (with all its networks and its pedigree), it's always possible to go back into the mainstream job market.

▶ David Skrilloff is Vice President of Gerard, Klauer, Mattison & Co. He received his BS in Electrical Engineering from Carnegie Mellon University in 1987 and an MBA from New York University Stern School of Business in 1992.

What do you do on the job? Describe a typical day.

My job is to advise companies on financial matters, particularly on how to raise capital. In my current position I usually have 4 to 8 companies that I am working with at any one time. The process of raising money is a two-step approach: (1) Prepare the company to go to the capital markets and (2) actually introduce the company to the appropriate market and raise the capital. My typical day consists of doing three things: (1) trying to identify and then pitch potential new customers, (2) working with senior management of the company to prepare them for the capital markets, and (3) talking to the potential investors in the companies we are representing.

How were you able to obtain this position? What steps led you to this?

I believe that my technical background along with my business experiences and MBA provided me with a combination that was desirable by Wall Street—the ability to understand technology and to understand what it would take to translate a technology into a profitable business.

What is your career history or prior work experience?

- Electrical Engineer in college.
- Started my own computer software company with a friend from school.
- Grew the company to $3 million in sales with 12 employees.
- Raised capital funding for the company.
- Sold the company and went to NYU business school.

- Worked for a venture capitalist member of NYU's board while at business school.
- Got current job after NYU, starting as an associate.

What are your favorite aspects of this job? Least favorite?

Favorite aspects:

- Seeing many different companies with very interesting ideas in technology.
- Helping a company succeed in its business by raising capital.

Least favorite aspect: Dealing with lawyers, accountants, and regulators to make sure that all securities laws and regulations are being followed.

What do people need to know to get into this field? What are the most important skills to have?

The most important skills are a strong understanding of accounting, very strong interpersonal skills, and a drive particularly in junior level positions when the hours of work are very demanding.

How can someone get your job?

The best way to get into this business is directly from undergraduate schools at entry-level positions and working one's way through the ranks. The other way is by establishing a specific knowledge that is desired by Wall Street (e.g., computers and the Internet).

What are your favorite books, trade journals, magazines?

My favorite books and magazines have nothing to do with my job. I like novels and outdoor adventure magazines. For my job, the most important piece of literature is the *Wall Street Journal*.

What motivates you to do what you do?

The ability to help entrepreneurs realize their dream by providing them with the capital needed to attain their goals.

What factors attracted you to your present career?

There are two pieces to my career. The first being investment banking and the second being a small firm. The investment banking career attracted me because I saw it as a step to becoming a principal. When I had my own firm, the area of expertise that I looked for was an understanding of finance. My job has provided me with that. I, however, never would have pursued this career if it was at a big firm. The camaraderie and atmosphere is a major factor toward the enjoyment of my job.

What resources did you use to identify specific job leads in your industry?

This industry, like all industries, particularly at more senior levels relies on contacts more than anything else. You just need to be bold and talk to everyone that you know and then talk to people that your initial contacts know. This is an industry of networking. Also, once one establishes a network from job hunting, that same network could be the single most important factor leading to success within the job.

What are the key points in answers to the question, "Why hire me for my ideal job?"

When hiring someone, I look for confidence, experience, and diversity. If someone has all three, I think they might make a good candidate. Also, I do not care if this is one's ideal job. I am only looking for someone who could contribute to both the success of the firm and to my success. The applicant needs to make believe that he or she could help me, not that I am helping him or her.

What sources did you use for identifying target organizations for your ideal job ?

It is tough finding a job, and thus I believe that all avenues must be pursued.

Who participated in the employment process for your job and what were their roles?

When I started there were only 50 employees. Therefore, most senior employees within the department or in areas in which I would work closely participated in the hiring process.

How did you find out about the employment process and individual roles?

I did not. I have to admit that prior to my initial interview I was unprepared.

What do you feel were the most unique advantages you had in obtaining the employment interview for your job?

I had done work as a consultant for the company and then when the company was looking to hire, they were familiar with my work and asked me to interview with them.

What do you think really got you your job?

I believe it was my experience. The contribution of a technical background and understanding along with a business experience got me the job. I also believe that the head of the department saw some of himself as a younger person in me.

Do you feel your work makes a difference to you, your family, and society?

I believe that my work makes a difference to both my family and society. In terms of my family, I have met a number of very interesting people who have become friends. In terms of society, I have helped companies succeed that have helped society with their products and/or technologies.

What are similar areas in this field that people might consider?

The investment community consists of two groups: the principal investors who invest their company's money into companies and the investment bankers who advise companies on how to raise capital. Within investment banking there are primarily three departments: sales and trading (people who buy and sell stocks), research (people who look at companies and recommend whether to buy or sell those companies' stocks), and corporate finance (people who actually advise a corporation on raising capital). Of these areas, sales and trading is probably the most intense with the best work hours, research is the most intellectually challenging and corporate finance is the most diverse. Also, most people within an investment bank specialize in a type of security (i.e., debt, equity).

What is your favorite quote?

There is more to life than work.

Any pearls of wisdom for people with similar aspirations?

Too many people go into this business because of the allure of money. If that is the reason one is aspiring for this industry, he or she should find a different job. The money is not always as good as one is led to believe and on a "$/hour" basis, it getting even lower. Aspire to a profession you enjoy.

How did your interest in this field originate?

I have always been an entrepreneur. I grew up in an entrepreneurial household and had started my own company. I knew that at the time of finishing business school, I did not want to start another company (at least not without a large amount of capital), but I did want to work with and help small companies. That is exactly what I get to do.

What do you see as the most challenging issues in your industry?

My industry has a number of challenging issues ahead. First, the industry is going through consolidations and mergers (particularly with commercial banks). As this occurs, the companies are becoming more bureaucratic and less flexible. Since my business is very relationship oriented, it will be interesting to see if the relationships can be maintained as the companies become a part of a much larger organization. Second, over the last several years, a lot of money has poured into the stock market, even a lot of money that does not belong, investors who are heavily at risk. If there is a major hiccup, a lot of investors could lose a lot of money that they cannot afford to lose.

Where do you derive your inspiration?

My inspiration is derived from my ability to help small entrepreneurial companies grow to successful companies. My other inspiration is simply my ability to earn enough money to provide a lifestyle for my family to which it is accustomed to living.

Who is part of your team?

My team consists of myself and one other senior banker, two junior-level bankers (both two years out of college) and two research analysts (one senior and one junior) with expertise in telecommunications. My team also includes my wife, who provides me with a lot of guidance and her valued opinion.

Where do you see yourself in 5 to 10 years?

I see myself acting as a principal investor with a pool of money to invest in growing technology companies.

How does your position affect your after-work life?

I try not to bring my work home with me and I believe that I am fairly successful at separating work and home. However, it is never possible to completely separate the two. I work fairly long hours (8 A.M.–7 P.M. on average, but occasionally as late as 9 or 10 P.M.) and travel fairly frequently (4–5 days/month) and thus do not get to spend as much time as I would like to outside of work. I am certainly developing a gut because I do not have time to go to the gym as much as I would like.

What are the international trends in your area of expertise?

The trends are definitely towards globalization and international companies. The trends are also toward the developing countries. Such countries are in need of a large amount of financing and my industry wants to help provide it.

FINDING YOUR WAY IN CONSUMER PRODUCTS

The profiles included in the consumer products sector cover a wide range of products: cosmetics, personal care, pharmaceuticals, food, software, sportswear, and fashion wear. The common theme in these product management profiles is the need for a general business, marketing-driven perspective. Other profiles bring in related fields such as market research, advertising services, and supplier to consumer product business, which also require the general business/marketing-driven combination. People are attracted to the consumer products sector because it is a dynamic field, subject to rapidly changing customer desires and needs. Also, there are great possibilities to see the results of your work in increased sales and profits. Finally, work in this sector combines a unique opportunity to use both creative and analytical capabilities—along with interpersonal skills.

▶ Alison Bard is the Buyer for Knit Collection Tops at Lerner New York, a division of The Limited, Inc. Prior to joining Lerner, she was the Merchandiser for Petite Sportswear at Ann Taylor, where she worked for 3 1/2 years. She received her BA degree in Communication Studies from the University of California of Los Angeles in 1986 and her MBA from New York University Stern School of Business in 1993.

How would you describe your current position? Describe a typical day.

I manage a retail sportswear business. I am responsible for product development and for achieving financial goals. I direct product sourcing, financial planning, and distribution of product to retail stores. I work closely with designers to develop new sportswear collections delivered to 180 stores. I edit the product line to fit the needs of the Ann Taylor petite customer and create a compelling merchandise assortment. I analyze current sales trends and present projections to upper management on a weekly and monthly basis. I develop and execute promotional strategies. I manage and develop assistant merchandisers. I coordinate the efforts of a team consisting of a merchandise planner and merchandise allocator.

A typical day is hard to describe because a merchant must always expect the unexpected. Business trends often dictate the focus of the day.

Each Monday is dedicated to analyzing the prior week's business. Each business or department has weekly, monthly, and seasonal financial plans. During weekly Monday night meetings, the sales results of individual styles and product categories are reviewed and presented to the entire merchandising organization. The balance of the week is spent meeting with vendors, the design team, merchandise planners, and trouble shooting delivery and other product-related issues and problems.

The first week of the month is focused on analyzing the prior month's performance from a sales and profitability standpoint. Financial projections from future months, usually the next 3 to 6 months, are also reviewed. Product meetings between design and merchandising usually occur on a weekly basis. Formal review meetings of product are scheduled on a quarterly basis. These meetings are attended by all merchandising executives and the president and/or CEO. The objective is to select and coordinate the merchandise that will come into the store in all product categories for a given season. Depending on the company, this meeting can take place anytime from 3 months to 1 year prior to actual delivery of garments to the stores. During these meetings all styles are selected, color and quantities are finalized, pricing and promotional strategies are presented and in-store positioning is decided.

What are your favorite and least favorite aspects of this job?

My favorite aspect of the job is that it allows me to combine my business and creative sides. I am rewarded for combining these two sides of my brain and making a profit for the company. As a merchandiser my scope of involvement reaches to every aspect of the business: design, planning, allocation, sourcing, marketing, and in-store merchandising.

While I consider my level of involvement a strong positive of my job, it is also the biggest built-in source of aggravation in my daily duties. Late deliveries, short/over shipments, quality problems, cost and retail changes, and accounting issues are all part of a merchant's day. There are other individuals and departments that focus their time solely on these problems. However, the merchants must also take part in solving these issues as it is their bottom line that is affected.

What do people need to know to get into this field? What are the most important skills to have?

An understanding of the fashion industry and of retailing is always helpful. An eye for fashion and strong analytical and computer skills are important. In my opinion, the most important ingredient is the passion for the business. Retail merchandising (in the fashion industry) is demanding of both mind and body. Long hours and the general craziness of the industry are the main reasons why people drop out.

Be prepared to become an assistant merchandiser and accept lower than MBA wages. Assistant salaries top off at $40,000–$45,000 for the experienced ones. The average salary is somewhere in the mid-$30s.

Another route into the industry is as a merchandise planner or merchandise allocator. These positions are focused primarily on the analytical side of the business. Requirements are strong analytical and computer skills. The merchandise planner is usually considered a peer to the merchandiser and is the most frequent career path for an MBA. The planner works closely with the buyer to plan and manage the financial side of the business. The merchandise planning function is relatively new to the apparel retail industry. As the industry moves forward, this function continues to grow in importance.

In some companies, an MBA might be started as a merchandise allocator. Allocators are responsible for distributing merchandise to stores. This job is considered a training ground for merchandise planning positions. Salaries for allocators are generally comparable to assistant merchandisers.

For those interested in pursuing a career in retail, I would recommend starting your search early. Although the fashion industry generally does its hiring on an as-needed basis, rather than on the typical MBA timetables, this practice is starting to change in a few companies. Regardless of a company's timetable, taking time to organize informational interviews in advance of your search is a great way to get to know the company, understand its requirements, and make contacts in the industry.

▶ Timothy Crew is Senior Director, Marketing and Business Development at Bristol-Myers Squibb. He received his BA in Economics from Pomona College in 1983 and his MBA from Columbia Business School in 1989.

What is your employment path since graduation?

My job history, all with my current employer, is as follows:

1989	Professional Sales Representative
1990–91	Sales Operations Associate

1992	Assistant Product Manager
1992	Associate Product Manager
1993–94	Product Manager I/II
1995	Senior Product Manager
1996	Director, Business Development
1997	Senior Director, Marketing and Business Development ($500 million line)

How would you define your career target at the time you were completing your MBA?

My career target was general management in the health care field and I saw marketing as a good path, although I was frequently off-target in accepting interviews in nontarget areas. Ultimately, the latter was a waste of everyone's time. I strongly endorse the principle of defining and committing to an ideal path.

How did you select your ideal career?

Prior to coming to graduate school, I realized my competitive advantage was being very good, but rarely the best, in many disciplines. The cross-functional nature of marketing appealed to me and appeared to be a good path to general management. I studied marketing and accepted a summer intern position in marketing and validated my hypothesis. Selecting health care was simply a matter of long-term demographics, healthy operating margins, and a personal philosophy of trying to make a meaningful difference in people's lives. For example, I personally find health care to be philosophically rewarding.

How did you identify target organizations for your career search?

The Executives-in-Residence were able to provide some great leads and helped establish early rapport with certain target companies. The career center's alumni list was also most helpful. A member of the faculty hooked me up with my present employer through previous placements from my school. My present employer did not actually interview on campus the year I joined.

What tips do you have for cover letters and resumes?

Keep them short and sweet, and use the telephone for further follow up. The person on the phone might be your boss soon, so you should be comfortable talking with him or her.

What do you suggest focusing on in preparing for an employment interview?

In retrospect, the most important thing I did in successful interviews was to establish rapport. Most who interview are reasonably qualified. You need to be able to articulate your abilities as they relate to the position, but people tend to hire qualified people they like. The points to address are why you want the job and why they should hire you. Present your superior qualifications as they relate to the position and then seek rapport, rapport, rapport!

▶ Erina DuBois is a Digital Commerce Analyst at Dataquest. She received a BS from Carnegie Mellon University in 1989 and her MBA from New York University Stern School of Business in 1995.

What do you do on the job?

I am an analyst with a large market research firm. My responsibilities are to track a particular industry (in my case, the Internet/Electronic Commerce industry) and write about the current trends that are prevalent in the industry. I make market predictions about which companies will succeed and about how each segment in the various markets will perform. I spend quite a bit of time meeting with companies (ranging from large companies such as Microsoft to start-up companies just formed over the weekend) to learn more about their product offerings and strategies. I help my clients (who are subscribers to our service) with their marketing plans and product offerings. I also spend time talking with the press, who are looking for information for their stories (usually they want quotes from us to print in their articles).

Describe a typical day.

Unfortunately, there is no typical day. Some days I spend meeting with companies. I am required to write a significant amount, so some days I sequester myself at home and write nonstop. I spend approximately 20 percent of my time on the phone with companies, clients, and the press. I spend approximately 60 percent of my time working alone (researching and writing). During a week, I spend 20 percent of my time conversing and brainstorming with peers.

What is your favorite aspect of this job?

I am able to meet with start-up companies (here in Silicon Valley and elsewhere) and hear and see their product offerings before the general public does. This industry is the most dynamic of any I have ever seen. The speed with which the technology of the Internet moves surpasses anything I have seen before.

What is your least favorite aspect of this job?

It is fairly difficult to keep up-to-date. I subscribe to and read over 20 different publications (not including newspapers) and I am perpetually surfing the Internet to feed my brain. Every day something is happening in the world of electronic commerce and you cannot slack off in the intensity of your reading and research.

What is your career history or prior work experience?

I worked for a large management consulting firm (Booz Allen & Hamilton) for several years right after undergraduate school. After that, I tried several different industries, including financial services (Halifax in London, and American Express), brand management (Kraft), and systems consulting (KPMG Peat Marwick). The common thread throughout most of my career has been my ability to leverage my technical background (i.e., engineering).

What factors attracted you to your present career?

The best aspects of this job are the nature of the industry and the autonomy of the job. I am completely immersed in one of the most dynamic industries and I meet the pioneers of the technology that affects this industry. Also, the job requires little to no supervision from anyone and I am free to write about the topics that I believe are relevant. There is still a great deal of teamwork involved when I forecast data and market trends, but overall the job is what I make of it.

What resources did you use to identify specific job leads in your industry?

I found this particular job through a combination of a newspaper advertisement and a friend at the company. In Silicon Valley, tenacity pays off. I was able to obtain interviews at large technology companies by cold calling (i.e., sending in my resume and cover letter without knowing anyone at the company).

 Robbie Kahn is a Senior Marketing Manager with Avon Products, Home Entertainment Division. She received her BA in Economics from the University of Rochester in 1982 and her MBA in Marketing from New York University Stern School of Business in 1984.

What do you do on the job? Describe a typical day.

I plan and buy all audio and computer software product for Avon's U.S. national catalogs, as well as video, books, audio, and games for Avon's Inspirational (launching first quarter 1998) and segmented African-American Catalogs. National catalogs are put out every other week, the African-American Boutique is distributed quarterly.

When buying product, I balance the product mix according to genre, price point, and seasonality. I negotiate cost and develop packaging. My division is very small, eight people in total. Due to our size and the nature of our business, we are able to make decisions quickly and react to current trends.

A typical day involves speaking on the phone with vendors, meeting with vendors, computer work, and interacting with coworkers. I also spend 15 percent of my time interacting with other associates in other departments, including art directors and copywriters. Overall, my time is distributed approximately as follows: phone—50 percent; meetings—20 percent; analyzing/writing—30 percent.

Is there growth potential or compensation potential for your job?

Marginal growth and compensation potential.

What do you like best and least about your present job, including pitfalls, challenges, and rewards?

I like best the small group and entrepreneurial environment. I enjoy planning successful programs, negotiating with vendors, and seeing the results (sales!). My least favorite aspects are not being able to reach people by telephone during the course of all the phone work I do.

How much do you work with computers, financial analysis, people, objects?

Over 50 percent of my job involves the computer and financial analysis.

What skills do you use the most?

Listening, negotiating, analytical, and organizational skills.

Who is part of your team?

Other buyers, merchandisers, and purchasing managers.

How can someone get your job?

A person could move over from other areas within Avon through an internal connection, or a person might possess skills and contacts that would enhance the business and be introduced through industry contacts or through Avon Human Resources.

What is your career history, or prior work experience?

After my first year of business school, I spent the summer in the Market Research Department at the American Stock Exchange. After graduation, I entered the Bloomingdales executive training program. I have now been with Avon for 12 years.

What factors attracted you to your present career?

The entertainment industry is exciting; my department is small, personal, and quick to make decisions; and the Avon environment is warm and supportive.

How did your education impact your career?

It got me started, and gives me a sense of security.

What training or education do you think is necessary for this career?

Industry and organizational experience are most important. Analytical abilities are also very important.

How did your interest in this field originate?

It began with retail. I like developing ideas and ways to sell things—and then seeing the results through sales.

What do you see as the most challenging issues in your industry?

Growth, technological change, and dealing with mass discounters.

What trends do you see in your industry?

I see increased CD penetration in our market, increased access to bigger name artists and movies, and continued growth as music and videos are perceived as a high-value gift item. I also see increased interest in computer software as home computer penetration increases.

What is key to getting into this field?

Be able to juggle many tasks and people. Develop strong people and negotiating skills. It is also important to have analytical abilities and contacts in the industry are helpful.

What are similar areas in this field that people might consider?

They might consider work as a supplier in a sales department; work in marketing departments at record, video, and publishing companies; positions creating product; or work at other catalog companies.

What is the outlook in your industry and functional area, and what are the most important tips for getting ahead?

The outlook is competitive. Tips: be outgoing, aggressive, quick, and a team player.

What personal characteristics do successful people in your industry share?

Easy going, yet aggressive. Flexible and patient.

Where do you see yourself in 5 to 10 years?

I see myself in an entrepreneurial department in a large company or in a top position at a small company. I see myself staying in the entertainment industry.

What are your favorite trade journals and periodicals?

Work: *Billboard* and *Ad Age*. Personal: *New York Times, People Magazine,* and *New York Magazine.*

What motivates you to do what you do?

Social and financial objectives, plus the challenge of being successful in a large organization.

How does your position affect your after-work life?

Happy during the day relates to happy after work.

What do you hope to achieve with your work?

Creative and financial satisfaction plus a feeling of accomplishment.

Where do you derive your inspiration?

From the need to accomplish and the desire for financial independence.

What steps led you to obtain this position?

I first met with Avon Human Resources during campus interviews at Stern.

What resources did you use to identify specific job leads in your industry?

Before coming to Avon I used the Office of Career Development at Stern. Once at Avon, I used mentors and contacts in other departments.

What sources did you use to identify organizations to target for your ideal job?

Personal contacts, school resources, newspapers.

Who participated in the employment process for your job?

Human Resources and managers in the individual departments.

What do you feel were the most unique advantages you had in obtaining the employment interview for your job?

At first, educational background and potential; later in my career, reputation, interviewing skills, and accomplishments.

How would you summarize your reasons for applying for your job at this particular company?

Industry and environment.

What do you think really got you your job?

I got my present job based on job skills and the good reputation at Avon.

Do you feel your work makes a difference to you, your family, society?

Yes. It makes me feel somewhat accomplished. It provides an income and security to my family. It provides quality product to customers, and the potential for income to the Avon salesforce.

If you wanted people to understand your profession, what would you want them to know?

The catalog industry is fast moving and fun. You have to be a team player in a large organization, and be patient with promotions and growth.

What are top three pieces of advice you would like to share with someone contemplating this kind of career?

Be flexible if you seek to advance to higher levels of responsibility and financial compensation; take some risks (which may include job changes and work for different companies); and build your portfolio.

What are the misconceptions people hold about this kind of work?

That you always have control. Many things that happen are upper management decisions and philosophies.

What is your favorite quote?

"Look for that right balance between home and work."

What other thoughts would you like to share ?

At each stage in one's career, one must decide what is most important (e.g., money, prestige, or homelife) and put that goal first. Prioritize goals and look for balance. If you go after them all you can be left frustrated.

▶ Margie Wong Kuo is an Assistant Marketing Manager with Pfizer Inc., Consumer Health Care Group. She received her BA in American History at Yale University and her MBA in Marketing and Finance from New York University Stern School of Business in 1996.

What do you do on the job? What is a typical day?

I am the assistant on Visine and our new prescription (Rx) switching to over-the-counter (OTC) product, OcuHist Antihistamine/Decongestant eye drops. I manage the budgets, expenses, production forecasting, sampling, and promotion programs for these two major brands. I also do analyses of the brands in terms of break-even points, and consumer responses to marketing programs (i.e., coupon analysis, scanner promotions). I have had the fortune of good timing in that I am working on the launch of the Division's first Rx-to-OTC switch product. I have been handling much of the professional detailing and sampling portions of the launch. I am responsible for giving design and creative guidance to our promotional agencies. This is perceived as training for more elaborate creative projects such as television commercial campaigns, of which I am part in the sense that my feedback is elicited, but I am not yet directing the process.

There is no such thing as a typical day at work for me, which is what I like best. I would hate to know exactly what I had to do every day. It would bore me. There are always some regular things that need to get done every week or month. These projects are a nice cushion/filler to fall back on when in a creative slump or while waiting approval on some other projects. I am constantly working on miniprojects and problems throughout the day, or bringing my manager up-to-date on the major projects that I worked on the night before. I am at my desk by 8:20 A.M. My manager leaves usually by 6:00 P.M. It is typically after he leaves that there is enough "quiet" time in which I can do the heavy-duty analytical work.

I am responsible for two minor brands as well, Visaclean and Rheaban. It is somewhat of a challenge and most frustrating for me managing brands that receive few marketing and promotional dollars along with little or no consumer data. Fortunately, I managed to finagle two full years of Infoscan data for these brands this past year to conduct two in-depth brand reviews that have shed new light on the management of these brands.

What are your favorite and least favorite aspects of this job?

My favorite aspect is working on different projects all at once, dealing with doctors and learning about the next or latest new technology and trying to market it. My least favorite aspect is the bureaucracy and conservatism of a pharmaceutical company.

What are the pitfalls and challenges of your position?

Not knowing the details and minutia that assistants need to track. The brand-manager relies on them for that information. Not following up on on-going projects, having to constantly compete for attention and time from the medical, legal, regulatory, and R&D departments. Not learning the bigger picture because you're drowning in the minutia.

How much do you work with computers, financial analysis, people, things?

I am constantly on the computer doing all sorts of financial analysis, but the temptation is to just sit at your desk and do only that. Half the battle is getting in front of the people from whom you need input, approval, and so on. Sometimes I spend my whole day meeting and talking with people. And it's only after the phones stop and the majority of people go home that I can get my work done.

What part of your day is spent doing what?

20 percent phone, 20 percent meetings (formal and informal), 10 percent administrative, 40 percent analytical work, 10 percent writing presentations and proposals.

What are the misconceptions people hold about this kind of work?

That it's not creative enough, and that they need a medical/science background. Or that brand management is a glamorous type of job. It certainly isn't in the first few years, but there are perks.

What training or education do you think is necessary for this career?

MBA, summer internship (especially if the full-time position doesn't come with a training program) and continuous reading of the *Wall Street Journal* and trade publications to keep up to date. Learn to analyze commercials. Take a media strategy course.

What is your career history or prior work experience?

In my first job out of college, I worked as a strategic planning analyst at The Boston Company, a subsidiary of American Express. Unlike my peers, I got to see the big picture first, without having to work through the ranks. Yet I realized how shaky my status was because I didn't have years of fundamental training. As a liberal arts major, I needed to play catch-up on marketing and finance fundamentals on-the-job. I did very well at The Boston Company, but once I hit the plateau on my learning curve there, I knew I had to move on to a different position within the firm, or change firms if that wasn't possible. I had become pigeon-holed as the person who could write really good presentations for senior management because I was able to grasp and distinguish what was important from what was not. However, I wanted to get involved in the actual implementation of strategies and concepts I helped to create.

I moved back to New York and looked specifically for a position at a smaller firm in which I could work on strategy and implementation. I think that sometimes the implementation of a strategy is more important than the strategy itself. A former manager once told me that it is better to have a mediocre strategy and execute it well, than to have an excellent strategy and execute it poorly. At The New York Botanical Garden, I worked on both, but realized quickly that despite the initial appearance of having control over my projects, I did not have enough control and power to create and implement the project plans because of hidden agendas, and ultimately, lack of funds. That year I also experienced what I still feel is the textbook case of limited managerial skills from the very top to the bottom. I enjoyed writing business plans for the revenue-generating projects the Garden had identified, so I took a chance and went to business school, so that I could make a proper and formal career switch to brand management.

I can't say I knew immediately after my first day at business school what type of marketing I wanted to do. I went in thinking that since I did not have the advertising experience many of my classmates had, I was going to have a much harder time making the switch into brand management. Fortunately for me, that was not always the case. First, I realized that anyone can be an assistant at an advertising agency, and that being one did not mean that they wrote any of the copy we hear and see on television. In fact, most of the product management companies were looking for people who had more diverse and more analytical experience—engineers, accountants, and bankers were hot targets. Moreover, it is my belief that recruiters favored students who really knew themselves, (e.g., those who really knew their strengths and weaknesses and had an answer for why those were their strengths and weaknesses and how they were dealing with them).

I think that introspection is very painful for some people. I believe it is a necessary pain that everyone needs to face. Once you can identify your weaknesses, you can build a plan of attack to circumvent those weaknesses. I knew that I did not have the marketing experience and "schmoozy" personality that some of my advertising agency classmates had, so I decided not to go after the more glamorous internships that others were seeking. I knew that I had to get a marketing internship for that first summer, no matter what, so that I could decide if I liked brand management. If I found I didn't like brand management after all, I would have another year to determine what other career path I could take.

I targeted the medium- to small-size product management companies and I read everything I could find about them in the news (the *Wall Street Journal, Brandweek,* etc.). I did not, however, and I'm proud to say, network and schmooze with the company representatives that came to make presentations. I personally despise networking for the sole purpose of getting a job, although that probably is the informal definition of the word. Nevertheless, it wasn't me, and I didn't think that was the way for me to make an impression on potential employers.

Instead, I really focused on my resume. Fortunately, I had a lot to work with, and I had a great counselor at Stern who worked with me on the resume and on my answers to tough interview questions. I tailored my resume by choosing words and phrasing my accomplishments in ways that a brand manager could identify with and could apply to what he or she was working on. I toned down the very macro, big-picture projects that I felt were important, but were inappropriate for a particular company's needs, and spent more "words" on those projects I thought they would be more interested in. I also tweaked and fine-tuned my resume for a company when I felt it was necessary to speak more about one project than another. I did not get invited to interview with any company the first year. I had to bid for every single one of my interviews. Nevertheless, I received three offers for that summer. I like to share this aspect of my interviewing process with first-year students who are feeling like the "second-class citizen" I felt like when I did not get on any interview invite lists. During my second year, however, I was on almost all the invite lists because I had a summer internship.

Bottom line: If you are making a major career switch, don't get too enamored with the idea of working for a huge, glamorous, well-known product management firm right away. Start out small, because there are fewer people competing for positions in a smaller, less well-known company. Look for companies that appreciate your background and are small-staffed enough so that you can get much more experience than anyone working in a huge company can.

This is exactly what happened with my summer internship at Warner-Lambert. The group I was in was short-staffed, so I got to manage the launch of a line-extension under the supervision of my manager. Ironically, I worked on a therapeutic product in a candy factory, Halls Cough Drops. I came to realize that I definitely did not want to market candy for the next few years. It was too "impulse" for me. I knew after my summer internship that I wanted to work on over-the-counter marketing. The learning curve is always moving with over-the-counter drugs as more prescription drugs switch over and the consumer is also a professional (doctor, pharmacist, nurse, etc.), which means marketing to a more challenging and intellectual consumer. Knowing this, I narrowed my search to only OTC companies during my second year. I think that this was an important first step. I guess it's analogous to method-acting. You have to really focus on being that one thing you want to be all the time, and not "fall out of character" ever. You can't stay in character if you are constantly playing different roles in front of very different audiences, thus diluting your performance.

The job posting for my current position came over the fax machine at the office of career development, and I was lucky enough to be standing by it as it came over. I faxed my resume and a cover letter back immediately, within an hour after receiving the fax. I had written to Pfizer earlier in the fall, but had heard that there was a hiring freeze, so I was elated when I saw this fax. I was called for an interview the next day and called back twice and given an offer, all within one week. In hindsight, I think the huge amount of preparation up front really paid off in the end when it counted most.

How did your education impact your career?

Getting an MBA was instrumental in my career change. It is a necessity in brand management. To a certain extent it's just a piece of paper that gets you considered, but on the job, you do apply some of the things you learned in school and the education gives you the confidence to compete and learn effectively on the job.

What skills do you use the most in your career?

My ability to quickly summarize the most important points of any issue and set a game plan based on that. Also, gaining support of functional staff and thinking analytically.

What factors attracted you to your present career?

I was almost premed. I went to a science and math high school and some close friends of mine are doctors. My personal belief is that a fulfilling job is one in which you can add value to something or some-one's life (i.e., not dealing with impulse items, but with medications).

Where do you see yourself in 5 to 10 years?

Senior brand manager or, preferably, in new product development, identifying Rx candidates for OTC switches, or overseas as a country manager.

What major pieces of advice would you like to share with someone contemplating this kind of career?

Be very sure you want to enter a niche field such as pharmaceutical OTC marketing. Company or industry switching is not that easy once you start in a niche field. Prepare to deal with the FDA and other bureaucracies; they are necessary challenges. Be realistic about what your role is during the first two years.

What do you see as trends in your industry?

More self-medication and OTC; the growth of Rx to OTC switches; more FDA involvement and regulation.

What do people need to know to get into this field? What are the most important skills to have?

You should know why you want to go into the pharmaceutical over-the-counter market. You need analytical skills, an ability to prioritize, interpersonal skills (you work with so many different types and levels of people), and good presentation skills.

What are the international trends in your area of expertise?

The OTC market is more flexible overseas in that more drugs are approved for Rx and for OTC uses. Thus, overseas markets are often test markets for products prior to their U.S. launch.

What advice would you impart pertaining to your industry?

This is a tough industry to crack. It is viewed somewhat (by insiders) as a "higher form" of marketing in that you are not just marketing to "Joe Schmoe," but also to intelligent consumers (i.e., doctors). Understand the issues surrounding such consumers and the health care industry. Be ready for the bureaucratic approval process. It is still a necessity and one needs to be patient.

How can someone get your job?

Get some real experience (via summer internships and classes) in the pharmaceutical, OTC, and medical fields. Read up on the industry and understand its trends.

What are your favorite books and trade journals?

Positioning by Al Ries and Jack Trout, *Drug Topics*, the *Wall Street Journal*, *Pharmaceutical Marketing*, *Brandweek*, *Kline Reports*, and *POV Reports*.

What motivates you to do what you do?

For me, my "work satisfaction barometer" is how quickly I wake up in the morning. If I wake up without a struggle (hitting my snooze bar, etc.) even after coming home from work around midnight, then I know that deep inside I am still enjoying my job, even when I have to work long hours and when certain things are not going the way they should be. I work longer hours than most of the other assistants, primarily because I have the largest brand in the division and I am the only assistant on the brand. I believe that you can only continue to work long hours if you enjoy your job enough.

Things do not always go smoothly at work, and every company has processes and people that can frustrate you, but as long as you can look past these blemishes, see the whole picture, and like what you see, you're still enjoying your job. Still, I have experienced major burn-out before, so I am careful to set aside time when I tell myself that it is okay not to think about work at all. My husband and I have an understanding that Saturday is our "Sabbath day." Also, my husband and friends know not to ask me about work because I don't want to discuss work outside of the office. This has become a policy with me. Not because I don't like my job, but there are so many other things in life to talk about.

When it comes down to what exactly makes me get up every morning, I guess it's the challenge of learning new ideas and new ways of looking at problems; and perhaps more so, it's the feeling that I can make decisions and implement them, a sense of control. I believe it is very important to feel that you have a certain degree of control over those projects that have been designated as yours. Otherwise the feeling of losing control starts a spiral of self-doubt and lowered self-confidence and inevitably a dislike for your job. Additionally, reinforcing comments from my manager help to fuel my drive where my self-motivation leaves off. However, I have learned one major thing recently: Not all managers know how to give positive reinforcement when it is needed, and that is when you have to pull from deep within yourself to keep plugging away in spite of the lack of encouragement. It also helps to have a peer group to vent with because you don't feel so alone on those days when nothing seems to be going right and people want to take it out on you.

Last, I enjoy the type of marketing I do. I view it as much more rewarding than the typical packaged goods marketing. With over-the-counter drugs, especially those that used to be prescription drugs, you feel that you are doing a service and adding value to people's lives by offering them a product that will provide them with some immediate relief to help them feel better. I find the science behind those products extremely interesting. I think it feeds my repressed high school desire to become a doctor. With over-the-counter drugs, I enjoy dealing with a more intelligent consumer (doctors, pharmacists, etc.), in addition to the public consumer, instead of trying to position products and commercials to appeal to the "lowest common denominator."

Any pearls of wisdom for people with similar aspirations?

Don't expect too much "glamour" in the beginning; the "boot camp" concept is still alive and well. Keep on top of the details, but be aggressive about learning the creative and strategic parts of the business as well. Learn to manage yourself, because you may not always get a good manager who knows how to coach and develop you.

What resources did you use to identify specific job leads in your industry?

I forced myself to really know myself. I worked with one of the best counselors at school to analyze my answers, my motivations, and my body language. I didn't network as much as people tell you to; it is not in my personality to network for the sake of networking. I put my best foot forward on a one-to-one basis.

What sources did you use for identifying target organizations for your ideal job?

I looked at all the companies behind the OTC products I knew and trusted. In a way, I felt that if I liked the product there was a good chance I would enjoy working at the company that manufactured it. I used "Infotrac" to search for names, and I read and collected *Brandweek* articles all year long (names often mentioned).

What were the most unique advantages you had in obtaining the employment interview for your job?

My unique advantages were my functional experience from my summer internship, my strategic planning background, and my knowledge of why and how I wanted to apply that background and experience to brand management. Pfizer HR was very into "targeted selection" interviewing, really drilling down to determine if you did do what your resume said you did. I was fortunate enough to have had a great summer internship at Warner-Lambert, where I launched a sugar-free extension of Halls Cough Drops. They were satisfied that I had indeed done what I said I did, and it was the type of experience they were looking for. I was able to defend and explain everything I did.

How does spirituality fit into your life and your work?

I believe that you can only be physically and mentally healthy if you are happy in what you do for a living because we spend so much time each day at work. When I don't enjoy my work, I get sick more often and lose my motivation to do things even outside of work.

Do you feel your work makes a difference to you, your family, society?

I definitely feel I do make a difference through my work. Educating consumers and professionals through marketing adds immediate value to people's lives. OTC drugs offer people immediate relief from symptoms that ail them. My job is to make sure that consumers know and understand how they can better their lives with the appropriate use of OTC products.

▶ Mary Lynn Maricucci is an Account Supervisor with Ogilvy & Mather. She received her BBA from the University of Texas at Austin in 1987 and her MBA in Finance and Marketing from New York University Stern School of Business in 1995.

As background what is your employment history since graduation?

Several weeks after graduating from Stern, I joined Newbridge Educational Publishing, a publisher of supplementary educational products for early learners, as Product Manager. After two years, I capitalized on an opportunity for a career shift into Advertising and I joined Ogilvy & Mather.

How did you identify you ideal career? What experiences, tests, contacts, and other sources were most helpful?

I studied marketing as an undergraduate, and eventually chose it as a career because it offered variety. Success in marketing requires a variety of skills from creative to financial, and with such a variety it is very difficult to be pigeonholed into one career track or to be bored. The first reference I relied on for information about the field of marketing was my college course catalog. By studying what courses would be required to earn a degree in marketing, I learned about the different options in the field and also began to determine which ones interested me the most.

How did you decide what key qualities and competitive edges you needed to offer your employer for your ideal career?

This is an ongoing process and I'm finding that I need to reinvent myself every 1 to 2 years to progress. I've relied on three sources to help me determine what qualities I need to be successful:

- On the job experience: I use my current job description and those of my superiors, observations about what makes colleagues successful, and information about what the competition is doing (and their success) to determine what I need to do to be successful in my current firm.

- Recruiters and advertisements in trade journals or newspapers: I rely on these sources to keep up-to-date on requirements outside of my current company. More often than not, there are similarities that enable me to discern industry trends.

- Trade journals (e.g., *Brandweek*) and other periodicals (the *Wall Street Journal, New York Times*): I read these to keep current on business news and developments in my field.

What special tips do you have for writing resumes and cover letters?

Other than the tried and true tips, such as use action words, quantify achievements whenever possible, use the active voice and limit the copy to one page:

- Think of the process of writing your resume as a game. Your challenge is to portray your background and jobs as the most exciting in the world, using as few words as possible.

- Read your finished resume and ask, "Does this sound like it was written by a person who loves his or her job?" If not, start over.

- Engage as many people as possible to critique and proofread your resume.

- Do not overstate your accomplishments, but do not downplay anything (even if you did it just once). As long as you can speak intelligently about a skill or achievement, put it on your resume and describe it in glowing terms.

- Make sure your letter is easy to read. Use bullet points to highlight accomplishments or reasons why you're perfect for the job.

- Personalize the letter as much as possible. If you are responding to an ad or a listing that spells out specific job requirements, make sure you address in your letter the ways you fulfill those requirements.

What special tips do you have for preparing for employment interviews? What were the three or four major questions from your prospective employers?

- Know what is important to you, and ask questions that will tell you whether a given job will provide you with what you need. For example, if you thrive with frequent feedback, ask how often and in what manner your performance will be reviewed. If you get an answer like "We'll let you know how you're doing," you may want to look for a company with a more structured feedback system. Likewise, ask questions about hours, training, or any other corporate policies you want to know about.

- Pick out from your resume one or two items that you want to talk about (e.g., your most significant accomplishment or most relevant experience) and highlight them in your conversation. Prepare messages on these strengths so you have ready, clear answers when the interviewer asks you about them.

- Practice speaking in a relaxed, very self-assured manner. This is probably most important for recent college graduates without much work experience who often get flustered during interviews.

- Know something about the company or industry. No one expects you to memorize the annual report, but you should know something.

- During the interview, listen carefully when the interviewer describes the position or company. This information can give you ideas for questions or can be useful when you have a follow-up interview.

- When you have a follow-up interview, weave information from your first round interviews into your conversations. This shows that you were listening and signals your interest.

- Try to determine how important politics are to an organization. Politics are often a hidden career maker or killer. It's tough to get a straight answer to the question "How important are politics?" but if you ask enough people you should get an idea. I like to ask "To what degree is your company a meritocracy?" That's a straightforward way of getting at a sticky subject.

- Insist on meeting at least one person who is not on a firm's regularly scheduled list of interviewers. This can increase your chances of getting straight answers.

Major questions from prospective employers:

1. Why do you want to work here? (I always get this one.)
2. Why are you looking to leave your current job?
3. Why did you get your MBA?
4. Tell me about a project that didn't go well and how you handled it.

What do you see as the challenging issues in your industry?

- Information technology (this issue is not limited to publishing). Most companies are relying on databases or technological infrastructure built years ago, before easy-to-manipulate software packages were available. Critical data are therefore locked up in archaic systems that are seemingly impossible to decipher. Devising marketing strategies and making sound business decisions is difficult without the adequate data.

- Devising offers that appeal to consumers who are increasingly savvy about buying through direct marketing.
- Responsibility without authority. As the agency, we are responsible for devising and executing strategies that will move our clients' business forward. However, we are often not given access to the information or key decision makers that would enable us to do so.

What do I think really got me my job?

Honestly, I believe I got my current job because (1) I had a varied "complete" direct marketing background, (2) my resume looked good (i.e., an MBA from a top school and experience at some well-known companies), and (3) I had an answer for "Why advertising?" and "Why Ogilvy?"

What do people in you industry share in terms of personal characteristics and industry skills that make them successful?

- Attention to detail. With complicated direct marketing programs to plan and execute as well as financial analyses that must be correct to be meaningful, it is imperative to be detail oriented.
- An understanding that advertising isn't just about creative execution. Without a good strategy you can't have good ads.
- A real commitment to quality work. In advertising, you live and die by the quality of the strategies and creative approaches you develop. They better be good.

▶ Tracy McNamara is Product Manager with Clairol, Inc. She received her BA from Colgate University in 1988 and her MBA from New York University Stern School of Business in 1995.

How were you able to obtain this position? What steps led you to this job?

Giving up a career and going back to business school was a big decision for me; both financially and emotionally. I had a successful career as a buyer for May Company (who owns Lord & Taylor, Filene's, Hecht's, etc.) and although I liked many elements of my job, I hated the environment I worked in. I decided that if I was going to make this big investment, I would not take looking for a job lightly.

To prepare for my job search, I did a lot of soul searching followed by extensive research. I looked at what I liked about the career I just left. The elements of being a buyer that I enjoyed most were that I was running a consumer-focused business and the results of what I did were quite tangible. I could walk into any May Company store and see consumers buying "my" dresses and every Monday morning I got a selling report telling me what was moving and what wasn't. This led me to brand management for a consumer products company.

I knew I wanted to have a traditional packaged goods experience, but I was not attracted to the really big companies. I had already worked for five years before business school and wanted to jump right in and take on responsibility, so I was looking for a company with an entrepreneurial spirit.

One can learn to market any product, but I knew that I would much rather work on products that consumers felt strongly about. Ideally, I wanted to work for a company with innovative, market-leading products that had a lot of brand equity and were somewhat image-driven.

Finally, the environment of the company was very important to me. I wanted to work with smart people from whom I could learn and who also had a good sense of humor and with whom I would enjoy working. After all, you spend a lot of your life working—you better enjoy it!

I went through the traditional recruiting process on campus to find a summer internship. Luckily, my background was very appealing to consumer product companies and I was able to get on many interview lists. I think what enabled me to turn so many of those interviews into job offers (I received six offers for a summer internship) was that I prepared extensively for the interviews. I read *Brandweek* and the *Wall Street Journal* religiously, attended all corporate presentations on campus and researched the companies. I went to the store and analyzed the products that companies marketed and their competition. However, the single most important thing I did was utilizing the alumni databases at Stern to do informational interviews with every company I interviewed with for an internship. I tried to do these in person but at the very least, I did a phone interview.

I gained two things from these informational interviews. They really helped me to understand each company's philosophy and get a feeling for the people and the environment and whether or not I wanted to work there. Second, recruiters were very impressed when they found out that I had traveled to their company headquarters to meet with someone. It showed initiative and a high level of interest in their company.

Although an informational interview is not a job interview, never underestimate the fact that you are making an impression on the person you are meeting. If someone likes you, they will very likely mention you to the people responsible for recruiting. People often either asked for my resume to "walk it over" to the people doing the interviewing or offered me names of friends at other companies that I could contact.

Two specific stories illustrate the power of informational interviewing: One of the companies I was interested in was Colgate. I had sent them a letter but had not gotten on their invitational list to interview. However, we received points to "bid" on companies to get on their open interview lists. I had a lot of points left and was confident I would be able to get on the open list so I had set up an informational interview with a Stern alumna who was a Senior Product Manager at Colgate. The morning of my informational interview, I was disappointed to learn that I hadn't bid enough points and I wasn't going to be able to interview with Colgate at all. I decided to go on the interview anyway because she might be able to give me contacts at another company and I knew I could still learn something.

We hit it off during the interview and I took a deep breath and decided to take the honest approach. I told her that I was very interested in Colgate, but had not been able to get on the interview list and asked if she had any suggestions (cardinal rule of informational interviewing: never ask directly for someone's help). Although she wasn't one of the product managers involved in on-campus interviewing, she took my resume and said she'd see what she could do, but was doubtful she could do anything.

Two days later, I received a phone call. The woman I met with had been asked to fill in for someone who couldn't attend the on-campus interviewing. She wasn't allowed to add someone to the schedule, but had been told that if she was willing to interview me on her own time, I would be considered. If I could be at her office in half an hour, she'd officially interview me. I got the offer.

My second story is how I got my job at Clairol. Clairol didn't interview at Stern the year I was looking for an internship, but I learned about the company from a second-year student who had been one of my orientation leaders. She had also been a buyer before business school and we were very similar personality types. She had spent the previous summer working at Clairol and had a great experience. In talking to her, it really sounded like the environment and philosophy at Clairol as well as the products they marketed were exactly what I was looking for. However, it's very difficult to get an interview with a company that isn't interviewing at your school.

Through the career office I got the name of an alumna who worked there and I called her. She was very busy, but we spoke at length on the phone. I asked her for suggestions as to how I could get an interview at Clairol. She gave me the name of the person to send my resume to and said I could use her name. I was brought in to interview during second rounds. I interviewed with four people and knew I wanted to work there. I was offered a summer internship and then a full-time position.

To summarize, my list of the most important things to do to get your ideal job:

- Identify what you liked and didn't like about your previous jobs.

- Know what motivates you with respect to type of environment, people you like to work with, level of responsibility and autonomy, lifestyle, and salary.

- Research, research, research. Read trade journals and the newspaper to understand trends and "hot buttons." Read the annual report. Know each target firm's strategy and that of its competitors. Understand the market in which the firm competes.

- When well-prepared, set up informational interviews with people who do the job you want. Come prepared with real questions on which you want their perspective, *not* a request for a job. Find out what they like and don't like about their job. How did they decide on this company and what other companies did they look at? What are the big trends in the industry?

- Write good, but short, cover letters. Mention the person you met with and what they told you about the company that made you interested. Tell the reader what you could offer the organization and why you would be an asset.

- During the interview, be interested. Realize that as stressful as it is, you are interviewing the interviewer, too. Look at this as an opportunity to learn more. Know your "story." Be able to explain everything you've done since college and how it's linked in to your master plan. Odds are you never had one to begin with but come up with one. Be prepared with questions. And whatever it takes, be confident.

- Follow up with a thank you letter. Odds are that they've made the decision before they receive it and many people never read them. But it's a guarantee that the one time you don't send one will be the one time someone factors that into their decision.

What is your career history or past work experience?

I went through the buyer training program at A&S Department Stores (which has since been merged with Macy's), spent a year as an Assistant Buyer and then a year as a Department Manager at its Brooklyn store. Having had enough of working directly in a store, I went to the corporate buying offices of Mercantile Stores, which owns department stores in the South and Midwest. I liked the atmosphere but wasn't being challenged enough or paid very much so I went to the May Company, at the time the largest department store chain in the country. I spent two years buying dresses and decided I had had enough of retail. May Company announced it was moving its corporate buying offices to St. Louis. Rather than move with May, I took the opportunity to go back to business school.

What are major things that make a great Product Manager?

- Leadership and the ability to motivate others. The ability to achieve your goals depends on communicating a clear strategy and then working with a team of people who don't report to you to manage the execution to achieve your strategy.

- A genuine curiosity. It sounds kind of trite but you need to be the kind of person who looks at commercials/products/promotions, etc., and tries to figure out the strategy behind them and whether you'd do the same thing. You need to be always thinking of different ways of doing things and asking questions, whether it's about consumer promotions, packaging, advertising, selling your product to the trade, distribution ideas, or ways to manufacture more efficiently.

- Ability to juggle many things at once while never losing sight of the big picture. As the team leader, you need to make sure that not only is everyone working toward the goal, but also that they understand the goal as well.

What is your favorite quote?

I have three that I alternate on my screen saver at work:

> "Nothing great was ever achieved without enthusiasm."—Ralph Waldo Emerson
>
> "Opportunities are seldom labeled."—John A. Shedd
>
> "May you live all the days of your life."—Jonathan Swift

If you wanted people to understand your profession, what would you want them to know?

This is a great question because most people have no idea what I do. At best, they think it's creating advertising. As a product manager, you are the marketing expert but you are also the team leader and a general business manager. Your brand is a small (or not-so-small) business within a larger company. You lead a team of functional experts that do not report to you, but on whom you rely to move your business forward. You are responsible for and held accountable for every aspect of the business from long-term strategic planning and the P&L to manufacturing, consumer promotions, sales, R&D, and yes, advertising.

What are your views on quality of life?

This is one I struggle with every day. When deciding on a career in business school, I looked into consulting and specifically decided against it due to the lifestyle. However, although I chose a "lifestyle" career, this is still an MBA level job. This means I work many late nights and (very) occasionally weekends. I chose a company that feels that having a life is very important, but you do have to accept that there are times when you are on projects that will mean many late hours. However, you have to find some way to get a balance in your life. I know I'm a driven person and want to achieve, but I also know that I don't want to look back on my life and have memories only of a career. The eternal struggle is to find a career you enjoy and a job with a company you like that challenges you, but still allows you to enjoy a personal life.

▶ Scott Nadison is National Accounts Manager with Mane, USA. He received his BA in Economics/Psychology from the University of Colorado in 1987 and his MBA from New York University Stern School of Business in Marketing/Management in 1994.

What do you do on the job? Describe a typical day.

V Mane Fils, the parent company to Mane, USA is the tenth largest manufacturer of flavors, fragrances, and aroma chemicals in the world. Its primary function is to service the beverage, cosmetic, food, pharmaceutical, and toiletry industries by offering them ways to improve the taste and smell of their products.

My job is to plan and direct all marketing and sales efforts to selected key accounts. I participate in the "pitch" to establish new relations with key accounts, oversee the daily management of these accounts, and look for ways to build on already established relations—and hopefully increase our share of their business.

On a daily basis, either in person or via the phone, I am in direct contact with my company's customers. I participate in advertising, marketing, and promotion teams to develop sales plans, define new product needs, and introduce new product concepts. I collaborate with Applications and Creative Laboratory staffs to develop products relevant to our customers' needs, and manufacturing staffs to produce products to meet their needs.

What trends do you see in your industry?

Consumers, customers, and competitors have all affected the way in which we do business today. First, consumers have become more knowledgeable and conscious of what they eat and what they want to eat as well as what they want to wear. As a result, greater demands for all natural beverages, cosmetics, and foods have forced new product lines to evolve. Second, as our customers "downsize" their product development staffs, the burdens of product development have become the responsibility of companies like mine—to the point where we do all of our customers' product development (without guarantee of compensation) and they have resigned themselves to project management. Finally, as with many other industries, mergers and acquisitions within the flavor and fragrance industry have created a few dominant companies in what was once a highly fragmented industry. The four largest companies control nearly a 70 percent share of the market.

What are the most important skills to have in this field?

The success of what we produce/sell is not necessarily dependent upon objective product performance measures, but rather product acceptance—a highly subjective criterion. Remember, my company produces scents and tastes for the cosmetics and foods consumers purchase. Therefore, to be successful on the commercial side (sales/ marketing) requires excellent communication skills. Not the least of which is the ability to listen. Understanding your customers' wants and needs is essential. It's unfortunate, but they are not always spelled out in detailed fashion.

What are the most important tips you have for students on preparing for employment interviews?

As with all job interviews, do some homework first. Know what's happening in the industry, the company, and its competitors. If possible, find out about the person who you will be interviewing with. If you know that person's interests and agenda, then you can frame your answers in a way that keeps them interested. Finally, understand the difference between confidence and arrogance. Too often I have interviewed candidates who appear to have an answer for everything—even the unanswerable. I have been more impressed by someone who admits to not knowing the answer to a question, but can formulate a method to finding out an answer, as opposed to someone who tries to "shoot from the hip." Fast-talking, smooth operators are not necessarily the best at sales and marketing.

What do you like best and least about your current work?

The best part about my job is that I have the ability to work on many projects with many customers across many industries. Currently, I am working with the confection, coffee, dessert, oral care, pharmaceutical, and soft drinks industries.

The worst part about my job is the time that it takes to see a project come to fruition. Particularly with pharmaceutical products, it can take as much as three years to realize some business.

What guidance would you like to give on trying to focus on an ideal career?

When you're thinking about your ideal career, do not think in terms of job title, or even job responsibilities, but think in terms of job functions.

Break down what you like to do most, whether it's work or hobby re-lated, and try to match those functions with those of a prospective ca-reer. You may be surprised just how many opportunities, regardless of industry, become available when you consider job functions first, title, and industry second.

What are your thoughts about paths to the ideal career?

Unless your chosen field is to be a doctor or lawyer, then there are not single paths to an ideal career. Always keep you options open and broaden your experiences as much as you can. Those who are most tal-ented in sales and marketing have the ability to offer fresh perspec-tives to unique situations. Therefore, a diverse background can be leveraged to your advantage.

▶ Robyn Rothke is Assistant Product Manager at Colgate-Palmolive. She received a BA from the University of Michigan and her MBA in Marketing and Finance from New York University Stern School of Business in 1996.

How were you able to obtain your position? What steps led you to it?

Through on-campus recruiting. I interviewed on campus and then on-site.

How would you summarize your reasons for applying for your job at this particular company?

Growth opportunities, training, reputation of the firm, location, and potential for finding industry mentors. I had a lot in common with Colgate's employees and I met the right people. Most importantly, I was myself.

How could someone get your job?

Beg, plead, prepare for interviews, network in the company, and never take no for an answer.

What factors attracted you to your present career?

I have always admired marketers. I like the spirit and focus of the best of the best. I also feel that marketing is the hub of all successful businesses.

What is your career history or prior work experience?

I have three and a half years of corporate sales experience, and I grew up in retail.

How did your education impact your career?

Without my MBA, I would never have been able to obtain my job.

What training or education do you think is necessary for this career?

An MBA and an understanding of corporate finance, management, consumers, and strategy.

If you wanted people to understand your profession, what would you want them to know?

Marketing is not just about advertising; it's about overall corporate strategy, profits, and losses. You are the CEO of your brand.

Where do you see job growth in your field?

I think I can utilize the skills I will develop at Colgate-Palmolive in a packaged goods, service marketing, or entrepreneurial career.

Where do you see yourself in 5 to 10 years?

Either as a director of a product division or as the owner of my own start-up firm.

What advice would you like to share with someone contemplating this kind of career?

Don't become a marketer if you want to work 9 to 5 and you want to know ahead of time what your work the next day will entail.

What trends do you see in your industry?

Power of the consumer and the customer. The uses of new media, such as shopping and advertising on the Internet.

What are the international trends in your area of expertise?

Product trends and consumer tastes are influenced by the fact that the world is becoming smaller and we share more ideals and desires now than ever before.

What are the most important qualities and skills to have in this field?

A strong personality, creativity, foresight, the ability to think "outside the box," as well as quantitative and analytical skills.

What is the outlook in your industry/functional area? What are the most important tips for getting ahead?

It is my belief, and that of many others, that the United States has to return to manufacturing. Marketing is critical. To get ahead you have to go above and beyond the call of duty.

Any pearls of wisdom for people with similar aspirations?

Choose a graduate program that top recruiters recruit from and where you will enjoy your two years of business school. Never take no for an answer.

What do you see as the most challenging issues in your industry?

The competition is constantly changing. You have to be on the cutting edge. Expect the unexpected.

What skills and personal characteristics do people in your industry share?

Interpersonal skills, self motivation, and perseverance.

What are the misconceptions people hold about this kind of work?

That the people who do this kind of work are soft-skilled, creative types.

What is your favorite quote?

Live for today, but plan for tomorrow.

What are similar areas in this field that people might consider?

Account executives or other jobs in service marketing (i.e., credit card, long distance telephone, Internet, or travel).

Where do you derive your inspiration?

I come from a family of strong, driven women. I intend to carry on the tradition.

Who is part of your team?

My team consists of my parents, siblings, and friends.

How does your position affect your after-work life?

It makes life a juggling act with the goal of balance.

What do you hope to achieve with your work?

I hope to wake up in the morning and look forward to going to work, and I hope to go home to a comfortable and happy family.

What resources did you use to identify specific job leads in your industry?

Everyone and anyone who could assist me—friends, family, counselors, other students, and alumni.

What are the key points in your answer to the question, "Why should I hire you for your ideal job?"

I am a proven leader, a true team player, and a creative problem solver.

What sources did you use to identify target organizations for your ideal job?

My business school's Office of Career Development, other students, alumni, and recent articles about packaged goods.

Who participated in the employment process for your job and what were their roles?

Initially, a product manager; later, a director, as well as other product managers, and a recruiter from the human resources function.

How did you find out about the employment process and individual roles?

Alumni network, programs at Stern, and friends.

What do you feel were the most unique advantages you had in obtaining the employment interview for your job?

Practice, practice, and more practice in interviewing skills, resume writing, and story telling.

What skills do you use the most in your career?

Interpersonal and creative skills are critical. A day doesn't go by that I don't do an analysis of Nielsen data.

What other thoughts would you like to share about choosing a job?

When choosing a firm, know the inside scoop. What is the turnover rate? Is there potential to grow as a woman/minority? Can you imagine working with the people there 50 to 60 hours per week? What companies recruit from that firm? What is the average period it takes to advance from assistant to product manager to director? How strict is the policy for upward mobility? Is there tuition reimbursement? Can you work abroad, and if so, how? Find out what the benefits are! A great job is not the job that pays you the most when you graduate, but one that prepares you to go where you want to go in life in the long run. Returning to my favorite quote, "Live for today, but plan for tomorrow."

What advice would you impart pertaining to your industry?

Know why you want to be in packaged goods, brand planning, and marketing; and know yourself.

What are your favorite magazines, books, and newspapers?

Magazine: *Brandweek.* Book: *All I Ever Need to Know I Learned in Kindergarten* by Robert Fulghum. Newspaper: the *Wall Street Journal* (Marketplace Section).

What motivates you to do what you do?

The never-ending demand for self-improvement, self-esteem, and accomplishment.

How does spirituality fit into your life and your work?

Spreading a friendly attitude and sharing feelings and emotions is the sort of spirituality I try to prevail.

Do you feel your work makes a difference to you, your family, society?

Most definitely. It is a source of pride for me and my family. I take pride in the fact that I will help Colgate-Palmolive sell more product, employ more people, and provide products that serve customers' needs.

▶ Robert Scheckman is Director of Marketing with The B. Manischewitz Company. He received his MBA in Marketing from New York
University Stern School of Business in 1990.

What do you do on the job? Describe a typical day.

I initiate, develop, and execute marketing objectives, strategies, and tactics to help the company grow the top-line and bottom line. It's true that
marketing is the hub of an organization. However, I feel more like the
flame thrower to ensure that projects move forward with quality. Just a
sampling of what I might do during the day: Develop P&L's, review advertising creative copy, develop packaging copy, follow up on tie-in promotions, create Web site copy, develop sales material for new products,
review consumer comments, plan for focus group research, and much
more. There are never enough hours in one day to get it done. The key to
success: prioritize, re-prioritize, and then prioritize again. A typical day
in the office usually starts at 7:30 A.M. and ends at 6:00 P.M.

Who is part of your team?

An Assistant Brand Manager and Product Development Analyst.

What part of your day is spent doing what?

Phone 20 percent, analyzing 15 percent, writing 30 percent, meetings
30 percent, reading 5 percent.

How much do you work with computers, financial analysis, people?

I work with a computer every day for sales analysis, P&L analysis,
competitive information, Internet research, and so on. I work with
many internal departments and external suppliers each day.

How do you get paid? Is there growth potential or compensation potential?

I get paid a salary and a year-end bonus based on my performance and
my company's performance. There is very good growth potential.

What is your favorite aspect of this job? Least favorite?

Favorite: The need to utilize a diversity of creative, financial, analytical,
and managerial skills. The great thing about product management/mar-
keting is that at one moment you can be working on financial analysis
and another moment be working on creative ideas for advertising. You

can see your accomplishments and their impact on the bottom line of the entire company. Also the people I work with are professional and motivated to move the business forward.

Least Favorite: Not enough hours in the day. I also dislike when a product's performance does not live up to the company's objectives or expectations.

How does your position affect your after-work life?

I'll never watch a thirty-second commercial the same way that I used to before working in this industry. In fact, while many other people will get up to get a snack during commercials, I'll sit them out to critique the spots. I spend way too much time in the supermarket when I'm food shopping because I'm looking for new ideas and conducting research. A trip to the store for ten items can take an hour before I am finished.

How were you able to obtain this position? What steps led you to it?

A professor at NYU once mentioned that the key to success is to get the "Initial Stamp," the stamp of a large well-known company in the field of your interest. Easier said than done! I was able to get an internship at Nabisco Foods during my last summer as an NYU student simply by keeping my ears open and being at the right place at the right time, and then capitalizing on it. The internship led to a full-time position as an Assistant Product Manager at Nabisco Foods. The key to obtaining this full-time position was not only to do a great job during the internship, but also to make sure that I was in close contact with key managers while I was finishing my MBA. An opportunity at Manischewitz was presented to me by a recruiter, and I acted on the opportunity. After lots of hard work that led to steady company growth, I was promoted to Director of Marketing.

What is your career history, or prior work experience?

After college, I worked in direct marketing (telemarketing, direct mail, etc.) for three years. Then:

- Stern School of Business, full time for my MBA.
- Nabisco Foods Company.
- The B. Manischewitz Company.

What factors attracted you to your present career?

Diversity of work keeps it exciting. There is a good balance of creativity and number crunching that keeps it interesting. I enjoy the fact that every day is different, and that I deal with a variety of people, from workers in the plant to advertising executives. One needs to be flexible enough to know his or her audience when working with these different groups. Another key attraction to my career is that everything is tangible. You think of an idea, develop the product, the packaging, and the marketing plan, and then you can actually see and touch it on grocery store shelves. I probably would not be as happy in a service-related business.

How did your education impact your career?

Case studies we covered at Stern have been the most useful to me because they provided a method to analyze, focus, and develop recommendations to address a situation. Actually, the biggest impact on my performance now is my involvement with Stern. I am involved with the entrepreneurial exchange, frequently go to seminars, participate in the career advisory program, and keep in close contact with marketing professors. I also have used the library on occasion.

Where do you see yourself in 5 to 10 years?

Vice president of marketing for a consumer package goods company.

If you wanted people to understand your profession, what would you want them to know?

Marketing is not rocket science. It is the ability to coordinate with other departments and outside suppliers to identify opportunities to grow a business or businesses, and to identify areas to improve efficiency. It is marketing's job to make these potential opportunities and efficiencies a reality that affects the top and bottom line.

What advice would you like to share with someone contemplating this kind of career?

To be a successful marketing professional you need to be able to: (1) manage at least 20 different projects at once and finish them all on time with quality, (2) motivate people in other departments who do not report to you, (3) sell your ideas up the line in a professional manner, (4) weed through the vast sea of information to find the most important data for drawing conclusions and making recommendations, (5) be persistent and organized at following up on projects to ensure completion, and (6) step back and look at the big picture.

How did your interest in this field originate?

A direct marketing project in college where I researched insurance policy expiration dates for an insurance agent showed me the real power of marketing. The insurance agent converted approximately 10 percent of my leads into renewed policies.

What is the outlook in your industry and functional area?

The food industry will always be stable because people need to eat. The successful companies will capitalize on consumer trends such as fat-free and low-fat foods. The key to success with these trends is to provide great tasting, lower fat foods. Even though there is a growing number of consumers who sacrifice taste for a healthier diet, the potential for increased volume will be greater with tastier products.

What misconceptions do people hold about this kind of work?

A good marketer does not sit in an ivory tower. A good marketer rolls up his or her sleeves and talks to the consumer, makes visits to manufacturing facilities, and so on. Some people think marketing does not require a total understanding of the consumer and that is why sometimes decisions can be made in a vacuum. A good marketer needs to understand how all the pieces fit in the puzzle to provide correct direction for the company.

What trends do you see in your industry?

- Within any category, the #1 or #2 brands will crush the #3 brand because of limited shelf space, unless the #3 brand has unique positioning and product.
- Trade will gain more power because of consumer data collection. Leading manufacturers should continue to conduct consumer research to stay current.

What do people need to know to get into this field? What are the most important skills to have?

- Flexibility, the ability to work on many tasks at once with a variety of people.

- Analytical ability.
- Creativity.
- Resourcefulness to solve problems.
- Enthusiasm to sell your ideas.

Where do you see job growth in your field?

Trade or account specific marketing and Internet marketing, opportunities at larger firms.

How can someone get your job?

To get this job you need an MBA in marketing from a reputable graduate school, and five to seven years of related marketing experience.

What are similar areas in this field that people might consider?

- Market research.
- Advertising agencies.
- Consumer promotion agencies.

What resources did you use to identify specific job leads in your industry?

My network, my friends. Keep your ears open. The opportunities are usually right in your backyard. I was lucky enough to hear about the Nabisco summer internship through a friend, and I capitalized on it. That eventually led to a full-time position with Nabisco. Other resources were trade publications. For example, look in the trade publications section listing people who have recently been promoted, and shoot them a resume. You never know.

What are the key points in your answer to the question, "Why should I hire you for your ideal job?"

I am a strategic thinker: analytical, creative, decisive, and energetic.

What do you feel were the most unique advantages you had in obtaining the employment interview for your job?

CAP—Career Advisory Program, of which I have been a member since I graduated from Stern. It enabled me to actually go to the office and see what marketing professionals are doing. This is also a great networking tool, although it is positioned as an educational tool.

How would you summarize your reasons for applying for your job at this particular company?

To work in a small company with less bureaucracy, and yet still be able to utilize my classical food marketing background was an irresistible combination. The organization is relatively flat, so I work very closely with the president and chairman. That really appealed to me. Also, I work much more closely with other departments and outside suppliers than I would in a larger corporation. For example, it is unusual for a director of marketing to go to new product packaging runs or manufacturing runs, but in this environment it is critical to be there to stay on top of your business.

What do you think really got you your job?

A strong consumer products marketing background with a high quality company such as Nabisco. Also, the number of things I've accomplished in a very short period of time.

What motivates you to do what you do?

- An increase in salary and bonus.
- A sense of accomplishment.
- The pride of seeing something through from idea creation to execution.

What do you hope to achieve with your work?

I hope to contribute significantly to help the company meet or exceed company objectives; leverage the strong Manischewitz brand equity by introducing new products that everyone can enjoy and continue to develop marketing plans to achieve the company's goals.

Where do you derive your inspiration?

My inspiration is somewhat self-motivated. However my dad is the real foundation of my inspiration. He was a successful Wall Street executive with whom up to this day I enjoy discussing business. His success did not come easy. He did it the old fashioned way. He earned it with honesty and hard work. Although I had no desire to work on Wall Street, I would like to follow in his footsteps.

What are top three things that make a great director of marketing?

- Creativity.
- Assertiveness.
- Analytical abilities.

What are your favorite books and trade journals?

Favorite Books: Robin Cook novels and *One Up on Wall Street* by Peter Lynch.

Trade Journals: *Advertising Age, Brandweek, Food & Beverage,* and *Modern Grocer.*

What is your favorite quote?

Work hard, play hard, and have fun.

Any pearls of wisdom for people with similar aspirations?

It is important to be detail-oriented, but the key to achieving your goals is to focus and act on the meaningful things.

Virginia Stults is a Marketing Manager with Shiseido Cosmetics (America) Ltd. She received her BA in Economics and International Relations from Tufts University in 1989 and her MBA in Marketing/International Business from New York University Stern School of Business in 1994.

What are your job responsibilities? Describe a typical day.

My responsibilities are typical of an associate product manager for any type of consumer packaged good. The primary difference is that, due to Shiseido's relatively small sales volume in the United States, I manage all the product lines sold under the Shiseido brand, giving me greater breadth of experience. Typically associate product managers are only responsible for a single brand or a certain category (e.g., eye makeup). In addition, because Shiseido's Marketing Division is so small, the Vice President of Marketing and I handle all the product management. I am involved with projects that I would not be assigned in a larger company.

Because my responsibilities are so varied, there is no such thing as a typical day in my job. That's one of the reasons I chose a career in product management. My responsibilities include:

Business Planning

- Developing, writing, and presenting annual marketing plans.
- Developing, writing, and presenting marketing strategies for new product launches.
- Planning promotions (working with the Creative Services and Purchasing Departments to ensure that necessary promotional materials are completed in time for a scheduled promotion, and developing alternative plans if there are delays).
- Developing an advertising strategy and copy, graphics and promotional materials (working with the Creative Services Department and the advertising agency).

Business Analysis

- Forecasting (working with the Finance Department to develop annual and monthly projections for sales, production).
- Analyzing sales results and also identifying trends, potential problems, and the like.
- Evaluating the success of promotional programs.
- Evaluating the sales potential of new products.
- Managing the marketing budget (i.e., tracking brand expenditures, reallocating funds, looking for opportunities to reduce expenses and related activities).

Consumer and Market Research and Trend Monitoring

- Monitoring and evaluating promotions, new product introductions, sales results, and market shares to identify competitive threats and opportunities.
- Monitoring social, fashion, and economic trends and evaluating how these trends might affect Shiseido's business or present opportunities for new products and promotions.
- Analyzing market research studies and consumer focus group results to draw sound conclusions and actionable recommendations.

- Writing a monthly market updates for senior management and making suggestions to New Product Development for new products and product enhancements based on my research.

Special Projects
- Overseeing the test marketing of a point-of-sale database.
- Manage a campus marketing program that includes sales through the Internet.

What do people need to know to get into this field? What are the most important skills to have?

Communication Skills: Marketing is ultimately responsible for the profitability of the brand. However, the marketing strategy cannot be successful if it is not properly communicated to the support groups responsible for executing the strategy. For example, if the people in sales don't clearly understand the goal of a promotion, it won't be presented correctly to the retailers, who in turn may not agree to participate in the promotion. Therefore, a large part of my job is communicating the marketing strategies to other departments and senior management either in formal written and oral presentations or in informal brainstorming meetings. In addition, I must keep the other members of the team informed about the status of projects. The ability to persuade and motivate others is extremely important. For example, in order to launch Staying Power lipstick ahead of schedule, Marketing needed to convince Operations to agree to run double-shifts in the factory to produce enough product in time for the earlier launch date and convince Finance that the additional costs were justified by the additional market share we would gain by preempting the competition with this early launch. Written communications skills are necessary for writing the marketing plans and launch guides for the sales force, as well as for summarizing key issues for senior management.

Analytical Skills: The ability to figure out the meaning behind the numbers and how this interpretation will affect the business is key. Also critical is the ability to evaluate a competitor's activities and anticipate that competitor's next move. Proactive responses require identifying opportunities and threats to your business as early as possible.

Creativity: Beyond being able to evaluate an advertising campaign or choose a package design, one must be able to think outside the box and come up with innovative ideas for promotions and new products. In today's highly competitive environment, finding new ways to get customers' attention and stand out from the competition is essential to the success of a brand.

Strategic Thinking: The Marketing Department makes all the decisions relating to a brand. It is important that one have the ability to take into account the long and short-term ramifications of each decision and see the impact of a decision on all parts of the business. Also, one has to come up with solutions to unforeseen problems or unexpected changes in the market place. Another critical ability is to anticipate competitive activity in order to respond proactively. Finally, one needs the ability to anticipate consumer behavior and develop the appropriate marketing programs.

Ability to Work in a Fast-Paced Dynamic Environment: Marketers need to adapt constantly and quickly to changes in the marketplace, modifying a promotion that isn't working and responding to competitive threats. Since cosmetics are driven by fashion trends, changes are especially fast in this industry. In addition, the rate of new product introductions is extremely rapid, thus changing the competitive environment constantly. Also, unforeseen problems arise that require the marketing departments to alter plans at the last minute. Some days, I never get to my "to do" list because I'm too busy putting out fires. There are never down times because we are constantly planning for the future.

How can someone get your job?

Knowledge of the Cosmetics Industry: An awareness of products, companies, promotional trends, retail trends, fashion trends, and so on, is also extremely important for successful interviewing. This knowledge will demonstrate that you are serious about pursuing a career in cosmetics and will reassure potential managers that you will be able to hit the ground running when you start the job.

Persistence and Patience: As with any "fun" industries, it is difficult to break into cosmetics marketing because there are relatively few positions and a large number of people trying to get them. While a few of the larger companies such as Procter & Gamble and Cosmair have organized on-campus recruiting, the majority of the cosmetics companies hire on an as needed basis and often it is impossible to anticipate what future hiring needs might be. I received calls in August and September from three companies I had sent letters to during the previous February. They had kept my resume on file until they had a hiring need.

My advice to anyone interested in a cosmetics marketing position would be to contact as many people as possible in all the companies you would like to work for. Try to arrange meetings with people in the company (especially in the human resources department and the marketing department) even if no position is available. If you impress the people you meet, it is likely that they will consider you when they do have an opening or pass your resume to someone else in the industry. As with any job search, it is important to pursue every approach because you never know where it might lead.

Most cosmetics companies look favorably on traditional product management experience and some even prefer to hire people with a few years of prior marketing experience. Therefore, I would also recommend pursuing other product management positions particularly in the personal care products category. This type of position will help you switch into cosmetics later on. Be sure to stay in touch with your contacts within the cosmetics industry so that they know that you are still interested in positions that open up. After accepting a position outside the cosmetics industry, a friend of mine periodically kept in touch with a major fragrance marketer with whom she had interviewed. Six months later a position opened up in the fragrance company and my friend was immediately called in for an interview and got the job!

What are your favorite trade journals and magazines?

Cosmetic World—a weekly trade magazine.

Beauty Fashion—a monthly trade magazine.

Women's Wear Daily, especially its "Friday Beauty Report."

Allure—a monthly consumer beauty magazine.

What are similar areas in this field that people might consider?

Within the cosmetics industry:

- Sales/account management.
- Training (conducting training programs for in-store beauty consultants).

- New product development.
- Public relations (working with beauty editors, planning launch parties, organizing special events and tie-ins with retailers and magazines).
- Advertising.

Outside the cosmetics industry: Product management for health and beauty products (i.e., haircare, suncare, soap, dental care, and the like).

What do you feel were the most unique advantages you had in obtaining the employment interview for your job?

My banking experience reassured potential employers that I had the necessary analytical and quantitative skills required for the job. My summer internship at Revlon gave me hands-on cosmetics marketing experience, insight into the industry, and demonstrated to potential employers my commitment to a career in cosmetics marketing.

What do people in your industry share in terms of personal characteristics and skills that make for success?

- Personal interest in the products. Most people I meet were "cosmetics junkies" even before they worked in the industry (e.g., they love using cosmetics, experimenting with new products, and browsing stores' cosmetics departments).
- Ability to identify fashion, cultural, and economic trends in their early stages and to anticipate what trends might evolve in the future.
- Ability to relate to one's customers and to understand the way they think, to put oneself in the target customer's shoes in order to develop marketing programs which appeal to her. Ability to put aside one's personal taste and preferences and listen to the target customer.

What are the misconceptions people hold about this kind of work?

Myth: Cosmetics marketing is glamorous. Since cosmetics is a high image, fashion-driven category, people often think that cosmetics marketing must be very glamorous. They are under the impression that I spend my time going to events, runway shows, and advertising shoots with super models, celebrities, and makeup artists. It is true that product launch parties and industry functions for cosmetics tend to be more glitzy than those for other traditional packaged goods, but the whole time I worked at Revlon I did not catch a single glimpse of Cindy Crawford or Claudia Schiffer. And no, I do not have a personal makeup artist to apply my makeup every day!

On a day-to-day basis marketing cosmetics is not much different from marketing cereal or laundry detergent. When analyzing the results of a promotion, forecasting sales volumes or reallocating funds in a budget, it doesn't make a difference what the product is. While marketing programs for cosmetics might be less traditional than those for household or food products, the same amount of work is required to plan and execute them.

Nevertheless, marketing cosmetics (as opposed to other product categories) does offer some unique benefits, especially to a "cosmetics junkie" like me. Many things I would be doing for pleasure such as trying new products and keeping up-to-date on fashion trends, are part of my job. I also like the fact that I have more leeway to be creative with promotions and advertising for cosmetics, especially makeup products, because they are not serious or practical items.

Myth: Cosmetics marketing is creative, but not analytical. Consumers today demand products that perform. It's not enough for the product to come in a pretty package or be a trendy color. It has to offer meaningful benefits. Technological and consumer research have become critical to developing products that appeal to consumers. The most successful product introductions in recent years have been innovative, high-tech products that offer unique benefits to the consumer or offer a solution to a common beauty problem (e.g., lipsticks that don't transfer onto coffee cups and moisturizers that protect against the environmental causes of premature aging).

What advice would you offer pertaining to your industry?

Move to New York (or at least be willing to do so)! New York is the headquarters for cosmetics marketing in the United States. Being only a subway ride away will make it easier to set up informational meetings and may even give you an advantage in being selected for interviews (i.e., you are available to meet at a moment's notice and the company will not have to incur relocation expenses). Nevertheless, there are cosmetics companies in other parts of the country (e.g., Procter & Gamble, Bath & Body Works, Neutrogena, and Freeman Cosmetics) if living in New York does not appeal to you.

Be proactive and persistent if you are serious about getting a position as a cosmetics marketer. There are positions available, but you have to find them by sending out resumes and networking.

▶ Scott Tucker is Vice President of Product with Montrail. He received his BA from Middlebury in 1986, his MS from the University of Washington in 1988, and his MBA from University of Washington Graduate School of Business in 1993.

What do you do on the job? Describe a typical day.

Product development is a big part of my job. I work with key customers, consumer focus groups, and designers to create new products and improve existing models. I manage the factories that produce the product and monitor inventory and sales to adjust production. I forecast sales and create financial plans, including capital requirements and expense budgets.

Who is part of your team?

There are only 10 people at Montrail, and we all work together. We each have functional areas of responsibility, but everybody is involved in big decisions.

What are your favorite and least favorite aspects of this job?

My favorite aspects of this job are the diverse responsibilities, the autonomy, and the challenges involved. My least favorite aspect is the hours of number crunching, such as updating the inventory model.

How much do you work with computers, financial analysis, people? What part of your day is spent doing what?

I am on the computer all day and employ financial skills constantly. I interact with and manage people and projects. On an average day, I spend three hours writing, one hour on the phone, three hours in meetings and two hours in analysis (unless I'm testing product on Mt. Rainier in which case I just have fun!).

What are three things that make a great vice president?

You must be organized, able to plan ahead, and able to use creative "out of the box" thinking. Knowing how to influence the president is also key.

How does your position affect your after-work life?

It really doesn't, except for the travel. Overseas travel really takes it out of me.

How were you able to obtain this position? What steps led you to it?

I was able to obtain this position through networking and personal contacts.

What is your previous work experience?

Prior to my job with Montrail, I was an environmental consultant—very technical work with no creativity.

What factors attracted you to your present career?

The outdoor industry fits my lifestyle. The work environment is supportive and challenging. I also get to work with like-minded people.

What skills do you use the most in your career?

Project management and process flow, with occasional flashes of creativity.

What training or education do you think is necessary for this career?

MBA, college degree, and mathematics.

What are three pieces of advice you would like to share with someone contemplating this kind of career?

Get an MBA, just get started in any position, and search for a good mentor.

Where do you see yourself in 5 to 10 years?

Spending more time on the big picture; analyzing markets; creating opportunities.

Where do you see job growth for yourself?

Job growth will come as the company grows. As we expand our product line and venture into new markets, my responsibilities will grow and change.

How did your interest in this field originate?

I have been interested in outdoor activities since childhood.

What trends do you see in your industry?

The trends I see are more frequent style changes, retailers pushing inventory risk back onto suppliers, and dominance by a few big retail companies (like Nike).

What is the outlook in your industry and functional area, and what are the most important tips for getting ahead?

The outlook is strong if you are able to constantly figure out what consumers want. Being innovative is the key.

What are the most challenging issues in your industry?

Intruders such as Nike, Adidas, and Reebok.

What advice would you impart pertaining to your industry?

Plan conservatively and use guerrilla marketing tactics if you are small.

What do people need to know to get into this field? What are the most important skills to have?

To enter this field you would need a basic business education and good people management skills (i.e., an ability to manage vendors, consultants, agents, factory reps, and others).

How can someone get your job?

Network with footwear professionals, work in retail or become a footwear buyer.

How did you find out about the employment process?

I learned about it through the school job placement center.

What resources did you use to identify specific job leads in your industry?

Contacts! I thought about everybody I knew and started asking for contacts.

How would you summarize your reasons for applying for your job at this particular company?

I was attracted to Montrail because of their strong growth potential, and the fact that they had an opening. But mostly I just wanted to work on outdoor retail projects.

What do you feel were the most unique advantages you had in obtaining the employment interview for your job?

I believe my most unique advantage was my special educational background and my participation in outdoor activities. You need to be authentic and really care about what you are doing.

Who participated in the employment process for your job, and what were their roles?

The CEO interviewed and hired me.

What do you think really got you your job?

They needed my skills. I had an inside line.

What are the key points to address to answer the question, "Why should I hire you for your ideal job?"

Experience and aptitude, but mostly ability. With a little work you can gain experience, but you cannot learn aptitude.

If you wanted people to understand your profession, what would you want them to know?

How hard it is to predict the future. You need to spend lots of time and money to get market data that will help you make predictions.

What do you hope to achieve with your work?

I hope to achieve responsibility, control, and influence in key decisions in my job, but mostly I hope to create some really great footwear that people love to wear.

What motivates you to do what you do?

I am motivated by creative impulse and the joy I get from making products people will use.

Where do you derive your inspiration?

I derive my inspiration from my kids.

What are your favorite books and magazines?

My favorite business books and magazines are *Seven Habits of Highly Effective People, Sport Trends,* and *Outside.* For pleasure I am currently reading Tolstoy.

How did your education impact your career?

It allowed me to change careers. My undergraduate education was the most important in giving me the skills to succeed.

What is your favorite quote?

Stop and smell the roses.

Any pearls of wisdom for people with similar aspirations?

It is good to learn computer software and hardware systems, but you need to constantly work on writing skills and public speaking.

FINDING YOUR WAY IN ENTERTAINMENT AND MEDIA

This section on entertainment/media includes the broadest range of profiles of any of the sectors. The survey field includes entertainment media research, talent buying, entertainment production, specialty entertainment products, music clubs, television channels, video/Internet access, internet marketing services, and custom publishing. These career fields are difficult to break into and demanding of those who make it in. Almost universally, a passion for the particular product or services is the most important success factor. These businesses "touch" the consumer in special, personal ways. Typically, the glamour image is overrated. More realistic is the need for special mixes of creative, analytical, technical, and interpersonal skills—to deal with the volatile complexities and unique personalities in this sector. The profiles convey the excitement of working in these businesses along with the skills and actions needed to realize these special opportunities.

▶ Lisa Fink is a Manager in Music Marketing at Columbia House Company. She received her BA in English and American Literature from Brandeis University and her MBA in Marketing from New York University Stern School of Business in 1996.

What do you do on the job? Describe a typical day.

I develop and implement marketing and promotion programs for a direct-to-consumer music club. There is no typical day. Though we publish our catalogs on a regular basis (19 cycles per year), during each cycle there are different promotions, music features, problems, and so on.

What are your favorite and least favorite aspects of this job?

My favorite aspect of my job is the variety of responsibilities. The job is both analytical and creative. I must understand sales statistics, offer strategy, analyze budgets, and so on, while also overseeing the editorial and graphic content of our catalogs. I also enjoy the diversity and the fact that it is challenging. I get to be creative (i.e., in product design), listen to CDs, and watch MTV at work! I also work with good people.

My least favorite aspect of the job is the very bureaucratic environment with its many layers of management. It can get very bureaucratic with a rigid organization and parts of the job can be very repetitive.

What part of your day is spent doing what?

I spend a lot of time in meetings because my job involves coordinating work among several different departments. I also spend a lot of time writing, reviewing creative materials, and talking on the phone.

How much do you work with computers and financial analysis?

My job is pretty computer intensive, particularly because I'm responsible for some Internet marketing. We also use a companywide computer network for file sharing, and I work on several different computer programs (e.g., MS Word, Excel, and Quark). I don't deal too heavily with financial analysis, but I do deal with finance related to sales data and I deal with statistical analyses from research reports.

Who is part of your team?

My team includes:

- Three Marketing Managers (myself included). We're essentially product managers, each of whom is responsible for a particular market segment. I handle the "core" segment, which is: Rock/Pop, Country, Jazz, Light Sounds, and Easy Listening;
- One Marketing Director who oversees all market segments and Marketing Managers;
- Marketing analysts who analyze sales data, demographics, etc. and work with Marketing Managers on pricing, offers, sales strategies, and so on;
- Creative services, editorial staff and graphic designers who create the music catalogs

What is your career history or prior work experience?

I was an Advertising Sales Assistant at ABC Television Network in New York City for one year. I assisted three Account Executives in the prime time Television Ad Sales Department, handled all of their daily administrative work and worked with clients (advertisers and agencies) changing ad schedules.

I worked for one year as an Assistant Media Buyer at an advertising agency, Lowe & Partners, in New York City. There I analyzed all network television media buys for three national advertising clients. My duties included determining cost per thousand for all buys, evaluating media plans, and preplanning media buys.

I worked as an Account Executive with George Trescher Associates in New York City for three years. I planned and executed special events for corporations and nonprofit organizations, and handled everything from start to finish. I created the concept of the events, and selected and over-saw all creative executions (i.e., location, invitations, decor, food, music, and the like). I also developed and presented pitches to new clients.

Prior to working here at Columbia House, I worked with WME in New York City as a Marketing Manager for two and a half years. I developed and executed marketing and promotion strategies for six direct-to-consumer music programs. I was involved in the launch of four of these programs; developed ancillary marketing efforts (e.g., Internet and branded merchandise); and produced television advertising, trade print advertising, and compilation CDs and videos. I managed the creative execution of six music publications, editorial, and graphic design.

How did your interest in this field originate?

I've always been interested in entertainment. I had college internships in TV production at the ABC TV affiliate in Boston and with Continental Cablevision. I ended up in music sort of randomly. I was looking for a summer internship at a media/entertainment company while at Stern, and got an offer from WME. It was either that or a job with a credit card company, so I went with WME.

How did your education impact your career?

My undergraduate education has been surprisingly helpful, mostly because as a Liberal Arts student I had to study a variety of subjects. Since my job involves working in many areas rather than honing in on one area, my diverse background is an asset. Also, it wasn't until I got to business school that I realized my writing skills were above par, a quite critical skill in a business career. Business school gave me the analytical foundation I was missing from my undergrad experience. It also gave me that piece of paper, my degree, that puts me a step ahead of other job candidates.

What training or education do you think is necessary for this career?

I think an MBA helps but is not necessary. I've noticed that my MBA has given me a small edge over my coworkers with things like understanding sales and research data. But I think that someone with a natural marketing sense can succeed without the degree. For direct marketing, some experience in production helps.

What skills do you use the most in your career?

Creative thinking and planning, strategic thinking, and people skills.

What trends do you see in your industry?

I see more competitors. As technology improves, one-to-one marketing will play an even greater marketing role for mass products. Columbia House has one direct competitor (BMG Music) and numerous indirect competitors such as CD Now, other music Web sites, and music retailers. Many of these competitors did not exist five years ago.

What do you see as the most challenging issues in your industry?

The entertainment industry is very dynamic, especially now. New trends constantly crop up. New competitors enter the market while old ones unexpectedly drop out. One needs to really keep on top of what's going on. One also needs to know about what's going on in related fields, not just one's own (i.e., paying attention to all trends in entertainment, not just in, say, music). Businesses and businesspeople need to be able to react quite quickly.

Where do you see job growth in your field?

Direct marketing is a growth field, particularly in online/interactive marketing. Entertainment companies are heavily invested in new media and everyone is launching a new media product of one type or another (most conspicuously the Net). The music side has been going through some growing pains. While new labels keep cropping up, CD sales went down in 1995 and will probably continue to decline. The late 1980s and early 1990s brought huge growth as people switched from vinyl and cassette to CD. Now that CD player penetration has peaked and people have replaced the majority of their vinyl, the market will continue to shrink until they come up with a new format. This hurts anyone in related fields (such as labels, retail, and catalogs).

What do people need to know to get into this field? What are the most important skills to have?

It is important to be analytical, to have an ability to understand sales data, budgets, and strategic planning, and also to be creative, to be an idea generator with an eye for detail—and to be a good manager.

What is the outlook in your industry and functional area and what are the most important tips for getting ahead?

The outlook is somewhat fuzzy. There's increasing competition in the market, and there are changes (e.g., as middle management continues to get squeezed out of organizations, any middle management job is vulnerable to downsizing). I think sticking to the basics can keep you ahead of the pack. Perform your job well. Understand all aspects of the business so you're not pigeon-holed and maintain your relationships with contacts both inside and outside your firm.

What do people in your industry share in personal characteristics and skills that make for success?

Most people share a love of entertainment. At record labels and music marketing companies, people are generally working there because they are music fans and have a passion for the product they're working with. To really be successful, it probably helps to have a somewhat aggressive or assertive personality. There are thousands of people out there trying to get ahead and it helps when you can get yourself noticed. Also successful are creative thinkers, not just creative in an artistic sense (though this is often the case), but people who can think out of the box, who are risk takers, and who can continually come up with new, innovative ideas.

What are the misconceptions people hold about this kind of work?

I think that for the music industry the misconception is that everyone is young and ultrahip. Sure there are plenty of people like that, but there are plenty of people who are not so cutting edge. They're just people who love music and understand how to create it, market it, and so on.

What are similar areas in this field that people might consider?

People might consider:

- Product management at a record label or a consumer or packaged goods company.
- Account executive positions at an ad agency (both traditional and direct marketing agencies).
- Marketing manager positions at any direct marketing company (i.e., credit card, catalog businesses, and the like).

What pearls of wisdom do you have for people with similar aspirations to yours?

Make as many contacts as you can in the industry. Try to find someone who can be a mentor to teach you about the business and introduce you to other worthwhile contacts. Take on internships while you're still in school to gain experience and make contacts.

How can someone get your job?

Every prospective employee must go through Human Resources for a first interview round. Columbia House hires lots of MBAs for full-time jobs.

How would you summarize your reasons for applying for your job at this particular company?

The reasons I applied and the reasons I took the job are not the same. I applied because I needed a job, the businesses were similar, and I was asked to submit a resume. I wasn't sure at the time I applied that I wanted to work for a company that is more widely known as a direct marketing business than as a music/entertainment business. After I went through rounds of interviews, learned more about the business, considered my other options, and considered my future career path, I decided this was the move to make. Primarily, I decided it was important for me to develop a level of expertise in a specific area. This job would add to my previous experience in direct-to-consumer entertainment marketing, which is a growing field. Also, looking ahead three to five years, I figured I'd have more hands-on experience in this area than most people at my job level, which would pay off in the long run.

What do you feel were the most unique advantages you had in obtaining the employment interview for your job?

The most important factor, or really the first qualifying screening factor, was my professional background. My previous job experience was very similar to what they do at Columbia House. Another key factor, I'm sure, was a personality fit with the people I interviewed with. When I met with the Director of Marketing, we had a laid back, friendly interview that I think was critical in getting the job. People want to work with people they get along with.

What are the top three pieces of advice you would like to share with someone contemplating this kind of career?

If you want a job in entertainment I'd say:

1. Make contacts. In this industry, maybe more than in any other, it's as much about who you know as what you know.

2. Keep on top of what's going on in all areas of media and entertainment. If you're interested in music, that should be your area of expertise, but all areas of entertainment overlap so much that it's an asset to know what's going on in film, television, interactive, publishing, and so on.

3. Be willing to make some sacrifices. Working in entertainment, especially for people just starting out, can mean long hours, basically, paying your dues. Have patience.

If you wanted people to understand your profession, what would you want them to know?

This is a hard one. When I get calls from Stern students I usually try to explain how my job is a combination of music marketing and direct marketing. I need to know a lot about the music I'm selling and the trends in the industry. On the other hand, I need to know how to reach my club members through direct marketing. I must be able to interpret demographic and sales data and use that information to determine the kind of music I will offer, as well as how that offer will be presented. I think that it's better to have a strong background in marketing than it is to have one in music. It's easy to read the trades and listen to the music to learn about what's going on, but understanding everything that goes into marketing a product isn't always so obvious and takes much longer to learn.

What are your favorite books, trade journals, magazines?

The magazines I try to read on a regular basis (though I obviously don't read all of these every week cover to cover) are the trade publications *Billboard, R&R,* and *Brandweek* (I think these three are "must-reads" every week, at least to skim through for important information), *Gavin, Hits, CMJ,* and *Variety;* entertainment publications *Entertainment Weekly, Rolling Stone, Spin,* and *Premiere;* and among other publications, *Wired* and *Time Out.*

What major things make a great job?

Things that make any job great:

- Having interesting, diverse responsibilities.
- Working with good people who are compatible, smart, and fun to work with.
- Feeling like you are actually accomplishing something.
- Taking on challenging projects.
- Knowing that there are opportunities for growth (e.g., moving up in the company and adding to your knowledge and skills).

What other thoughts would you like to share?

What constitutes being in a great job is a very individual concept. If you get up in the morning and you feel good about going to work you know you're in the right job. I'm most satisfied when I'm working on challenging projects, when I've got so much to do that the first time I look at the clock it's already 5:00 P.M., and when I go home at the end of the day feeling I've actually accomplished something or learned something.

▶ Jeffrey B. James is a Research Manager with MGM/UA. He received a BFA in Film and TV Production from the New York University Tisch School of the Arts in 1986 and an MBA in Marketing from New York University Stern School of Business in 1994.

What do you do on the job? Describe a typical day.

Here at MGM/UA I am setting up a research department for international distribution from scratch. In my previous position at Warner Bros. (WEB), with a research department already set up, a typical day consisted of answering questions from the overseas salesforce regarding the performance of WEB programs in the United States and overseas; creating regular product performance reports using overseas television audience measurements information; creating program pitch books (i.e., sales support tools that give audience research highlights on either U.S. or overseas markets) for the various television markets where WEB programs are sold; and working on special projects initiated by the Vice President of Marketing & Research.

Who is a part of your team?

Here at MGM/UA it is me and my boss. At Warner Bros., it was primarily me and my assistant.

What skills do you use the most in your career?

Math, creative writing, deductive reasoning, and analysis.

How much do you work with computers, financial analysis, people, things (objects)?

I work a great deal with computers. Much data is stored on a computer. Translating the data into usable presentations for salespeople and pointing out a program's best audience attributes is important. Data analysis is also part of the job. I have to read the numbers and interpret them. If the numbers don't say anything exciting, I have to hunt down more numbers until I find those that work, and then for those that don't, I have to put the best spin possible on them because I am helping the company to sell programs to clients.

What are your favorite and least favorite aspects of this job?

My favorite aspect of the job is the hunt—how to make the ratings and audience information exciting so that a salesperson can use it to help sell a show or movie. If the show is not a great performer how can I make it sound good? It's part detective work. Hunting through audience information to find that the show is #1 in its time period with adults of ages 18 to 24 as opposed to be #4 with adults of ages 25 to 54, is fun and challenging. I like challenge. At Warner Bros., I enjoyed the challenge of meeting deadlines and getting material and quality analyses out to the field for use. At MGM/UA my job is creating materials and helping to set up a department.

Another of my favorite aspects in research is focus group testing of a program that I have only observed. The professionals who do this have my highest respect and regard, because they are able to pull out of people, from children to adults, what they feel and think about a program. It is a special talent.

My least favorite aspect of the job is difficult to say. Sometimes getting the information is boring. At Warner Bros., the monthly product performance report was time-consuming and monotonous. The report format was set, and much of the research was checking lists to see what programs were or were not WB programs. This work required no creativity whatsoever. The reports were very cut and dried and presented information with no analysis; they said "show x did this in country y for month z."

What is the outlook in your industry and functional area and what are the most important tips for getting ahead?

There is potential for growth, but not as strictly a media researcher, because the higher up you go, more responsibilities are added that are not purely research-oriented. With growth, one progresses from finding information (as a research analyst and as a manager) to using it (as a marketing research director and higher). Compensation for the entertainment industry is likely to be lower than some other industries because of what I call the "Glamour Factor." It will always be a buyer's market rather than a seller's market because more people want to be in the industry than there are places available for them.

What are the top three things that make a great media researcher?

- Knowledge and the skill to find it.
- Ability to interpret and use that knowledge.
- People and communication skills.

How can someone get your job?

Someone can get my job by networking, reading the want ads, and having the skills needed to do the job. One cannot walk off the street and do my job without prior experience. No company or studio will hire you without prior media research experience. Studios are not training grounds for research analysts. One already needs to know how to read audience information because you will be dealing with people who do not know how to read and interpret the information. They hire their media research people to get the information for them and translate it so that they can read and use it.

How were you able to obtain this position? What steps led you to this opportunity?

I got my position here at MGM/UA because the Vice President of Marketing & Research was formerly with Warner Bros. (i.e., International

Television's International Channels). We knew each other because I had done some work for her at WEB. When a newly created position opened up at MGM/UA and I realized it was a chance to work with her, so I called her. Also, because I had previously applied for another position at MGM/UA my resume was still in the human resources resume file and unbeknownst to me, human resources passed my resume to her as well, recommending me as a suitable candidate. The personal connection greased the wheels and within a few weeks I had the new job, a nice raise in salary, and a sizable promotion less than two years after I arrived in Los Angeles with Warner Bros. Without question, this is very much a people business and my knowing people made the difference and sped the process along.

How did your education impact your career?

My education had an impact on my career because the combination of BFA and MBA degrees is not common. Film school was what I had been working for since elementary school, though I didn't know it at the time. In high school, I knew the film school was the college education I wanted. I applied to NYU's film and TV program as a transfer student from USC and earned my BFA from that program. NYU's Film and TV program was one of the greatest experiences of my life up to that point.

After several years in the workforce, I realized I followed the business side of the entertainment business with as much passion and love as I followed the creative side. I applied to one MBA program, Stern, and got in. My writing ability may have been the reason I got in. At my interview, the interviewer mentioned that the committee hadn't seen such well written essays in a long time. Writing was and is one of my strongest skills, in part because of my creative background. When I came to Stern, my thought was to change careers, but when I tried to change my field by drastic means, it didn't work. The BFA in Film and TV Production limited my choices. Corporate recruiters didn't look at a BFA-MBA degree combination as positive to their company's hiring needs and goals. Fortunately, I decided that the entertainment business was still the choice for me. Perhaps if my MBA had been in accounting or finance instead of marketing, then the career change might have happened. But marketing was my goal for my MBA and in hindsight, it was the right thing for me.

I earned an MBA to learn the skills and earn the certification necessary to show the business community that I had the background and experience to be taken seriously in business. My undergraduate degree nevertheless did keep me out of areas that MBA graduates traditionally pursue, such as brand management and marketing. Corporate recruiters did not connect the dots between film school and business school. Many didn't understand that the two degrees are more compatible than not.

Most BFAs in production pursue a career in production. If I had gone from graduation to being a low-paid production "gofer," then after seven years I might have moved up the production ladder. But after deciding to go the corporate route, and then staying with a market research firm for seven years I was not about to go back and be a lowly paid gofer (one of the unsung heroes of the entertainment industry). The MBA was the best source of action to move beyond my station in life at that company and move up the ladder without leaving and going back to square one and starting my career over.

What pearls of wisdom do you have for people with similar aspirations?

Be prepared to work. Be prepared to think. Be prepared to bust your ass when necessary. Be prepared to deal with many different people who need many different things and be ready to juggle projects. Love it or leave it. Keep a flame of passion for the job. If it goes out, so will you.

Be passionate about your chosen industry or field. Love it as you would love another person or yourself. Passion for something makes it easier to do. And people will see it. Don't do the 9-to-5 job that you hate unless it's for a higher purpose. Use your strengths to get in the door the best way you can. Don't make lateral moves if you can avoid them because lateral moves waste your time and your life. Lateral moves only help if you're getting pushed out or fired and need to land a quick job.

Don't alienate people on your way up because they sure aren't going to help you when you're on your way down.

Like your job. Don't stay if you're bored out of your mind, unless it's part of your master plan (i.e., to rise through the ranks). If you're bored, superiors will find out because boredom will be reflected in your work.

Network your ass off. Meet people. So what if they can't help you now, they might in the future.

What do you see as trends in your industry?

This industry is changing all the time. What will not change is the demand for U.S. entertainment product exports. That demand will continue to be strong for decades to come.

Satellite-delivered networks will enable U.S. studios to set up their own channels all over the world, which means guaranteed distribution of their product. That means these gigantic distribution entities will need more and more original programming. Many countries are making the leap almost overnight from 2 to 3 terrestrial channels to 50 to 100 satellite-delivered channels. Many territories will skip the development of cable and advance from broadcast to digital satellite within several years, if not months.

What is the outlook in your industry and functional area and what are the most important tips for getting ahead?

The outlook for MGM/UA is growth. My division is expanding into international channels and eventually co-productions, in addition to continuing to sell the library. Research will play an important role and will be part of my job. As international television platforms grow, demand for programming will grow. Distribution is like a shark that needs to be constantly fed product. Research will help companies differentiate their product for their clients from that of the other suppliers.

What do you see as the most challenging issues in your industry?

Increased competition and more regulations designed to protect local programming interests from U.S. programs. Local production companies in various countries will soon match the quality of U.S. programming, which means more local competition. As some countries close their ranks to U.S. programming, studios will have to set up their own channels to guarantee access to foreign markets. This will shut out the smaller U.S. production companies, which will have to align themselves with large U.S. production companies. There will be an oligopoly among the largest players in the industry, and then there will be a second tier and a third tier of production companies, which will fight among themselves for the scraps left after the large companies finish. Huge media powerhouses will expand into every corner of the world. This trend will force smaller program suppliers to either sell out their foreign rights or spend more to get their products into the international marketplace. There is and will continue to be a battle among the titans, aligning and fighting over every TV set in the world.

What do people need to know to get into this field? What are the most important skills to have?

People need to have a basic understanding of the entertainment business and they have to be passionate about this industry. Media research is such a specialized field that people need to gear their research interests to media research, as opposed to packaged goods or brand research. No matter how much the entertainment industry wants to establish brand-like status for their products, with a few exceptions there is no such thing as guaranteed brand-like status. To succeed, one needs to know an almost encyclopedic amount of information and one also needs to know how to use that knowledge. After knowledge, people and communication skills are the next most important things to have. One has to deal with creative people all the time. Egos run rampant. Dealing effectively with people above and below is a key to success.

Where do you see yourself in 5 to 10 years?

I don't know where I will be in 5 to 10 years. If it's in research, it will be as a vice president of research, if not for MGM/UA then for another studio, network, or program supplier. If not in research, then in program development and scheduling either in the United States or overseas.

Do you feel your work makes a difference to you, your family, society?

My work helps me provide for my family. I like my job and the work I do. It is challenging. I can make and hope to have made a difference for the companies I have worked for and the people I have worked with. We all bring ourselves to our work, and if I've made a difference with a workplace friendship, that's good. I'd like to say that what I do will have a lasting impact on the human condition. It doesn't. Does it give me great understanding? On a snapshot level perhaps because it says that at this point in time, in this country, these different people were being entertained by these programs.

Do you consider yourself spiritual?

I consider myself spiritual, but more importantly, ethical. I have personal integrity. I believe in taking responsibility for my actions. I have to be able to look myself in the eye and live with my actions. I also believe that I should do unto others as I would have them do unto me. I believe that what goes around comes around in a cosmic justice system. If one wrongs people or is a "bad," unethical person, one's lack of morality and ethics will catch up to oneself. I've seen it happen. People passing off work done by others as their own, have gotten "it," maybe not for the original offense, but in other ways. It goes back to the expression, be nice to people on your way up, otherwise they'll spit on you on your way down.

Each of us has talents that can be developed or not. People need to know themselves before they can get others to know themselves. They have to be honest with themselves. If one has screwed up, face it and accept the responsibility. Too many people pass on the blame for their actions. If all this means that I am spiritual, then yes, I am very spiritual.

How does spirituality fit into your life and your work?

My philosophy toward employment is that no one put a gun to my head and said I had to work for a certain company. If I have an unresolvable problem with a superior, my attitude is to either work it out or leave. No one is forcing me to work for this company or this person.

Anything that takes time away from accomplishing my goals wastes time. I'm not saying that I am a workaholic. I'm not. I like relaxing more than working. I'd rather spend a day playing with my son and daughter at the park than going to work, but if I don't go to work, no one's going to do it for me.

What motivates you to do what you do?

Love. Love motivates me to do what I do. I couldn't have lasted as long as I have lasted or advanced as far as I have advanced and will advance without that passion. I love the entertainment industry, but my love for this industry is not blind. The entertainment industry can be cutthroat. It is dominated by egomaniacs. One has to be thick-skinned to survive. One has to be able to network and socialize on many occasions. Los Angeles is an industry town for entertainment in much the same way, I would imagine, that Detroit is an industry town for automobiles.

What are the misconceptions people hold about this kind of work?

The biggest misconception is that just by being in the industry you get to meet stars. Nope. Research and distribution is one facet of show business, and seeing "stars" is rare because this side of the business is the business side.

What other thoughts would you like to share?

I would like to share the following thoughts about the entertainment industry. After almost two years of working for Warner Bros., I still got a thrill from walking on the "lot." It is magic to be a part of the entertainment industry. Sometimes I can't believe it. One of my goals in life was to work for a studio and I worked for one of the biggest, and now here I am working for another. Both companies are rich in history. If I hadn't been a film major as an undergrad, I would have been a history major. It's important to learn from the past. Knowledge of the present and the past can give you insight into the future. By seeing and understanding patterns and being able to read the clues, one can identify potential problems and work to resolve them before they become real problems.

I read and have read a great number of books about the entertainment industry, in part because the more information I can absorb the more it will help me. I think that to succeed in any industry, one has to love it and have passion for it. It can be anything. I have spent most of my life to bring me to this point in my life and it is a never-ending learning experience. I still feel the drive that helped me realize this was the industry that I had to be a part of. One cannot just jump into the entertainment industry unless you bring something to the table that no one else has or have something that you do better than anyone else.

Creativity and business are not mutually exclusive fields. A film degree and a business degree complement each other. Sometimes creative solutions are better for a business problem than any "business solution."

Luckily, the entertainment industry can recognize that a BFA-MBA combination is valuable. The entertainment industry is not for everyone.

Finally, remember this. You are ultimately responsible for your life and the actions you take. Luck doesn't exist. When people say that someone is lucky because he or she was in the right place at the right time, I don't agree. Luck had nothing to do with it. It was being in the right place at the right time, but also acting on the opportunity. Seizing the moment and running with it. That's my definition of "luck." People make their lucky breaks. It doesn't just happen. You should train and learn about what you're doing and when the opportunity presents itself, go for it. Is that luck? You can't wait for things to happen. You have to make them happen. You make your breaks.

Many people told me I was nuts for wanting to be a part of the entertainment industry, but I love it. I wouldn't want to be in any other industry.

▶ Paul Jelinek is a Manager in International Development with Discovery Channel International Networks. He received a BA in History from Vassar College in 1988 and an MBA from New York University Stern School Business in 1995.

What do you do on the job in your current position? Describe a typical day.

It is difficult to describe my typical day at Discovery Channel International Networks because each day varies quite substantially. Nevertheless, I do have some specific responsibilities. First, I was hired to perform two essential jobs; one was to manage Discovery International's business operations in the Middle East and India, and the second was to co-manage the budget and business planning process for all our International Networks during the summer. The jobs are quite different.

The first role, managing business operations, entails two primary functions. In the Middle East, it is more of an "affiliate relations" type job, because Discovery has a distributor relationship with one "operator" that distributes Discovery as well as other programmers' channels throughout the Middle-East region. Much of my time can be spent on the phone working with our affiliate to ensure that (a) there are no problems with distributing our channel and (b) Discovery is being branded effectively in the region. In addition to spending time on the phone with our distributor, I also work internally with our marketing, press, and production people to effectively promote Discovery in the region.

My responsibilities vis-à-vis India are to work with our India-based staff on all aspects of our strategy, which can entail helping them with business planning, analyzing the costs and benefits of specific projects, or strategizing with Indian staff on a specific aspect of their business, such as their distribution system. With respect to India, I am more of a facilitator, and the "eyes and ears" for senior management (based in Bethesda) on what is happening in the region vis-à-vis our office, as well as the competitive situation in the region.

My responsibilities during the summer in my second job are truly "number crunching" and information gathering. I work with every department (marketing, press, production, programming, etc.) to find out what their goals and objectives are for the next year for each network we serve, and then to determine how much those plans will cost for the year.

Who is part of your team?

Our international team is based in Bethesda, Maryland, although we have staff throughout the world, located in London, Singapore, Hong Kong, India, and Miami (for our Latin America operations group). Reporting to the head of our international division are General Managers for our Asian office, for Latin America, and for India. All have extensive experience in the industry.

How much do you work with computers, financial analysis, and people?

I work with computers every day. I perform financial analysis frequently, but it is not anything close to what I did in my MBA program. That is not to say that studying finance was not useful. On the contrary, the finance skills that I used in my finance, marketing, statistics (and other) classes all helped me to develop my problem-solving abilities and to be able to use financial analysis to develop an argument. I would say that while I use my computer daily and perform financial analysis often, I spend most of my time discussing ideas and working out problems with other people. I spend much of my time in meetings and on the phone, and I think that these are skills that one develops over time. I feel that the combination of my MBA education and my professional experience enable me to work effectively with people.

What do you like best and least about your present job, including pitfalls, challenges, and rewards?

My favorite part of the job is thinking strategically about how Discovery Channel should position itself in a particular region of the world, or thinking about potential competitors in a particular industry, or holding development meetings to determine with whom Discovery can work (distributors, affiliates) to grow the business. The least attractive part of my job is dealing with the little things that are essential to the job, but not the most exciting (e.g., sending a wire transfer and sending materials to a particular region). But even in these instances, I try to understand that these tasks are essential to running a business, so they are not mind numbing to perform.

I love the people that I work with. I tell this to many people, but I truly feel that I lucked out in terms of the people I work with. The people at Discovery International are smart, creative, warm, aggressive, and genuinely interested in what they are doing. Undoubtedly, working with these people, learning from them, has been a great experience. In addition, I have had the opportunity in only four months to travel to India, Dubai, and Rome. Traveling is wonderful exposure, especially for business. Even the mundane, trivial aspects of my job (e.g., making copies if I have to, filling out forms, and sending those wire transfers to our India office), while not terrific, are part of my job, and, when viewed in the context of a larger whole, I embrace them.

Is there compensation and growth potential in your job?

I don't get paid as much as someone would normally make starting out with an MBA, but there is tremendous room to make a very good living and opportunity to grow. I would suggest that if you really want to be in an industry, bite the bullet a little bit (if there is room for growth), because the money will come if you love what you do and are in an industry that is growing and potentially lucrative. I believe that I am in such an industry, and will be compensated in time if I am successful.

What steps led you to this opportunity? How were you able to obtain this position?

When I went to business school at Stern, I saw many large, homogeneous companies coming on campus to conduct interviews. Some things definitely attracted me to these firms: the money, the prestige, the security, and so on. In addition, there was this embedded "follow the pack" mentality, where everyone was speaking about who had what jobs, and so on. I knew that I wanted to do something international, and I was leaning toward doing something in the entertainment industry, but I was still drawn to the idea of an investment bank or the big consulting firm.

After my first year, I went to work for an investment bank, and found that the money was nice, but I just didn't care for the product, the business of making money for the sake of making money. After I graduated, I had an offer from a consulting firm, but I knew that my heart was not in it.

I graduated, and decided that I would make an effort on my own to find an entertainment company that appealed to me and where I might do something international. I started contacting everyone I knew and requesting annual reports of companies that interested me. I wrote letters to people who were listed in the annual reports of every major company and then I called them. Much to my surprise I was not always rebuffed.

During one conversation I had with a fellow Vassar graduate who now works at HBO, she mentioned that one of the heads of Discovery International also graduated from Vassar. I wrote to that Discovery International executive, called her and got an interview. Two months later I was hired, moved down to Washington and began working for Discovery International. Much of landing my job, I admit, was luck, but I also believe that much of it came from reflecting about what I wanted to do with my life and having the guts to wait and not grab the first thing that came my way.

What is your career history?

My prior work experience has been for American Express, Morgan Grenfell, and Weil, Gotshal & Manges. At American Express, I worked for the International Travel division doing special projects for the head of that division. At Morgan Grenfell, an investment bank, I performed equity research for the emerging markets division. At Weil, Gotshal & Manges (a law firm) I was a legal assistant. In each job I always concentrated on doing something international and on finding a skill that was transferable to any other job I might have in the future.

What impact did your education have on your career?

I think that my MBA was extremely valuable in developing my functional skills, my overall perspective about international business, and my ability to work effectively with people from different backgrounds and cultures. I also think that majoring in history (something other than business) in college was valuable in giving me a broader perspective and thereby developing my business acumen.

Where do you see yourself in 5 to 10 years?

One of the exciting things about Discovery International is that there are many options for a career, especially internationally. My goal is to spend a good number of years in Bethesda learning, in detail, how this company operates, and how to manage each international network. Once I have gained that ability, and, I hope, contributed to the company, I could envision working in Affiliate Sales/Business Development for one of the regions where we are located abroad.

What training or education do you think is necessary for this career?

I think one simply needs to be smart and aggressive to succeed. As our company grows, I think an MBA helps one get into the company, but I don't think it is vital. I do believe that my MBA helps me everyday in solving problems, but I also believe that there is an enormous number of people in this company without MBAs who perform very effectively because they have broad industry experience and are simply very smart.

What trends do you see in your industry?

There are many trends in international media, too many for this page. The two main trends are a continued expansion in programming content and constant changes in distribution technology. The first trend is something you notice every day. Programming companies in this business are constantly finding and developing new cable channels to offer consumers. We are fast developing into a society that will have specific programs for each demographic group. There are sports channels, travel channels, educational channels, and the list goes on. This constant competition for shelf-space is occurring internationally as well as in the United States. Equally as important as content is how consumers receive their channels. Distribution is undergoing dramatic changes and consumers are being bombarded with constantly changing methods of receiving Pay TV (e.g., direct-to-home vs. cable and analog vs. digital). Content and distribution are the name of the game and they are changing constantly.

What are the international trends in your area of expertise?

If you look at the major players, both cable programmers and broadcasters, they are doing two things: Creating product-line extensions (new channels) that enable them to secure additional shelf-space and expanding internationally. This is not surprising, because many international markets are untapped and are increasingly becoming the main revenue generators for large global media companies. Take India, for example, as an international market. India has a population of almost 900 million people, four times that of the United States. Currently, there are approximately 40 million households in India with TV's and 14 million of these have multichannel capacity. That may not be close to U.S. levels, but it represents a huge source of potential growth. If India eventually had 70 million households with multichannel capacity, that would represent only about 8 percent of its population, and yet would still surpass U.S. levels.

What do people in your industry share in terms of personal characteristics that make for success?

I think most of the people I work with are young, aggressive, and very smart. In addition, most of them love what they do and are extremely interested in international media in particular. I feel that I have been fortunate to have found a group of people who are not only interested in what they are doing, but are also a particular pleasure to work with.

How can someone get your job?

No one can have my job—just kidding. If you want this kind of job, find out what companies are in the field, who the people are, and write to them, then call them. Being aggressive has always helped me. Too often, people think that there are many, many people calling and writing. The truth is, yes, many people write letters, but not a lot of people make the required calls and really get in peoples' faces.

What are similar areas in this field that people might consider?

Each company is structured differently so I really can only speak about Discovery Channel. The names that I discuss below might be different at other companies, but the types of jobs probably do not vary that much. There are a number of different fields for people in the media industry. If you are creative, you might want to work in production. There are positions in programming, where one essentially evaluates potential product for distribution and creates program schedules. People who have a technical bent, can work in technical operations or satellite strategy. There are positions in management, advertising sales, affiliate sales (which essentially serves distributors), finance, accounting, and business development. There are many, many opportunities for anybody with a desire to work in media.

What do you feel were the most unique advantages you had in obtaining the employment interview for your job?

I think my skills were important, but in addition my personality fit very well with the group that I interviewed with. The more I meet people and interview, the more I realize that people want to hire people they want to work with, as long as they are also intelligent and motivated.

What are the key points in your answer to the question, "Why should I hire you for your ideal job?"

I always pitched several things about myself that I believe I am very good at and that are difficult skills to copy (essentially, I try to differentiate myself): (1) I play up my MBA and the fact that I can perform any kind of financial analysis; (2) I highlight my communications ability, and usually bring writing samples with me so that I can show my work; (3) I pitch my professional and academic experience as someone who comes from a nontraditional background who is well-traveled and who is able to communicate and work effectively with people from different backgrounds and cultures; and (4) I make it my business to know about the company and industry of the job that I am interviewing for, so that I can impress my interviewer with company and industry specific questions.

What do you hope to achieve with your work?

I don't know, honestly, what I hope to achieve with work. I would like to do my job well, make good friends in the process, and be able to explore a large portion of the world through many professional experiences. It would be nice one day to head a company or start my own international media firm, but I just don't know what I hope to achieve that far down the road.

What are major things that make a great job?

The major things that make a great job and life are: (1) enjoying the people that you work with; (2) being passionate about the industry you are involved in and the product or service that your company produces; and (3) having a job that enables you to grow.

What is your favorite quote?

Ambition is the last refuge of failure. (Oscar Wilde)

What pearls of wisdom do you have for people with similar aspirations?

Don't assume you know more than anyone else.

What are your favorite books and magazines?

I love reading nonfiction books (e.g., political, travel, and biographical), and I read "The Economist" religiously.

How does spirituality fit into your life and your work?

Spirituality does not fit into my life, although a deep interest in Woody Allen, Chinese food, and Schubert piano sonatas does.

Do you feel your work makes a difference to you, your family, society?

Work definitely makes a difference to me. Enjoying work and working hard helps me to appreciate other things in life such as having time off, being able to spend an evening at a classical music concert—not only earning the money to do those things, but also being able to appreciate and savor having free time. When I reflect on times when I was dissatisfied or depressed with my life, it seems that those times usually occurred during a period when I did not like my job.

What advice would you impart pertaining to your industry?

Someone with whom I work gave me a good piece of advice. In media, don't ever think that you know everything because it is always changing. Humility, in terms of your knowledge base, is key.

▶ Susan Lopusniak is the Nickelodeon and Nick at Nite Brand Director with the Viacom Retail Group. She received her BA in Visual Arts from the College of the Holy Cross in 1989 and her MBA in marketing and International Business from New York University Stern School of Business in 1996.

Tell me about your background and what attributes got you to where you are today?

I graduated from college during the peak of the U.S. recession with a degree in visual arts. Although I didn't know what I wanted to do (I realize now that was due, in part, to the fact that I didn't even know what jobs existed), I did know what I didn't want to do, and did know myself pretty well in terms of the disciplines in which I excelled and those in which I did not.

I am in the business of building brands. My personality, interests, and prior experiences have crafted my current position in brand development for one of Viacom's emerging and most promising businesses. How I got to where I am will undoubtedly play a role in where I go in the future. I attribute my success and current job to a few principles I've gathered throughout my tenure in the entertainment field: know yourself, set high standards, take pride in your reputation, and be willing to take risks.

How did you go about targeting companies?

I targeted firms in industries whose performance and growth would not be negatively affected by the country's recessions—cosmetics and entertainment. On a whim, I accepted an interview for an entry-level position at MTV Networks, part of the Viacom family. I researched the company, prepared pointed questions, and sent timely thank you notes.

What was your career path at Nickelodeon?

I spent the first four years in Nickelodeon's licensing department in New York, rising through the ranks from assistant to manager. I entered this area as the industry's size burst to $60 billion per year. My responsibilities ranged from contract negotiation with external parties (manufacturers and retailers) to creative product development and design. I found that I liked the combination of businesses, from shoes to glassware. Over the years, I developed an animation art business for Nickelodeon, drafted our company's merchandising agreements for theme parks, and designed gift products based on the cult program, "The Ren & Stimpy Show." I worked closely with companies such as American Greetings, Marvel, and Mattel and crafted a rolodex of active contacts.

What made you decide to get an MBA?

It was during this time that I explored furthering my education. The field of licensing was booming and both start-up and well-established companies were exploiting the trend, integrating their trademarks into products ranging from apparel to video games. Although the majority of industry executives did not have advanced degrees, I felt an MBA could give me a competitive advantage and would provide insurance should I choose to switch jobs in my field. I decided to pursue my degree at night so that I would not be out of the swift-moving entertainment field for two years.

The discipline and time-management required for the part-time pursuit of my MBA made me perform better at my job. I understood that although I was traveling constantly, I needed to return every phone call and turn in assignments on time. I became better able to prioritize work and integrate play. I began to see how my role with my department fit into Nickelodeon's larger, more strategic picture. My positions and the associated results were rewarding because I believed in the company's philosophy of developing brands that reached their audiences in unique ways. I became emotionally attached to Nickelodeon's kid-first, empowering brand whose attributes held meaning for me.

These prior jobs as well as my current one are pretty demanding. Twelve-hour days are common as is extensive travel, often to small cities as well as major metropolitan ones. The social nature of the entertainment industry blurs the lines between your professional and personal life, because many events take place on nights and weekends. You need to roll up your sleeves to get the job done, because executing a glamorous event often translates into tactical activities, lots of hard work and many trips to the mailroom.

On a whim, not unlike that which I followed to get into this industry, I applied for an overseas study program through Stern. My acceptance into this program required me to take four months off and move to Australia in order to participate. Although I did not want to leave the industry, I knew I wanted international exposure and viewed this as a unique opportunity to simultaneously reflect on my career and pursue my MBA. I requested, and Nickelodeon agreed to, a leave of absence for four months.

Being away allowed me to broaden my horizons and really think about how I had spent the past four years. I evaluated the impact of my education on my job and thought about my next career move. I realized that I needed to hone new skills that would improve me as a manager and increase my ability to move ahead at Viacom or any other company. Perhaps more importantly, I began to think about different options beyond my small world of licensing.

Upon my return to New York and Nickelodeon, a position that fit well with my skills and desires opened in the network's marketing department. I was quickly promoted to director, responsible for creating and executing promotions with external and intracompany partners. Nickelodeon, like all of Viacom, was growing quickly, as was my exposure to different facets of the company. My Rolodex grew to include new contacts from these divisions as well as from Stern. I continued to nurture important industry relationships through cocktail parties, seminars, informal chats, and written communication.

What skills do you need to succeed?

The need to communicate well is important in the entertainment industry because many deals are struck through colloquial and friendly conversation. A certain amount of business etiquette peppers these exchanges. A congratulatory note to a colleague or tickets for an executive's favorite concert are gestures that are welcomed in this industry, but must be delivered sincerely. My Rolodex contains the names and ages of many contacts' kids. I am, after all, in the kids' business. Holiday time is usually spent writing personal notes on the inside of several hundred Christmas cards because that type of individual attention matters. I learned through experience that I'm not only in the business of marketing the Nickelodeon and Nick at Nite brands, I'm also in the business of marketing myself.

During my last year of business school, Viacom announced the birth of a new division charged with creating owned-and-operated retail stores, to extend the awareness of all of the company's brands. Nickelodeon asked me to spearhead brand development for both Nickelodeon and Nick at Nite in this venture, Chicago's Viacom Entertainment Store. While the job promised excitement, career growth, and challenges, it also required me to move to Florida during my last semester of school. Sensing the opportunity to meld my prior experiences and drive a highly entrepreneurial process for brands with which I truly identified, I accepted the job and commuted to Stern for the remainder of my graduate education.

Flexibility is an important skill, too. After a year in Florida, my division relocated with our parent company, Blockbuster, to Dallas, Texas. I'm traveling now more than ever between New York and Dallas, and am realizing how well my background and prior experiences prepared me for this new challenge.

Describe a typical day. What is the scope of your work and its challenges?

This job has no typical day. My responsibilities include translating these brands to products, a retail environment, advertising, promotion, and special events. These responsibilities are as tactical as writing copy for a hangtag and as strategic as positioning Nickelodeon's preschool properties to a consumer audience. Because of this division's entrepreneurial nature, I wear many diverse hats, often several at a time. The ability to juggle many projects simultaneously remains important, as does the ability to focus and perform on many projects. My familiarity with and passion for these brands motivate me. If I didn't believe in the validity of this project and the application of these brands within this new retail concept, I couldn't succeed.

The field of entertainment retailing that charges each outlet to engage consumers in brand-relevant activities and to sell product commemorative of the experience is hot. Warner Bros. and Disney have created this field, and companies such as Nike and Viacom, among others, have quickly entered it. The race is on for all of us to design interactive, revenue-generating retail experiences that push our brands further than we ever imagined. My involvement in this process, as an individual and as part of a team, leverages my experiences in both licensing and marketing and the skills and knowledge I gained through earning my MBA.

Throughout these experiences, I've found it important to know my skills, my strengths, and my weaknesses, as these form the standards I set for myself and my work. Brand development, for brands whose attributes mesh with my own, is an exciting field and one in which I excel. My most developed assets, however, are my mind and my rolodex, and both will take me where I want to go.

▶ Doug MacKay is Director of Custom Publishing at Gruner + Jahr. He received a BA from Vassar in 1982 and an MBA from New York University Stern School of Business in 1992.

What do you do on the job? Describe a typical day.

I manage the Custom Publishing business for Gruner + Jahr USA Publishing. My company is the fifth largest publisher in the country, publishing seven major women's service magazines: *Family Circle, McCall's, Parents, Child, Fitness, YM,* and *American Homestyle and Gardening.* Custom Publishing creates single sponsored magazines, either one-tie issues or on-going projects, for corporations usually using one of our titles as a tie-in.

For example, my key client is Target Stores, the discount store chain owned by the Dayton Hudson Corporation. I publish their magazine, *Target the Family*, four times per year. Each issue contains editorials about home decorating, entertaining, family living, and fashion as well as celebrity interviews. Where appropriate, we feature merchandise sold at Target. Half the issue is the magazine and the other half is Target's catalogue for that quarter (it looks like a Spiegel catalogue). I hire the editors and art director, serve as the key liaison between Target and Gruner + Jahr, and coordinate the ad sales, manufacturing, and distribution. When I'm not working on this project, I'm managing our magazines for Nordstrom and Gaylord Entertainment as well as prospecting for new clients.

A typical day involves some meetings with internal contacts (like the production staff) to ensure our schedules are running smoothly. I spend lots of time on the phone with the various freelance editorial staff and with the clients putting out fires, running approvals, and coordinating production schedules. More time is also spent on follow-up calls for new business and lunch appointments with people to discuss potential projects.

Who is part of your team?

My team changes constantly depending on the project on which I'm working. However, I usually have a freelance staff of 6 to 8 editors and art directors. My assistant is invaluable for keeping track of everything.

How much do you work with people, computers, and financial analysis?

Most of my time is spent with other people who create our projects with technology. All of our layouts and editorials are created on screen and shipped between us and our printer via America On-line. I also spend many hours per day at my computer (and with a laptop, on the weekends) writing proposals and cranking out spreadsheets for project profitability reports. And I'd be nowhere without voice mail and e-mail, both inside and outside of the company.

What part of your day is spent doing what?

I spend half my day on the phone or in meetings. The other half is divided between writing internal and external correspondence, reviewing and signing off on expenses, analyzing profitability statements, and thinking about new projects. I also travel quite a bit, so another chunk of my time is spent in taxis, rental cars, hotel rooms, airports, and airplanes. I travel with a laptop sometimes and I always bring magazines from work, which I read and then discard on the plane.

What do you like best and least about your present job?

The best part of going to work is the autonomy. I'm in a department with two full-time employees, and I have wide latitude in planning and implementing my projects. It's also incredibly creative. I'm constantly coming up with new magazine ideas for prospective clients and am involved with creative problem solving for existing clients. This makes my work day unpredictable. I never know what will pop up or how long it will take to fix, but at the end of the day it's my work and I'm accountable for its success or failure. Plus, it's fun to see your name on a masthead.

The down side of this is that we are a renegade group within the company. I report directly to the CEO. He worries about lots of other problems, so getting his attention and input is sometimes difficult. Similarly, being the point person for these projects means that all the problems cross my desk. I deal with the personality conflicts, delays in the processing of bills, the snowfall that halts delivery—everything. It's a real juggling act. The least favorite part of the job is the turnover. I've reported to four people in less than two years, which is frustrating.

How do you get paid? Is there potential for compensation growth?

My compensation is a combination of salary and bonus, based on the net income that I generate during the fiscal year. I stand to increase this amount significantly if I bring in additional business or increase business from existing clients.

How does your position affect your after-work life?

Most of my friends are in book or magazine publishing so we talk a lot about work outside of work. My hours aren't too bad, but the travel schedule is sometimes difficult. However, if I come home late from a trip, I'll go to work late the next day or take off early on Friday. Because my department is so small, I feel some responsibility for checking in while I'm on vacation. I rarely take work with me, but I'll call in and I always leave an address and phone number in case anyone needs me. I'd much rather take 10 minutes to solve a problem from a phone booth in the Caribbean than walk into a crisis the first morning back at work.

How were you able to obtain this position? What steps led you to it?

I owe this job to Stern. The woman who had this job before me was a year ahead of me at Stern. After I graduated, I met with lots of people, including her, to talk about various career options. She saved my resume and called me 18 months later to tell me she was moving and to ask me whether I would be interested in her job. I followed up, went through a four-month job interview process (they were in no hurry to fill the opening), and got the job.

What is your career history?

I spent several years in advertising before business school. Starting as a media planner at a whopping $10,000, I moved on to account work and account planning. I enjoyed advertising, but I felt that the real power and business decisions were on the client side. After finishing Stern, I joined the client side as a marketing officer in a private bank. Boring, boring, boring, but a nice vacation schedule and free checking.

What factors attracted you to your present career?

I was intrigued by the overall opportunities and by the chance to learn about an entirely new industry. Although I knew a bit about the logistics of magazines from my advertising days, I'd never created one. Plus, as I continued the interview process, I realized that the prospects and upside of custom publishing were incredible.

How did your education impact your career?

As an undergraduate majoring in English, I honed a love of words and learned to study a project carefully and thoroughly. In business school, I gained an appreciation for the accounting skills, financial equations, and marketing concepts involved in a successful business. However, what really came in handy were the management information system skills and the organizational management courses because communications and interacting are fundamentally at the core of my job and are skills I use every day.

What training or education do you think is necessary for this career?

An MBA isn't required for this job, but it helps in preparing and analyzing financial data and in writing presentations about marketing objectives and strategies. An introductory course in media planning would provide a solid introduction to what a publisher faces from an advertising agency and some technical overview of production would make the first six months much easier.

Where do you see yourself in 5 to 10 years?

I'll still be in publishing, I'm just not sure where. If the online craze continues, I'd be interested in going there. Custom publishing at another company like Time Inc. or Conde Nast is another option. However, as I get older, the appeal of owning my own business, either starting a magazine or joining a new magazine—increases.

What major pieces of advice would you like to share with someone contemplating this kind of career?

Major pieces of advice: be prepared to work a lot for a little until you get noticed, then you'll work a lot for a little more; never be afraid to ask a question, but just be careful who you ask; and know when it's wise not to repeat information to somebody although you're busting to tell.

What trends do you see in your industry?

The magazine industry is recovering after several bad years, resulting from high paper prices, shrinking print-advertising budgets, and a glut of magazines. The growth potential for custom magazines is excellent, as corporations realize the viability of owning their own publications and as they see how this marketing tool ties them closer to their customers. As this attractiveness increases, so does the competition. Many more magazine companies offer custom publishing as an added value program to an advertiser. For example, if Mercedes increases their ad spending in *Car and Driver*, then the publisher might create a custom magazine for Mercedes for next to nothing. I can't compete if the profit point is too low.

What are the international trends in your area of expertise?

Internationally, custom publishing is burgeoning. Gruner + Jahr is based in Hamburg and is active in German custom publishing projects.

Other Western European and Australian publishers also have viable custom businesses. Many of these are stand-alone companies, meaning they only do custom publishing and aren't connected to a larger magazine company. This approach is in direct contrast to the trend in American custom publishing, where most custom publishing is done by major magazine entities.

What do people in your industry share in terms of personal characteristics that make for success?

We're all team players, which sounds hokey, but it's true. Without the support of all the various departments, we'd never publish a magazine on time. We're also good communicators, because we need to explain carefully and thoroughly what the assignment is, how to approach it, and what needs to happen in order to get it completed on time. The second part of that skill is being a good listener and processing what people are telling us. And we never underestimate the importance of having a sense of humor; it's crucial for getting through the day without killing someone.

What are the misconceptions people hold about this kind of work?

Custom publishing is often seen as the ugly stepsister of magazine publishing. It's not. It's a great way to present information to a consumer in a long and structured format, that is completely controllable. It has more impact than just a magazine ad and more longevity than a television spot—plus it's a lot cheaper. To be good at custom publishing you need to know more about magazines than about advertising, because you're creating editorial content first and then wrapping around and incorporating a marketing message. It's also a lot more fun than people expect.

What are the most important traits and skills to have to get into this field?

Someone breaking into this magazine field should have an innate love of magazines. I knew I was a magazine junkie when I realized I received more magazines in my mailbox than junk mail. Knowledge of the industry and a keen interest in it are key. Hanging out at Barnes & Noble is a great way to browse new magazines, see what topics are hot, and notice who's writing what.

The most important skills are the ability to sell a project, knowing how to motivate others to support your projects, budgeting the expenses of the project, and a fearlessness in tackling all the problems that arise during the development of the project.

Where do you see job growth in your field?

Assuming that it continues to grow as quickly as it has, online offers the greatest growth potential. If magazines figure out how to put their editorial on line without repeating a story and make money from ad sales, then it looks like a golden opportunity for growth.

How can someone get your job?

Land a job in custom publishing by talking to people who do what I do at other publishers, by reading trade magazines like *Folio* and *Media Week*, and then by doing great follow-up.

What are similar areas in this field that people might consider?

Similar jobs in magazine publishing are working in advertising sales, in the marketing department of a magazine, or a corporate marketing department. Editorial experience is another option because you can develop solid writing skills and a good sense of the mechanics of magazine work.

What is the outlook in your industry and what are the most important tips for getting ahead?

The forecast is good because as the magazine industry continues to improve, so will custom publishing. Tips for getting ahead in this business are pretty similar to business tips in general. A few of the golden rules are: Never speak ill of your boss; always introduce yourself to higher ups; be nice to your support staff, because without them you're screwed; and, most importantly, be self-confident because then everyone is likely to assume you're wildly capable, even if you feel otherwise.

What do you hope to achieve with your work?

I hope to achieve a reputation for producing quality, profitable work that I'm not embarrassed about, and that provides a decent salary and sense of satisfaction. It sounds easy, but there are a lot of schlocky custom magazines out there.

How does spirituality fit into your life and your work?

I equate spirituality with a sense of calmness and serenity. Often I attempt to incorporate this into my work life by trying not to panic at every crisis and by maintaining an evenness of temperament throughout the day. This also means treating my coworkers kindly and avoiding finger-pointing when problems arise. At home, I meditate sometimes and I take a yoga class once a week, which helps me maintain my sanity in a 500-square-foot one-bedroom apartment. Working out four or five times a week also strengthens my inner self, my resolve, and my abs.

What are the key things that make a great manager?

The key characteristics are: listen to people's complaints, maintain profitability, and don't be afraid to make a mistake.

If you wanted people to understand your profession, what would you want them to know?

Publishing is glamorous in that you work with writers and photographers, go on shoots, and fret about color registration and printing mishaps. But it's a business like any other. We worry constantly about the bottom line, operating profit margins, budgets, and accounting minutia. The underpinnings can be as boring as those of banking or pharmaceuticals, but the cast of characters is more fun and that makes all the difference.

What resources did you use to identify specific job leads in your industry?

In looking for work, I relied heavily on the Stern network, my Vassar network, my friends, their friends, and want ads in several publications. I'd write to people who were listed in the alumni listings and go talk to them, even if they weren't involved with areas I was interested in. I figured I had nothing to lose, and often they referred me to contacts in areas I was interested in. Similarly, I got really good at working cocktail parties and other social events for leads.

What do you feel were the most unique advantages you had in obtaining the employment interview for your job?

Besides being a friend of the woman who was vacating the job, I also offered a combination of relevant work experience and education. In addition, I really prepare for interviews by gathering as much information as I can find. In this case it meant finding annual reports, reading the current issues of the magazines and calling my friends to see if any of them knew anyone there. Coincidentally, the woman who hired me for my first job in advertising had become the research director for this company. So it always pays to keep up with people.

Who participated in the employment process for your job, and what were their roles?

I interviewed with three people: the director of the department, the COO, and the CEO. The director gave me the lowdown on the job and outlined all the responsibilities. I really needed to mesh with her in order to move up the interview ladder. The COO was a young German who, although pleasant, was very technically oriented. He grilled me about my job history and quantitative capabilities. I literally sweated like a race horse through this interview because his office was overheated and my seat was in the sun. Last, the CEO and I met for an hour. I knew before the interview that we had a mutual friend, so I called the friend and asked him to put in a good word for me. Having this introduction immediately put the CEO at ease and we had a great talk. I now report to him directly, so the good impression lasted.

What do you think really got you your job?

What I tried to communicate in all the interviews was my enthusiasm about the job, my willingness to work, and my determination to get the job. I pitched myself as the only logical candidate. I wasn't arrogant, but I made it evident that I really wanted this job and that not hiring me was a mistake they shouldn't make.

What are the key points in your answer to the question, "Why should I hire you for your ideal job?"

Hire me because I'm articulate, give good presentations, and understand the importance of a deadline and a budget. In my interview, I also stressed my understanding of the business from my time in advertising and drew in the relevant business school coursework.

What pearls of wisdom do you have for people with similar aspirations?

Focus on what your goal is and force yourself to do something every day toward that goal. Make a phone call, write a letter, join an industry association, or go to a lecture. Also, as you go through the interview process, there are several pointers that can come in handy:

always write a thank you letter that's punchy and compelling, ask your interviewer what two things they would change about their job, and shine your shoes (nothing says spiffy better than well-cared for footwear).

Where do you derive your inspiration?

It's corny I know, but I get my inspiration from my father, who went into business for himself in 1968 and today owns a very successful marketing consulting business in suburban Chicago. He proved that hard work, a clear sense of direction, and a fearless approach to air travel can push you toward success.

What are your favorite trade publications, business periodicals, and books?

For work I read lots of trade magazines. In addition to *Folio* and *Media Week,* I read *Ad Age, Media Industry Newsletter, Inside Retailing,* and *Discount Store News.* I religiously read the *Wall Street Journal* and the *New York Times.* I rarely read business books; I guess I should read more, but it seems like such work. However, I usually read two books a month for pleasure. This builds my vocabulary and provides a wonderful escape from office life.

What is your favorite quote?

Never say never.

▶ J.B. Miller is Co-President of Empire Entertainment Incorporated. He received a BFA in Television and Film from New York University Tisch School of the Arts in 1987 and an MBA from New York University Stern School of Business in 1993.

As background what is your employment history since graduation?

- Ron Delsener Concerts, NYC, Booking Assistant.
- Late Night with David Letterman, Talent Booking Assistant.
- MTV Studio Production, On-Air Talent.
- Overland Entertainment, Head Talent Buyer, Producer, Vice President Sales and Marketing.
- Empire Entertainment (my own company), President, Talent Buyer, and Producer.

How did you identify your ideal career? What experiences, tips, contacts, and other sources were most helpful?

I did what I enjoyed most and the career opportunities just sort of developed around me. I did do a few internships, which exposed me to the people who later hired me in my first two jobs.

What key qualities and competitive edges did you need to reach your ideal career?

There were no key qualities. You either offer skills that get the task at hand done or you don't work out.

How did you identify target organizations for your ideal career?

I did no formal research. I have always focused on doing the best possible job, and opportunities just arose. However, it helps if you're in a job where you're speaking with many people and have some profile.

What special tips do you have for writing resumes and cover letters?

Spell everything properly on your resume and have it ready to fax if someone asks for it. Don't let the conversation or interview be only about your resume. Make the interviewer confront the person, not the piece of paper. Resumes are not truth.

What special tips do you have for preparing for employment interviews?

I have never failed to get a job offer in an interview. Prepare as follows: Ask yourself if you 100 percent want the job offered. If the answer is anything less than 100 percent, don't bother going on the interview. If the answer is yes, don't leave without convincing everyone in the room that you'll do the job better than they could.

What do you think really got you your job?

Being able to do the work that was needed.

What do you like best and least about your current work?

Best: variety, stimulation, money, prestige, travel, and being at the center of happening things.

Least: long hours and people who get in the way of my doing what I want to do.

What part of your day is spent doing what?

80 percent on the phone, 10 percent in meetings, and 10 percent writing.

What skills do you use most in your career?

Relationship building, chatting, and negotiation—all people skills.

What are your favorite books, magazines, and trade journals?

Books: Buddhist and history books.

Magazines: *National Geographic, New York,* and *Spy.*

Trade Journals: *The New York Times* and *Pollstar.*

What do you see as the most challenging issues in your industry?

The Internet is making professional information available to amateurs. Information without expertise does not create experts.

What do people in your industry share in personal characteristics and skills that make for success?

They are people who crave stimulation, are always looking for the next big thing, and are fun at parties.

How can someone get your job?

Work for my company.

What are similar work areas in this field that people might consider?

Special events producers or corporate entertainment industry liaison.

What other thought would you like to share?

Don't think that anything is beyond your capabilities or experience.

Having completed this questionnaire, is there any thought you would like to add?

If you don't enjoy the work, change your job.

▶ Philip Sidel is a Marketing Manager at American Express Travel Related Services Company, Inc. He received a BA in Economics and a BA in Drama from Tufts University in 1991 and an MBA from New York University Stern School of Business in 1996.

What do you do on the job? Describe a typical day.

I am a manager in the Interactive Services Group at American Express. My group is responsible for all Internet and online initiatives for American Express worldwide. My job centers around bringing American Express products and services onto the Internet. I act as an internal consultant for various groups within American Express.

Who is a part of your team?

My team consists of me, a director of marketing, a vice president on the marketing side and depending on the project, various business development and implementation people.

What part of your day is spent doing what?

I spend about half of my day (if not a little more) in meetings and spend the rest on the phone, on the Internet looking at new concepts and ideas for our sites, or responding to e-mail.

How much do you work with computers and people?

I work most with computers, then people. My job centers around computers and creativity. I'm constantly in meetings checking out at the "look and feel" of a site, or figuring out how to make static information more dynamic.

What are your favorite and least favorite aspects of this job?

I love being able to apply knowledge that someone just learned about the Internet to my job the next day. And I hate having to write marketing copy. I love the fact that I will come into work every morning and have a completely new problem facing me. Since this is such a new environment, it is always a challenge to get people to agree on a direction or even a basic goal for a specific task.

How does your position affect your after-work life?

I end up talking about American Express and the Internet at every party, bar, and restaurant that I go to. It seems that everyone has billing questions and wants to talk about the Internet.

What are the major things that make a great manager?

Creativity, willingness to learn, and ability to work in an unstructured environment.

How were you able to obtain this position? What steps led you to this opportunity?

I was extremely lucky in landing this job. I had been rejected by three divisions within American Express and, after the let-down finally wore off, I called all of my contacts and asked them if there was anything else I could do. One Stern grad knew of a friend hiring for a part-time internship position with Interactive Services. He forwarded my resume and I got the job. That job then turned into a full-time summer internship, a part-time job during my second year at Stern, and now a full-time job after graduation.

What was your prior work experience?

After I graduated from Tufts, I moved to East Greenwich, Rhode Island, to restore an old vaudeville movie theater from the 1920s and create a nonprofit center for the performing arts. I worked for three years recruiting volunteers, raising funds, and producing at the newly minted Greenwich Odeum.

How did your education impact your career?

I have to be the candidate for the "Got the most out of business school" award. I would never be here today if I hadn't gone to Stern. In business school I learned some basic skills that revolved around technology and I was able to leverage them into this incredible job.

What factors attracted you to your present career?

I love the adventure and creativity of working with the Internet, and the freedom of marketing using this channel.

How did your interest in this field originate?

My uncle is a computer distributor and ever since I can remember, he used to bring home computers for my cousins to use. I used to go over to their house and play adventure games on the computers, so it was ingrained in me very early that computers went hand in hand with adventure. I see my job as an Internet "adventure," so I guess I'm just doing the same thing I've always done.

What do you hope to achieve with your work?

I would like to gain enough expertise to manage an entire corporate Web site and have the skills to make it interesting and vibrant enough to draw consistent consumer attention. I also am hoping to learn more about managing resources.

What skills do you use the most in your career?

Creative thinking, critical thinking, time management, and management of office politics are probably the main personal skills I use. I also work in the Excel, Word, and Powerpoint software programs every day.

What major advice would you like to share with someone contemplating this kind of career?

(a) Surf the Internet daily to see what the latest technology enables companies to do online; (b) try to get something that relates to technology on your resume; and (c) create your own web page.

What training or education do you think is necessary for this career?

It is necessary to have some formal marketing experience and a lot of knowledge about computers and the Internet.

What are similar areas in this field that people might consider?

Business development for companies on the Internet and market research for all interactive services.

What do people need to know to get into this field? What are the most important skills to have?

They need to know how the Internet works, and need to be conversant with web culture. Probably the most important trait to have is the desire to experiment and explore. I don't think you'll last long in this business if you like seeing the same thing every day.

What do you see as trends in your industry?

The Internet is going to affect every aspect of our lives in the next few years. Every company that is serious about doing business is going to have to employ Internet-savvy marketers and managers.

What are the international trends in your area of expertise?

They mirror what's going on domestically, except that there are greater pressures to keep business materials in their original language.

What do you see as the most challenging issues in your industry?

Security and misinformation are the two major issues facing the Internet and all interactive services. If this technology is going to spread throughout the United States and the world, programs need to be written that will ensure the privacy of the information transferred via the Internet. Also, the media needs to educate itself about the realities of the Internet. Until the U.S. population is given the message that this environment is safe and easy to use, the Internet will continue to be a playground for the education and business elite.

What do people in your industry share in terms of personal characteristics that make for success?

Everyone seems to be bright and to love a challenge. I've never heard anyone say "It can't be done" when referring to an idea for a site.

What is the outlook for your industry and functional area and what are the most important tips for getting ahead?

It looks as if the Internet is going to exceed everyone's expectations as a growth industry. I think that people with expertise in marketing on the Internet will be in constant demand because businesses will consistently want access to this expanding market. To get ahead, it is essential to know what developments are happening today so that you can plan accordingly for the future.

What pearls of wisdom do you have for people with similar aspirations?

As long as you surf the web consistently and can tell a good story that shows why you should be in this industry, you shouldn't have that much trouble. The problem that most people have is that they are interested in the interactive world, but they don't do their homework. You've really got to explore the Internet and understand what is happening "out there" before you can get into this field. Whereas the desire to get into this area used to be enough, now you have to back that up with some real experience.

Where do you see the most job growth in your field?

There will be incredible job growth in the secure transactions, secure identities, market research, and interactive marketing fields.

What sources did you use for identifying target organization contacts for your ideal job?

I looked on the Internet for companies that did things I thought would be fun and then bothered my friends and family until I found contact names at all of these companies.

How would you summarize your reasons for applying for your job at this particular company?

I applied for a job at American Express for several reasons. First, after my experiences in the nonprofit world, I wanted to work in the comfortable setting of a big corporation for awhile. Second, although I wanted to be involved with the Internet and online services, I felt very wary of working for a smaller company that might be bought, be sold, or out of business in the first few months of my working there. Finally, if the Internet didn't develop as anticipated, I would still have the marketing experience at American Express on my resume.

What do you feel was the most unique advantage you had in the interviewing process?

My advantage (as I was told after my interview) was that I was able to relate experiences that I had had in the past to situations currently facing the marketing team in the Interactive Services Group. By making each interviewer feel as if I had been in situations similar to theirs and had survived to tell about it, I was able to convince them that I could do a commendable job working with them.

Who participated in the employment process for your job and what were their roles?

In my first two interviews, I met directly with the decision makers, each of whom had the ability to "ding" me. When the first liked me, I was interviewed by the second, and was hired on the spot at the end of my second interview.

What are the key points in your answer to the question, "Why hire me for my ideal job?"

I answered this question by showing how the skills associated with this new job were similar to those I used in previous jobs. For example, I showed that I was creative, was an able manager, worked well in an unstructured environment, and liked dealing with the unknown.

What do you think really got you your job?

I was told by the vice president for marketing for our group that I got this job because I was "nice." So I would suggest to anyone who is interviewing to remember to smile and pay attention to what the interviewer says. A sincere comment like, "Wish your child a happy birthday" just might get you the job.

If you wanted people to understand your profession, what would you want them to know?

I would want them to know that I'm making their computer worth the investment.

What are the misconceptions people hold about this kind of work?

I'm not sure whether people know how much fun this line of work is.

Do you feel your work makes a difference to you and society?

I think that the work I do makes people's lives a little easier. I like the idea of doing simple tasks online such as paying an American Express bill or finding a good restaurant in New York. I also feel this job will take me somewhere. We're just seeing the beginning of what this new technology can do and by working with it now, I think I'll be prepared to take advantage of some major developments in the future.

What motivates you to do what you do?

I guess what truly motivates me is the desire to make an impression. I would like the work I do to affect a lot of people.

What are your favorite books, trade journals, magazines?

My favorite magazines are *Forbes* and *Business Week,* and the best trade journals are online, such as *Seidman's On-line Insider.*

What is your favorite quote?

I am that.

How does your spirituality fit into your life?

For now it just helps me keep things in perspective. I practice yoga daily and incorporate a lot of the spirituality behind it into what I do. Two of the "teachings" are that you have to be "present" in what you're doing, and you have to breathe. So, although it's difficult sometimes, I try to focus on what's going on right now and not to worry about the three other meetings that are coming up in the next few hours. I find that if I do that (and remember to breathe) I can get a lot more quality work done than when I'm flying around the office.

From where do you draw your inspiration?

I draw my inspiration from my desire to make a difference.

Where do you see yourself in 5 to 10 years?

I hope to be running my own business on the Internet.

What other thoughts would you like to share?

I believe very strongly in sharing contacts and helping other people. I would never have landed this job if someone wasn't willing to help me, and I've tried to do the same with my peers. With all the uncertainty surrounding this business, I think it's essential to stay in contact with everyone you know who is in interactive services and to help them out whenever possible.

What advice would you impart pertaining to your industry?

Surf every day.

▶ Caroline Turner graduated from Princeton University in 1982 with an AB in English and spent 12 years working as an administrator in professional theatre. She then attended the Stern School of Business at New York University where she received an MBA in Finance in 1999. She is now Supervisor, Business Affairs at MediaVest Worldwide, Inc.

What do you do on the job? Describe your current position. Describe a typical day.

My title is Supervisor, Business Affairs for MediaVest Worldwide, a media management company. My job has two components: contract administration and financial analysis. The contract administration piece involves negotiating and drafting contracts and managing the contracting process for a variety of contracts, ranging from research agreements for the company to development deals for made-for-television movies. The two most complex agreements are joint ventures that a client has with other companies, which I manage. I have also done revenue forecasting and monitoring for the company. A significant portion of a typical day is spent on the phone with clients and with attorneys. I also meet regularly with senior management on the status of the joint ventures. I also spend time reviewing contracts and dealing with various other people within the agency.

How were you able to obtain this position? What steps led you to this?

While I was in business school, I became interested in media and entertainment, which seemed a logical extension of my work in the theater business. I had always loved negotiating contracts so business affairs for an entertainment company seemed like an interesting option. I wanted to work in the entertainment business during the summer between my first and second years of business school; I thought that the summer would be a great time to try something new out and if it wasn't right for me, I would have the second year of business school to figure out my next step. I did a great deal of informational interviewing using every possible lead that I could come up with: alumni from my college, business school alums, friends, my hairdresser . . . I got my summer job (which became my permanent job) through a friend from college whose father wrote a letter on my behalf to the person who hired me. I worked part-time for MediaVest during my second year of school as well.

What is your career history or prior work experience?

I spent 15 years in professional theater management working primarily in nonprofit regional theaters. My last job in the theater was as the general manager of a Broadway show. After realizing that I had progressed about as far as possible and feeling disenchanted with commercial theater (Broadway), I decided to make a career change. This was a long, difficult process which included career consulting and working as business manager for a program for mentally ill, homeless women. This long transitional period resulted in my decision to seek an MBA.

What is your favorite aspect of this job? Least favorite?

My favorite aspect of the job is negotiating deals. My least favorite is the fact that I don't really have any peers so I sometimes feel isolated.

What do you see as trends in your industry?

Consolidation (e.g., The MacManus Group, MediaVest's parent company had merged with The Leo Group, another large advertising/media company), vertical integration (e.g., Viacom's acquisition of CBS), and the increasing importance of the Internet as a media outlet.

What do people need to know to get into this field? What are the most important skills to have?

In business affairs, one would need to have a working knowledge of contracts. Often business affairs professionals are lawyers (I'm not). Understanding the fundamentals of the television business is important as well. Key skills include interpersonal strengths, high motivation, ability to work well without a lot of supervision, attention to detail, and negotiating talent.

How can someone get your job?

Intern in a business affairs office and network. It's all about getting in the door in some way.

What are you favorite publications?

Variety, Entertainment Weekly, Entertainment Industry Economics by Harold Vogel.

What motivates you to do what you do?

I like the complexity of the process of making deals. Each time, it's a different process and therefore new in some way. It's usually interesting and often exciting.

What are things that make a great supervisor?

Giving clear guidance and feedback; articulating a direction/vision. Ability to set priorities. Being approachable and responsive to subordinate concerns.

How did your education impact your career?

My undergraduate major was in English. That was an advantage in terms of gaining writing skills but combined with a theater career, it made the transition out of the arts very difficult. I was viewed as "artsy" with few transferable skills even though my theater management jobs involved accounting and budgeting. This was my primary reason for getting an MBA in finance. I needed the credential to make the career change out of the arts.

What are similar areas in this field that people might consider?

People might consider a job in finance within a media/entertainment company, perhaps as an analyst. Some of what I do is similar to what analysts do.

What is your favorite quote?

Life would be no better than candlelight tinsel and daylight rubbish if our spirits were not touched by what has been. (George Eliot)

Any pearls of wisdom for people with similar aspirations?

Explore every avenue when going after your first job. The entertainment business is all about relationships. You never know where that first opportunity is going to come from.

How did your interest in this field originate?

During my time as a theater manager; I negotiated many different kinds of contracts and got involved in negotiating collective bargaining agreements with the theatrical unions. Those duties were always the ones that I enjoyed the most so when I decided to make a career change I looked around for a job which would allow me to do the same kind of things.

What do you see as the most challenging issues in your industry?

The impact of consolidation, new media, the changing role of the networks in television.

Who is part of your team?

I work with attorneys, other business affairs professionals, senior management for the agency, our clients, and many other people within the agency who legal review of agreements. One of the great things about the job is the variety, both in job responsibilities and the people that I have contact with.

Where do you see job growth in your field?

In media/entertainment because of the demand for content, more deals are being made which means more demand for people who make the deals.

Where do you see yourself in 5 to 10 years?

I see myself still at MediaVest working in business affairs but with more responsibility for bigger deals.

How does your position affect your after-work life?

It can be difficult to get out of the office in the evening because I'm on the phone with people in California which is 3 hours behind New York. They're just coming back from lunch when it's 5 P.M. here.

What do you hope to achieve with your work?

I hope to provide the best possible service to our clients.

What factors attracted you to your present career?

I was most interested in the kind of work that I would be doing. The work environment is relatively casual; upper management is approachable. That made a difference to me, as well.

What resources did you use to identify specific job leads in your industry?

Networking/informational interviewing is the way to approach finding a job in media/entertainment. These companies don't usually recruit on campus and often aren't a priority for a business schools' career development office.

What sources did you use for identifying target organizations for your ideal job?

I used all the sources listed. I relied primarily on personal contacts and alumni from both business school and college. I really believe that exploring these contacts is the most effective way of finding a job.

Who participated in the employment process for your job, and what were their roles?

Above and beyond the normal channels, I was fortunate to have access to senior management through a personal connection. I was interviewed by two executive vice presidents and had a final interview with the CEO.

What do you feel were the most unique advantages you had in obtaining the employment interview for your job?

A personal recommendation from a former colleague of my boss.

What do you think really got you your job?

My background in contracts and the personal recommendation.

If you wanted people to understand your profession, what would you want them to know?

I spend a lot of time synthesizing and presenting information so that others can make decisions. I have to think a great deal about my "audience" and how to present issues clearly and concisely.

What are three pieces of advice you would like to share with someone contemplating this kind of career?

(1) It's easier to maneuver after you get in the door at a company. There are often lots of opportunities that are available but only after you've found a way in. (2) Be aggressive about going after projects. Speak up if you want to be involved in a project. Don't wait to be asked. (This is especially true for women.) (3) Try to maintain the contacts that you made during informational interviewing after you have a job. It's likely that you will need to use them again at some point in your career and it's easier if the connection isn't stone cold.

How much do you work with computers, financial analysis, people, things (objects)?

30 percent—computer work (writing, editing).

40 percent—people, talking on the phone, or meetings.

20 percent—financial analysis.

10 percent—working with hard copies of contracts.

What skills do you use the most in your career?

Writing skills and financial skills (including ability to construct and manipulate spreadsheets)

What training or education do you think is necessary for this career?

The MBA has certainly been helpful; I took some media/entertainment-related courses which I have used. I don't know that an MBA is absolutely necessary for the job I do; I probably draw more from my previous on-the-job contract negotiation experience. Strong writing skills are absolutely essential; they come from a good liberal arts education. As I wrote previously, business affairs professionals are often lawyers so a law degree can be helpful.

Is there potential for increasing your compensation?

People interested in this business should know that business affairs is a support function; it isn't revenue-generating. This limits your compensation potential.

What are the misconceptions people hold about this kind of work?

People often think my job is glamorous because I work in television. It has its moments, but I spend way too much time poring over contracts for glamorous to be an accurate description.

What other thoughts would you like to share?

Changing careers is a difficult thing to do. It can take a lot of time and work to make a transition. It can be frustrating and exhausting to invest time and effort in something that has an uncertain outcome. But it has its rewards: you really learn a lot about yourself in the process and it's immensely rewarding to accomplish your goal.

What advice would you impart pertaining to your industry?

This is really for all industries. During my career transitions, I have done a great deal of networking and informational interviewing. Almost to a person, everyone that I have called has been extremely generous in terms of offering time and assistance. I keep reminding myself of this when people call to ask me for my time and assistance.

▶ Michael Whalen is Vice President of Finance and Acquisitions for People's Choice TV (PCTV), a wireless telecommunications provider of video and high-speed internet access services. He received a BS in Accounting from New York University in 1987 and an MBA in Finance from New York University Stern School of Business in 1988.

What do you do on the job?

PCTV's strategy is to own, develop, and operate wireless telecommunication networks to deliver digital video and high-speed Internet access service in large metropolitan markets. The company's operating and targeted markets are concentrated in the mid-western and the southwestern regions of the United States. Currently, the company provides service in six operating systems located in Chicago, Detroit, Houston, Phoenix, St. Louis, and Tucson, and controls wireless cable channel rights in three additional markets, Indianapolis, Salt Lake City, and Milwaukee, where the company expects to launch networks in the future.

What part of your day is spent doing what?

I am on the phone and in meetings 50 percent to 60 percent of the day.

How much do you work with computers, financial analysis, and people?

I work with computers 25 percent of the time, financial analysis 25 percent, and people 50 percent.

What is your favorite aspect of this job?

The job creation that occurs as the company grows. So far, the company has grown from 100 employees two years ago to over 500 employees as of 12/31/96.

How could someone get your job?

Build as many contacts as you can. It's always easier getting a job when somebody knows you.

What is your career history or prior work experience?

I worked for five years for Bank of Montreal, where I was director of the Media/Telecommunications Group and director of the Private Placement Group. A client (Matt Oristano, CEO of PCTV) asked me to join PCTV.

How did your education impact your career?

My MBA provided entry into the investment banking field.

What factors attracted you to your present career?

What influenced me was my relationship with Matt Oristano, founder and CEO of PCTV and my belief in his "vision" of the telecommunications world in 10 years. Information and communications will be transmitted primarily via a wireless platform rather than fiber.

What skills do you use most in your career?

Negotiating, financial modeling, and interpersonal skills.

What do you see as trends in your industry?

The deregulation of the telecommunications industry, which will make for interesting strategic alliances.

How did your interest in this field originate?

As a child and as a teenager, I was always interested in media, entertainment, and business.

What do you see as the most challenging issues in your industry?

Access to capital and complete deregulation of the telecommunication industry, so that we can enter additional businesses.

Where do you see job growth in your field?

Job growth will be in programming content in order to feed distribution pipelines (i.e., new cable TV channels and networks along with film production).

What do people need to know to get into this field? What are the most important skills to have?

People need to have knowledge of financial markets, valuation of assets, and deal structures as well as strong interpersonal and negotiating skills, and a strategic vision of the future.

What do people in your industry share in terms of personal characteristics that makes for success?

They are entrepreneurial and quick decision makers.

If you wanted people to understand your profession, what would you want them to know?

Entrepreneurial companies bring highs and lows in terms of achievements and failures. One can't dwell on failures.

What is your major advice for someone contemplating this kind of career?

Flexibility, focus, and persistence are key.

What resources did you use to identify specific job leads in your industry?

A personal relationship with a client of mine at Bank of Montreal.

What are the key points in your answer to the question, "Why hire me for my ideal job?"

I have a strong technical background in finance, I am a good negotiator, and I possess strong interpersonal skills and industry experience (i.e., as a banker I focused on the telecommunications industry).

Who participated in the employment process for your job?

No one except Matt Oristano, the CEO.

What do you feel were the unique advantages you had in obtaining the interview for your job?

I knew the industry and had a strong finance background.

What are your favorite publications?

The periodicals *Business week,* the *Wall Street Journal,* and the *New York Post* (for its sports section), and trade journals, including *Multichannel News, Variety,* and *Broadcasting/Cable.*

What motivates you to do what you do?

Being involved in a dynamic growing industry makes a mundane thing like finance fun and interesting.

Where do you derive your inspiration?

My family (wife and parents), my church, and "internally."

Where do you see yourself in 5 to 10 years?

In the rapidly changing telecommunications industry, I don't know where I will be in three to six months, much less five years.

How does your position affect your after-work life?

It is completely separate.

What do you hope to achieve with your work?

The creation of jobs, shareholder value, and I'd be lying if I didn't mention personal wealth (via incentive options I have in PCTV).

How does spirituality fit into your life and your work?

One needs a balance in life. Spirituality helps me find such balance between family, work, and other social activities. If you work 16 hours a day for 20 years you will one day be sorry for all the things you missed in life (i.e., family, friends, social events, travel, and the like). You can never recapture this no matter how much money you have made!

How important is work to you?

Work is important to me, but by far not the only thing. It would make a Top Five List, but probably not at #1.

FINDING YOUR WAY IN OTHER BUSINESS FIELDS

So far we have covered the major business sectors. There are many other, smaller sectors to consider. The profiles in this section include examples from real estate, high-tech, aerospace, chemicals, personal services, and automobiles. Exploring career options in these smaller fields typically requires more focused research and more networking than for the larger sectors. There might be less on-campus representation from these organizations and some of these industries are not well-known. The links of your undergraduate education to these industries might be greater than anticipated. Examples from the profiles include education in architecture, engineering, international studies, science, communications, and journalism. By definition, a wide range of industries and companies fall under other business fields, thereby offering you a broad opportunity to identify a job that is right for you. You can give full rein to your preferences for such things as physical environment, professional mix, working culture, quality of life, and even excitement. This narrower focus can take you to unexpected, but rewarding activities (e.g., the profiles include reconstucting a major railroad station, building wind power facilities, traveling abroad, identifying new businesses, starting a personal services venture, and promoting automobiles). The main message is to go beyond the major sectors to at least consider some that might be a great match to your heart-of-heart career objectives.

▶ Daniel Alter is an Associate with Lasalle Partners. He received his BA in Architecture in 1983 from the University of Minnesota and his MBA from New York University Stern School of Business in 1996.

What do you do on the job?

I am a real estate developer working in the Development Management Group for one of this country's largest real estate firms. The group oversees every aspect of the entitlement, design, and construction of corporate office buildings and large institutional or private development projects. The range of concerns that my group addresses on any project include the areas of finance, municipal approvals, architectural design, engineering, construction, leasing, management, logistics, and community along with municipal approvals. The goals established for me by my company vary depending on the project I am engaged with.

The goals always tie into budget and schedule concerns and performance is measured against the established goals. In order to reach my company's goals and my clients' goals, I must convince, persuade, cajole, form teams, consult, direct, analyze, and explain. I also must apply technical knowledge of construction methods, materials, process, design and building codes, accounting, and so on.

On my current project, I oversee the development of new retail space within Grand Central Terminal, where some 500,000 people pass through the terminal construction site daily. I work with existing tenants who are being relocated or inconvenienced, as well as with user groups who will be affected by the redevelopment (i.e., railroad communications, operations, maintenance). I am a liaison between the contractor, owner, consultants, tenants, and users and act as a single point of contact for the owner.

Who is part of your team?

The people who are part of this project team possess quite varied skills. The project executive has an MBA from an Ivy League school and has a background in development. His colleague is a former investment banker. Other project executives at this firm have backgrounds in architecture, engineering, or construction. The development side has two senior project managers. The first has an engineering degree; the second has no engineering degree, but has a strong background of work with a nationwide contractor. Supporting the senior project managers are a project accountant and several project managers who handle different aspects of the project. All seven of the project managers and senior project managers have a master's-level education in engineering or real estate or an MBA. Men outnumber the women, but new hires at the firm are just about 50-50 men to women. Within the Development Management Group, a number of women hold senior-level positions.

What is your favorite aspect of this job? Least favorite?

One of my favorite parts of this job is the fact that I am not tied to an office all day. I am really on my own the entire day, checking in at the field, spending some time in the office and attending meetings. I spend about half my time in the field inspecting construction in progress and monitoring the general status of the projects. I do this on a daily basis. I enjoy the interaction with a wide range of people: contractors, trades people, engineers, architects, and the client. It is also interesting to understand the specific needs of each client and how the client operates so that we can better satisfy these needs and operational requirements.

In the position of developer, I orchestrate the entire project and that is very satisfying to me. I enjoy tracking the budget and working with the different groups.

My least favorite aspect of this job is that, although we as developers have enormous control over a project, there are some aspects of it that are outside of our control. A contractor's skill and speed cannot always be improved if found lacking. Also, a client's wishes may sometimes contradict the client's goal for a project. The nature of this industry is cyclical, and I wish that this aspect were less so.

How much do you work with computers and financial analysis?

The industry is becoming more reliant on computers. The firm I work for is no exception. We have e-mail like everyone else. We also have a companywide database that includes major categories related to public relations, marketing, research, contacts, case histories of past projects, and contracts and forms to be used in the course of our work. We have group scheduling and project management software and specialized software for different functions within the firm. In addition, we have computer training at least once a year.

The amount of financial analysis depends on the phase of the project. In initiating and planning a project there is an enormous amount of financial analysis. As the project progresses, the intensity of that analysis lessens. In development management we also spend a lot of time looking at contract documents including drawings, specifications, plans, and leases.

How did your education impact your career?

My MBA education had a dramatic impact on my career. I probably would not be where I am today had I not had that training. My architecture background is a big plus. From my graduate schooling I learned a business outlook and the seeking of solutions from a business point of view. This attitude is the critical factor in convincing potential employers that I am able to make decisions that can positively affect a company's bottom line. A business outlook and way of analyzing problems are things I didn't have before I completed my MBA. These capabilities have nothing to do with smarts or qualifications; they have to do with how my training affected me. In addition, I am convinced that employers, including the "Big Six" consulting firms and my present employer, would not have given me a second look had I not had the training that I did. I often heard that my combination of education and experience was seen as unique and an attractive element to recruiters.

What factors attracted you to your present career?

A number of factors attracted me to my present career. I didn't want to make a complete break with my past. I felt that my background and MBA would be an asset in a real estate development career and that if I entered a different industry, I would be starting over in many ways. I have numerous skills, experience, and technical knowledge that are assets in this industry, but that might not apply in another industry. I enjoy the variety of roles one plays and the opportunity to go from an office/professional environment to a field/tradesman environment in the course of every day. There are personal rewards and professional advantages in this kind of daily variety of relationships and environment. One can learn quite a bit about potential pitfalls and fine-tune knowledge of the development/construction process through such daily interactions.

What trends do you see in your industry?

One trend in this industry is the emergence of big players who can attract large sums of capital to invest. The ability to do that has always been critical, but is becoming more so. In addition, the corporations who use our services have become more sophisticated about the different types of real estate services they desire. Many corporations are outsourcing and are seeking professional management to take over roles formerly performed in-house. Besides this, or maybe because of this, corporations are looking for one-stop-shopping for real estate services. Even mid-size corporate clients can have interests overseas and want one global player to serve their needs. There are consolidations driven by the need for capital and the requirement to be national or international to service all the needs of any one client.

A trend within companies is to have better integration between disciplines in the firm to provide better service. This change also enhances a firm's ability to cross-sell services—to sell one service to a client initially and then to sell other services. One example of this would be selling development management services to a client and then selling property management or investment services to that client if it has a portfolio of properties.

Another trend is greater reliance on industry research to bring value to a firm. The firm with better research on markets, etc. will have the ability to develop better strategies and more attractive products.

What do people need to know to get into this field? What are the most important skills to have?

People have to have a good understanding of the construction process, be able to understand construction documents, and be creative in proposing solutions to issues that arise. Also important are good communications and the ability to handle a number of different projects at once. At any one time there may be 20 issues which need an immediate solution. The resolution often must involve all the groups: contractor, owner, developer, architect, and so on. There are no long periods of time in which to focus on one issue because the product is being developed and built while the issues come up and wait for resolution. There are short periods of time available in which a solution must be proposed or a position relative to project impact must be taken.

People in my group have backgrounds in engineering, finance, architecture, construction, investment banking, real estate, and general project management and within each of these disciplines are useful skills for development management.

How did you find out about the employment process and individual roles?

I spoke to a number of people in the field regarding the firms I had targeted. Through those contacts I found out about the employment process and possible job openings. It was a little surprising for me to realize through my discussions that there were a multitude of functional areas within real estate and that a person performing one function was not always aware of what was happening in another functional area. For example, leasing people don't necessarily know what project managers do and tenant representatives may be unfamiliar with the development process.

For my own searches, I referred to the Stern telephone directory, which listed firms where people were willing to offer information about the company. I used a contact I had in Chicago to help set up a lunch meeting with a colleague of his in order to get additional information.

Once every couple months, I would try to get in touch with each contact or at least the ones with whom I had established the best rapport.

How would you summarize your reasons for applying for your job at this particular company?

The company that I targeted is one of the largest in the industry. The size of a real estate company is important and is becoming more so. The company is large enough that it has specific disciplines such as, advisory, leasing, investment, asset management, and development, whose employees are considered experts in their field. In addition, the company plans to continue to grow both internally and through acquisitions. I felt that this plan could strengthen the company and my position in it as time went on.

In economic downturns the company did not shed employees, even in the Development Management Group at a time when activity in the field dropped by approximately 50 percent. This happens to be an especially strong period for this industry and I wanted to be with a leader. The firm I signed with has one of the best reputations in the field. It has been around for nearly 30 years and has held itself to incredibly high standards throughout that time. The hiring process is quite long and appears to be very selective. I was happy to be one of the successful candidates.

If you wanted people to understand your profession, what would you want them to know?

Real estate is curious because many people don't really understand it or know what to think about it. Their only association with it may be through local real estate agents or brokers. For people interested in corporate real estate, I would want them to understand that it is a real business with all the attributes of any other service business. Furthermore, it is a business that today in almost all respects has shed the muscle-bound arm twisting salesman stereotype many people seem to associate with its practice. For a number of years now, a majority of the top firms have been hiring people with MBAs. The level of sophistication and professionalism has never been higher both in its practice and in how corporations and Wall Street view it. The same reengineering that corporations have been undergoing is now being demanded of corporations' service providers, including real estate.

Aside from all of that, I would want people to understand that the field is growing in depth as well as breadth. There are many functional areas, and one must investigate each function to find the best match for his or her personal interests and goals.

Although the real estate industry is undergoing a fundamental change in the services and sophistication it provides, it may still be a cyclical industry that follows the ups and downs of the economy. This may be hard for some people to accept or deal with. Almost all industries experience worker mobility and real estate may experience more of that than others.

▶ Reid M. Buckley is Vice President of Wind Energy with Tomen Power Corporation. He received his BS in Engineering Mechanics from Yale College in 1983 and his MPPM from Yale School of Management in 1989.

What is your employment history since graduation?

1989–1990	Fellow, Robert Bosch Foundation
1991–1992	Consultant, William Kent International
1992–1996	Manager, Business Development, Kenetech Windpower
1996–1997	Director, Business Development, Kennetech Windpower
1997–	Vice President, Wind Energy, Tomen Power Corporation

How did you identify your ideal career?

The key was knowing what I did like and did not like. Having worked in consulting, I knew I wanted to focus on a single industry and to stay away from consulting type staff jobs. I wanted a job with day-to-day decision-making authority. Also, I wanted an industry where I believed strongly in the products or services offered. This factor was most important in identifying my target industry. What industry would I be proud to say I worked in? What industry would I be excited about day in and day out? Using these criteria, I began discussions with friends and searched through my academic and work past to identify areas of real interest.

How do you suggest identifying the qualities one needs to pursue one's ideal career?

By understanding your target industry and by understanding the challenges and opportunities facing the industry, you can determine the kinds of profiles and skills needed and sought by the industry. This information does not come from reading career books or advertisements, but rather from studying trade publications and the general business press, and, most important, from talking to people in the industry.

Having settled on a target industry, how did you identify target organizations?

Personal contacts in an industry were the best source of information on specific companies in the industry. Trade journals and articles in the general business press on the target industry were also useful in identifying target companies along with their executives, strategies, and so on.

Who was in your search network and how did they help you?

My search network initially included friends and colleagues and rapidly expanded as I met contacts suggested by these people. It is important to ask each new contact for additional contacts (i.e., "Who else do you know whom I can meet?"). Executive recruiters can also be an excellent source of industry information and contacts.

What are your special tips for writing cover letters?

In cover letters, I try to do two things: (1) Make my past relevant and (2) state clearly what I can do for the company based on my experience and knowledge of the company and industry needs.

What are trends in your industry and what backgrounds offer the best opportunities?

In electric power, the key industry trend is deregulation, away from regulated monopolies to competing enterprises. On the marketing side, almost any marketing experience, especially in telecommunications, is viewed positively. On the power generation side, project finance work or real estate development are seen as valuable experience. Foreign language skills are also a plus because the key markets for power generation are offshore.

What do you like best and least about your current work?

What I like best is the opportunity to develop, finance, and build environmentally sound, cost effective, renewable power plants. What I like least is travel, which is a necessary component of project development work.

What values and objectives influence your career path?

My career thinking is governed first by consideration of how any specific job will affect my family life. I have to find work that allows time for my family. In addition, I want my work to be something that my family can be proud of.

Reflecting on your experience, what additional career search tips do you have for graduating MBAs?

Know yourself. Base your search on your own goals, personal and professional. Resist the temptation to measure yourself against your classmates, whose goals and values might not be your own.

▶ Laurena A. Ketzel-Kerber is an International Program Manager, Asia-Pacific Region with AlliedSignal, Aerospace Division. She received a BA in International Trade and Politics from Whitworth College in 1988 and an MBA in International Business from New York University Stern School of Business in 1996.

What is your career history or prior work experience?

After graduating from Whitworth College in 1988, I worked in the field of integrated global logistics. This term has come to include international transportation/freight forwarding (ocean, air, rail, truck), import/export, customhouse brokerage, warehousing, and freight insurance. I was involved in import operations for about three years and earned a Federal Customhouse Brokers license during that time.

In 1991, my husband and I traveled throughout Central and South America for a year with the purpose of checking out holistic community and economic development organizations and projects. Soon after that trip we returned to Central America, where we managed a semester-long study/service tour for 29 university students through my alma mater, Whitmore College. In between my work and these trips, I was able to find consulting projects with small businesses and often assisted in logistics and international issues.

Prior to entering the Stern School of Business, I returned to the integrated logistics field and moved into marketing and sales, where I worked for about one year.

After completing a year of the MBA program, I worked for the Overseas Private Investment Corporation (OPIC), a U.S. government agency in Washington, DC. I served as the Assistant to the Vice President for Finance, and worked on international project finance issues and projects all summer. Although I was not planning to focus my MBA studies on finance, I needed to augment my quantitative skills and knew that OPIC would give me great exposure in that area, as well as exposure to economic development, international issues, and government and bi- and multilateral agencies located in Washington, DC.

What do you feel were the most unique advantages you had in obtaining the employment interview for your job?

AlliedSignal actually called me and invited me to interview with them on campus. Previous to this, I had not really considered a manufacturing company, because I was still thinking more about international consulting or some type of economic development-related firm or agency. Given my logistics and operations background, however, I found that manufacturing firms in various industries were interested in my skills. This led me to consider other large manufacturing firms as well and I began to investigate those that had international operations.

During the summer in Washington, DC, I networked some, and asked numerous questions to help me define what I was looking for in a full-time job. All of the people I contacted were very helpful in answering questions and pointing me along in my journey. I conducted a number of informational interviews with Stern alumni as well as with other businesspeople I met through Stern faculty, and at various conferences I attended. I commuted daily from Princeton to Manhattan and did some networking at this time. When I began my job search in the fall, I contacted several of the companies that had offered me internship positions for the previous summer.

My real search, however, began around Christmas time and at the beginning of second semester. Although this was very late in the recruiting season to begin, previous to that time I was unsure on exactly which functional and industry areas I wanted to focus. I had given up the idea of being an international consultant due to concern for quality-of-life issues. Traveling away from my family for 80 percent to 90 percent of my time did not sound like a fun way to spend the next few years of my life. By Christmas, I had just begun to learn about the rotational management training programs that many large manufacturing firms offered and that sounded like a good option to pursue. I did apply to several development related firms and agencies, but nothing seemed to really "fit."

Who participated in the employment process for your job and what were their roles?

- An initial screen was conducted by a middle manager.

- Second round interviews were conducted by managers from around the country, from a variety of functions. Each voted/ "scored" me, and a group of managers decided who would receive offers.

- Once offers for specific locations/functions were made, on-site visits were scheduled and additional informational interviews were conducted by senior managers and local Human Resources people. Human Resources people didn't really make hiring decisions. Managers recommended candidates for specific positions and responsibilities and roles were more specifically defined.

- At the end of the day of various interviews with on-site managers, a Human Resources person met with me to review my preference for assignments. He then spoke with respective managers, and they offered me specifics later. This process took quite a few weeks due to communication lags and the need to get clarification about the specifics.

How did you find out about the employment process?

Mainly from library research and talking with current employees and interviewers. I also had a key contact with someone in another MBA program who was interviewing for the same company. We often swapped notes and compared all aspects of the respective offers we received. This was extremely valuable.

What do you think really got you your job?

Although AlliedSignal pursued me, I wasn't very excited at first because of the perceived lack of international activity in the company overall. After several site visits (i.e., including Headquarters, the Morristown, New Jersey office, and various offices in Phoenix, Arizona) I became much more interested, especially after talking with two international directors in the Aerospace Division. My background matched up well with what they were looking for and my passion for international work and my enjoyment of strategy were closely aligned with where the department and company in general hope to go.

When I began my job search, one of my main criteria was geographic. I wanted to be involved with international work and wanted to live and work outside of the United States for several years. Specifically, I was interested in Latin America. That did not work out. I started my search a little too late to get into recruiting cycles at some manufacturers that operate in that region, and it was too late to pursue other networking contacts I generated during the semester without the risk of having no offers and options until 5 to 6 months after graduation.

AlliedSignal's offer in international procurement gave me a strong introduction to that functional area and is providing a solid post-MBA experience on which to build for future options. An international assignment is not likely in the very near future. However, one never knows what might come up, especially in a large company like AlliedSignal and in a situation where my colleagues and superiors know I want to be stationed abroad as soon as possible.

What are the key points in your answer to the question, "Why should I hire you for your ideal job?"

I usually answered that question with some of the following points:

- I believe I'm qualified for the job because of my experience and education history:
  — Previous work experience
  — Previous international experience
  — Undergraduate academic training, a major in international trade and politics
  — MBA program and courses
  — Summer internship
- I believe the following personal qualities will enable me to add value quickly to your company and department:
  — Fast learner
  — Assertive and resourceful

— Genuinely enjoy teamwork and group projects, yet not afraid to lead and have several recent, strong examples of leadership roles from my Stern experience
— Enjoy people and have a positive outlook on life and work
— Enjoy hard work and can handle stress and multiple, simultaneous projects
— Self-directed and creative

I tried to back up each of the qualities that I listed with examples from work/academia, and personal life.

Since my background is slightly eclectic due to extended travel periods and work in a little known industry, I often had to explain my resume (e.g., Why finance at OPIC for the summer and you're not a finance major?). However, I had a tight argument and motives for each change and was easily able to explain each step in my journey. My story seemed to make sense and people were usually interested in how I ended up in business school, and Stern in particular.

How can someone get your job?

Network. Ask lots of questions until you can talk with the people who are doing international work.

Do you feel your work makes a difference to you, your family, society? What do you hope to achieve with your work?

I tend to be committed and loyal to my employer. I believe in working hard, making a contribution and making my work environment, my world, a better place because I'm there. That sounds corny, but I really do think that life is whether you're happy or enjoying things.

I firmly believe that people were and are made with a desire to work, be proud of their work, and derive some sense of accomplishment through their work. I don't think a people should achieve their identities from work. They can disappear or change in a flash. And, I believe there is a need for life outside of work. Nonetheless, work is an important part of contributing to society, as well as a way to earn a living.

Where do you derive your inspiration?

I have been inspired by several members of my family, including my great grandmother (a medical doctor in the early 1900s), my grandmother (whose faith is uncompromising and perennially aglow), and my parents (whose integrity, dedication, and thoroughness continually challenge me).

I have also been inspired by close friends who were and are mentors: Mr. Ken Hanson, former cofounder of Service Master, Inc; several faculty members at my undergraduate institution; and several colleagues at work. These few people have had a significant impact on my career decisions, including the decision to pursue an MBA and pursue it at Stern.

How does spirituality fit into your life and your work?

My spiritual convictions and beliefs form the basis for who I am. I try to daily live out my beliefs, which specifically impacts my behavior and decisions. I read the Bible, pray, and worship in a community setting and church, all on a regular basis. My spiritual beliefs really define who I am, though I don't go around talking about them all the time.

Interestingly enough, I'm married to a pastor. This often provides for good discussions because I love business and enjoy the corporate world for the most part. Many people see this as an extreme dichotomy—an assertive, goal-oriented MBA, married to a youth pastor. We, however, see our marriage and respective spiritual experiences as quite complementary. We help to balance each other and keep our perspectives on life healthy.

What other thoughts would you like to share?

People are key. You never know where you'll run into someone who knows some of the same people you do, who usually remember, good or bad. Networking really is helpful and some of the people I least expected to help me in my job search ended up being terrific resources. I'm very thankful for the wonderful support and encouragement I've been given. Don't be afraid to ask for help when you need it. You might get some great positive responses.

Be willing to help others. It makes life a great deal more interesting as well as a smaller community. When the MBA experience has ended and you're in a real job, don't forget what it was like to sit on the other side of the table. Experience the joy of helping someone else out in their job search.

One thing to remember—life is short and uncertain: Do what you enjoy, and enjoy what you do.

▶ Mary Passalacqua is a Market Development Manager with AlliedSignal. She received a BS in Chemistry from Tufts in 1984 and her MBA in Finance from New York University Stern Business School in 1991.

Why did you get an MBA?

I always knew that I would attend graduate school at some point. With my chemistry degree, two paths were obvious: more chemistry or business. After working for a few years in various laboratories, I realized that I did not want to pursue any more chemistry. So by elimination, I chose business school. I also became interested in how businesses are run while I was working in a quality control lab at Warner Lambert Co. My hope was, and still is, to draw on my chemistry background and apply that knowledge in a business setting.

How did the Office of Career Development (OCD) help?

I attended Stern Business School part-time. During my last year, it became clear that opportunities at the company I was working for were limited, so I decided to do some interviewing on campus through OCD. Although I was fairly sure that I wanted to continue working in manufacturing, I wanted to explore which jobs suited me best, so I began to meet fairly routinely with a counselor at OCD, who was very helpful by offering me tools such as the Meyers-Briggs personality test and setting up exploratory interviews for me with other counselors so that I could learn more, for instance, about consulting. In fact, one such discussion helped me realize that consulting was absolutely not for me. By mid-fall in 1990, I had selected a handful of chemical-related manufacturing companies to which I wanted to apply for financial analyst positions.

Counselors provided critical feedback on my resume and cover letter, and worked with me doing mock interviews that were videotaped. Now that I am involved in campus recruiting, I can say that it does make a difference: one-page resumes please! Since I was working full time, I had limited time to prepare for and attend interviews. I used vacation time and evenings as needed. When the interviews approached, I used a Stern Business School alumni reference guide and made telephone calls to people working at the companies I was interviewing with. I remember a woman from Merck who was extremely helpful for both my first and second interview there. She gave m   '
advice and plenty of time for questions.

How did you make the transition from a career in chemistry to one in business?

Having never worked a day in finance or even in a business setting (all my work experience was in labs or at plants), I knew that I would have to draw on my understanding of operations and my management experience. The latter was limited, but compared to that of other candidates, it may have been an edge. At that time, Total Quality was a hot topic and a common theme in manufacturing. I was a quick learner and tried to meet as many people as I could to help me become a useful part of the business team.

What do you do now on the job?

I am a market development manager for one of the specialty chemical businesses at AlliedSignal. One of my responsibilities is to evaluate new products and new business ideas. Working with our technical people, I perform market research/analysis and then develop preliminary business plans for management review. As part of a business development group, I am also working with our business leaders to build a robust new product/new business development process aimed at generating the double-digit growth and profitability performance that AlliedSignal and the investment community expects.

Prior to this assignment, I spent six years in finance where I held both operational and corporate-level positions. Beginning as a financial analyst and working my way up, I gained a wealth of knowledge about each of the businesses I supported, and also made many contacts throughout the finance function that cuts across all businesses at AlliedSignal. The experience I gained in strategic planning and analysis allowed me to transition from a finance role to marketing. I can now leverage both my undergraduate technical knowledge and finance experience while learning how to bring new business opportunities forward in today's competitive environment.

What do you do to stay current?

In marketing, you must constantly stay abreast of events, activities, announcements, and especially changes related to your business. Technology helps here. We have several newswires and clipping services available. We also read trade journals and use consultants as necessary. Attending trade shows, workshops, and other gatherings is also important.

In terms of improving our business processes to stay competitive, AlliedSignal has dedicated significant resources to bring us to the leading edge in operations and commercialization. These people are extremely knowledgeable in their fields and impart exciting concepts and learning to our organization. I also read *The Wall Street Journal,* the *New York Times,* or other business publications to keep up with current events.

How does recruiting work in your company?

University Relations is run centrally out of our corporate office. There are over 30 targeted colleges and universities. (The list is revised every few years.) A campus manager and a campus executive are assigned to each school. These people are responsible for establishing and maintaining relations with the schools, allocating company donations, managing the recruiting process, supporting selected student events and functions, etc. We do on-campus recruiting, followed by second round interviews. At the MBA level, we bring in the students for second round interviews on three selected days (23–30 students each day). With all the recruiters in attendance, we interview in teams in the morning, have lunch, send the students off and make hiring decisions in the afternoon. We have worked this process for a few years now and it gets better all the time. We also have an active summer intern program for MBAs. We hire about 50 percent finance MBAs with the remainder in marketing, management, operations, and information systems.

What skills are needed in your job to succeed?

The ability to look broadly at business processes and find ways to help businesses understand their performance and where/how to improve that performance. Some examples include: supply chain management, new product commercialization, operational excellence, and new business development. Computer skills are a must. We do a fair amount of analysis, and must be able to get to the right issues quickly. We work with executives and people who are very smart and very busy, so work must be presented clearly and concisely, often without the luxury of much lead time.

Communication skills are critical, both knowing how to communicate well and also with whom to communicate. Effectiveness really depends on making sure that all bases are covered and that the right questions have been addressed. We balance meetings, team work, and individual projects, and we write, analyze data, and deliver presentations. Since we have many locations outside our Morristown headquarters, we are often on the phone with people from other sites. Good finance people are more than just "numbers people"; they are excellent thinkers, delegators, and communicators. They share information, work with facts, stay ahead of issues, and address problems readily. Today in marketing, one of my most critical skills is to interview well and gather information to properly evaluate and select the right business opportunities.

What are the positives and negatives of your job?

Double-digit growth is a strategic imperative for AlliedSignal, so being part of the "growth team" is exciting. I do mostly project work, allowing for some flexibility, planning, and long-term thinking. I like working with our research and businesspeople, as well as our important customers. One downside of my current assignment is not being close to "today's" results and business activity. Before in finance, I always knew exactly what was going on.

There are days when I really like what I do, and other days when I wish I could work at something for which I really have a passion. It's hard to love working in a big corporate setting all the time, but the "pluses" include a lot of opportunities to learn new skills, rewards for high achievers, a nice setting (fitness center, day care, etc.), good benefits, and a lot of great people. As a woman with a working husband and one small child, I have found that my situation works very well for me. I am able to afford live-in child care and that makes my life less crazy when I need to be in early or work late. When it comes to work-life issues, our management is becoming increasingly sensitive to the need for flexibility, and I have not had any serious issues or conflicts. The key is to make sure you are reliable and to plan ahead as much as possible to minimize last minute surprises and issues. Right now, I have not decided whether I will be here 5 more years or 15, but it's nice to feel that at this point, it is my choice. And you really have to keep all aspects of your life in view as you plan ahead, to think about the implications of different career paths at different points in your life.

▶ Stacey Platt is President of her own company called Breathing
Space. She works with a number of clients organizing people's offices and home living environments. She received a BA in Communications from University of California at San Diego in 1989 and an MBA
from New York University Stern School of Business in 1996.

What do you do on the job?

What I do on the job varies with the client. Though I deal with all kinds
of organization issues, most often, I help people to set up systems to
manage the flow of paper through their home or office. That's the surface level—paper management. But the implications are far greater.
People call me when their lives feel out of control. The piles of paper
amount to stress and uncertainty—not knowing what they have, what
they need to do, where things are, what's important. When someone
calls me for help, they are making a statement that they want to
change. Some people want to change their physical surroundings and
that's a wonderful start. They are interested in getting some of what
the name of my company promises, breathing space. Other people recognize that the paper pile-up is a manifestation of some deeper issues
and are ready to change not only their physical surroundings, but also
themselves. On the surface, I do paper management; but on a deeper
level, I also often am called upon to be like an organizational therapist.

Describe a typical day.

There is no such thing as a typical day, although six days a week my
morning begins with a two-hour yoga practice. From there, I see
clients. I might spend the day in a gymnastics studio or at a horse farm
or in the penthouse apartment of an actress or getting a tour of the
neonatology unit at a New York City hospital where I am helping a
client reorganize her office.

How did you start your company?

I placed a two-line ad in *New York* magazine that said, "Get organized.
Call for a free consultation." and my home phone number. After six
months, I had to pull the ad because I couldn't meet the demand.

What is your career history?

I started out of college in a much sought-after position as an assistant
to a television talent agent at a major talent agency in Los Angeles.

Though there was some prestige to obtaining this hard-to-get job in the entertainment industry, I was essentially a glorified secretary. My college friend, who was doing the same thing at a television network, and I used to jokingly brag to each other about the ways we were putting our college degrees to use—"I can reduce on the copy machine!" After two and a half years and numerous attempts at quitting, which were all thwarted by my very persuasive boss, I was informed by him that he was leaving the agency and forming a management company. He invited me to join him in a slightly elevated status. So for nearly two more years I provided a little office organization and managed a few actors. But my heart wasn't in it. My boss, who I'm still very close to today, had the good sense to fire me.

At a Grateful Dead concert in San Francisco, I had an epiphany that the entertainment industry was not where I was going to find the fulfillment of my life's work. I felt that the work, though glamorous at times, had no real connection to me and to my life. I could not find meaning in what I was doing. The epiphany, however, did not include where exactly I would find such meaning. I did know though that I could not possibly flourish under the lifeforce-zapping glare of fluorescent office lights and the 9 to 5 regimen of a structured work week. More importantly, I had had a malignant melanoma removed a year prior and knew that I needed to reduce the amount of stress and environmental toxins in my quotidian life.

To start, I went to Guatemala where I lived for several months with a Guatemalan family while studying Spanish and then traveled around Central America with a backpack. Somewhere between diving the coral reefs off the coast of Honduras and trekking the rainforests of Costa Rica, I had another epiphany. I could see no other alternative than to work for myself. I needed to go to business school to acquire a skill set that I did not yet possess. As luck would have it, I got robbed in Costa Rica and had to cut my trip short. I made it back to the United States in time to get my business school applications in for the following school year.

I took an unheard of semester off while at Stern to do something even more unheard of—go to India to study yoga. This was before yoga had made its big debut on the trend scene. India was actually the 4½ month culmination of a 10-month journey through Australia, Thailand, and Vietnam. The journey changed my life. The practice of ashtanga yoga under the compassionate guidance of my then 82-year-old yoga teacher taught me lessons more valuable than anything I would learn in business school—lessons in commitment, faith, courage, love, trust, and surrender.

Back in New York, remembering my goal of wanting to work for myself, but not quite knowing what I would do, coupled with financial pressures, I got caught up in the interviewing frenzy. I landed a number-crunching position in a human resources consulting firm where my job was to create incentive schemes for sales forces. I felt like a stranger in a strange land. Each morning when I sat down at my desk in my windowless, fluorescent-lit office, I imagined a deep voice that said, "and the role of the consultant will be played by Stacey." My boss didn't like my work, my attitude, or the way I dressed and after nine miserable months, he mercifully fired me.

I had absolutely no idea what I would do. A friend described to me the job of a friend of hers who helped people get organized for a living. A light bulb went off in my head and I intuitively knew this would be a lucrative and rewarding career for me. The job seemed to encompass all the parameters that I was looking for—helping people, the ability to create my own schedule, continual change, and a way to capitalize on my extreme penchant for detail. Fear of having to work in a traditional office job is what drove me to immediate success.

What is your favorite part of your job?

My favorite part of the job is the intimate relationship that develops between my clients and me. I love that I am able to give a person a system or some tools that quite literally change that person's life for the better. I am hard pressed to come up with a least favorite aspect of my job.

What trends affect your business industry?

Two trends that affect my business are the increase of people doing business from home and the proliferation of personal computing devices from the desktop computer on down to PDAs such as the Palm Pilot and the new Handspring electronic organizer. Both increase demand for my services.

What skills are important for success in your field?

The most important skills to have to do my job are a calm exterior, compassion, patience, the ability to listen, a linear thought process, neat handwriting (or a good label maker), and, of course, an innate and logical sense of organization.

What motivates you to do what you do?

I am motivated by my desire to help people. I like doing this because I provide a service for which people are very grateful. The work I do changes their lives on a very basic level, but the implications have a far greater reach. I am motivated by the responses I get from my clients, for example:

"You've changed my life."

"This is better than therapy."

"You end up feeling a lot better than if you had gone to a spa."

I am also motivated by the lifestyle that this work allows me to lead. I usually work about 25 to 30 hours a week, yet I earn more than what I was making at a job working 50 to 60 hours a week. I am able to practice yoga for two hours ever morning. And this year I have taken a total of three months off to travel to London, Rome, India, Maui, and Los Angeles as well as a 10-day silent meditation retreat in Massachusetts.

Did your education, including the MBA, help you in your current job?

My formal education did not impact my career as much as my informal education in the areas of yoga, meditation, Hinduism, and Buddhism. When I first started my business, I had also begun to teach yoga. The similarities between the two were profound. In organizing and in yoga, it's all about creating space. In creating physical space, both by getting organized and on the yoga mat, we are also creating the quality of space that allows for new possibilities to enter. I tell my clients that a cup full to the brim with water cannot receive any nectar. Both methods of creating space give way to greater clarity and peace of mind.

Any related areas of interest for others to consider?

Related areas in this field are interior design and Feng Shui.

What is your favorite quote?

Life shrinks or expands in proportion to one's courage. (Anais Nin)

What pearls of wisdom do you have for those embarking on their own career path?

For anyone who wants to do this or anything in their life—JUST DO IT!

What is the most challenging issue facing you in your current position?

The most challenging issue I face is getting people to change their behavior. Some people are ready for real change and they just require the guidance. Other people want to become organized, but are not yet willing (or able) to make the behavioral changes necessary to sustain the work that we do together.

Where do you get your inspiration?

I derive much of my inspiration from the work that I do on the yoga mat every morning. So much of what I learn from practicing yoga is a metaphor for life. At one very difficult point in my practice that lasted several months, my yoga teacher said to me, "You don't *have* to do these postures, but you have the *freedom* to." It was liberating for both my thought process and my practice. I passed the wisdom along to a client who was berating herself for not maintaining the level of organization that we had established. She did not *have* to be totally organized, but she had the *freedom* to be. That comment in itself created a spaciousness—an allowing, rather than a demanding; a nurturing, rather than a scolding.

Will you expand your current business?

Job growth is possible in many directions. I can expand my operation and hire a staff. I can get more heavily involved with corporate work. I can lecture, write books, or lead workshops. I've also thought of marketing a funky line of office products. The possibilities are endless.

What do you hope to achieve with your business?

What I hope to achieve by helping people get organized is really to help them gain clarity and a sense of peace and fulfillment in their lives. A direction that my work has started to take is that I am getting more involved with life management issues whereby I aid clients in clarifying what they want their life to look like, creating a mission statement, identifying and removing obstacles (whether physical or emotional), and then setting goals and identifying action steps to achieve their goals. I'd also like to write a book on life organizing from a spiritual perspective.

What motivated you to do what you do?

What motivated me to start my own business was my complete and utter inability to work under someone else—as evidenced by my multiple terminations. I don't like being told what to do, how to do it, who to work with, what to wear, what to say, what not to say, when to come to work, when to take vacation. My boss at the talent agency used to have to remind me that *he* was the boss. A casting director whom I worked for briefly while waiting to be admitted to business school screamed at me one day in a mad frenzy that she felt like I was trying to take over her business. I was fired from that job, too. But somehow, despite all this, I am willing to give everything of myself to my clients. I feel as though I have chosen them in as much as they have chosen me.

Where do you see yourself and your company in 5 to 10 years?

I feel some pressure to grow, expand, make more money, and all that, but I ask myself what that would entail and do I want to sacrifice my valuable resources of time and freedom to achieve those ends? The answer in my heart right now is no. I am very content with the work I am doing and I feel strongly connected to it, but I also value my time and freedom to pursue my other interests such as yoga, traveling, and photography. I choose quality of life over quantity of life. I am reminded of a story about a fisherman:

> He lived on a sparsely populated tropical island with his wife. He'd spend most of his day fishing for the day's meals. And in the late afternoons, he'd make love to his wife. And life went on like this and he was quite happy. One day, a businessman came to the island on business. He met the fisherman and pointed out that he could live so much more efficiently; that he could fish for more than one fish at a time, take the surplus into the village and sell it. The fisherman said, "and then what?" The businessman said, "and then with the money you make, you can buy more boats and hire some people and increase your daily catch and sell even more fish." And the fisherman said, "and then what?" And the businessman said, "and then you could buy a barge and distribute your fish to other islands and to the mainland." The fisherman thought for a moment and said, "and then what?" The businessman responded, "well,

then you could set up a corporation and have a fleet of fishing ships and a packing factory and begin to deliver frozen fish to supermarkets." "And then what?" asked the fisherman. "And then, you could market frozen fish dinners and advertise on television and become a major name on the frozen foods scene," replied the businessman. The fisherman said, "and then what?" The businessman responded, "and then you could take your company public and retire!" "And then what?" asked the fisherman. "And then you could move to a tropical island, fish all day, and make love to your wife!"

▶ Laura Diane Viola is a Management Associate with BMW of North America. She received her BA in Journalism from New York University in 1990 and her MBA in Marketing from New York University Stern School of Business in 1996.

What do you do on the job? Describe a typical day.

I am currently in the Management Associate program, a 12 to 18 month training program where Associates rotate throughout departments of the company for periods of 3 or 4 months at a time. The program enables me to experience several disciplines to get an overview of the total operation of BMW. We are given projects that challenge our abilities and expose us to different facets of management at the company. BMW's North American headquarters is located in Woodcliff Lake, New Jersey, and we have four regional offices throughout the United States to facilitate regional sales and marketing efforts. We are encouraged as Management Associates to spend one of our rotations in a regional office to gain some exposure to the retail side of the business.

To date, I have worked in three areas: Financial Planning, Professional Development, and our Southern Region Headquarters in Atlanta. Financial Planning oversees the entire budgeting process for the company. Professional Development creates and implements retail training programs and workshops for all sales, service and parts personnel. Some of the projects I have worked on are described next.

Visionwerke, the BMW Network is an internal television network that broadcasts announcements, industry news, training courses and product updates to employees at all of our retail offices, regional offices, centers and headquarters. I believe it is unique because it offers "interactive distance learning" where participants can communicate with each other even though they may be miles apart. My television production experience helped on this rotation as I got involved with casting, story ideas, programming, enrollment, publicity and all other aspects of running a small network.

The BMW Academy is a unique two-week intensive training course which welcomes people to BMW. The Academy introduces sales specialists, service advisors and parts counterpersons to BMW history, brand values, ethics, selling skills, service expectations, buyer motivations, operations, and product knowledge. The Academy is a "trendsetter" in the industry, boasting high interest levels and rave reviews from participants and dealership management. I was able to attend as a participant as well as a presenter, facilitator, and logistics coordinator. "BMW Day" is part of an effort to encourage more women and minorities to become interested in career opportunities with BMW. The day involves product displays, lectures and workshops on the industry and its trends, and includes influential people from within BMW and from Spelman College where "BMW Day" was held. I helped coordinate "BMW Day."

During my rotation in Atlanta, I have had the opportunity to work on local projects throughout the South. I have visited dealerships to sit in on sales meetings; attended finance and leasing meetings, car auctions, marketing events, and inventory allocations; prepared and given presentations at various dealerships; and spent time at the car preparation center to see how vehicles are prepared for sale. I will also be spending two weeks at a dealership here in Atlanta to understand the entire operation and I will be expected to sell cars for a few days as well!

What is your favorite aspect of this job? Least favorite?

My favorite aspect of my job is that I am encouraged to learn and see as much as I can during the training process. I am exposed to many areas of management and I am getting a solid understanding of how all the areas of the company interact and affect each other. It is excellent knowledge to have and build on.

How were you able to obtain this position? What steps led you to this?

Over winter break during business school, I came to school when no one was around and sent a mass mailing to every marketing company on this side of the world. I think I spent my entire break creating mailing lists and cover letters and different versions of my resume. Our Office of Career Development had supplied us with a huge directory of companies and their addresses and by the end of break I had contacted every single one of them. I spent weeks waiting. Then the rejection letters started flooding in. Sometimes I would get ten in one day. I actually got a rejection letter from BMW. I figured it was because I had never worked in the auto industry before.

Then there was a career fair at school. There was an unbelievable snow storm the night before and I trudged half of the day through two feet of snow to get there, only to find that half of the companies didn't even make it because of the weather. BMW was one of those companies, but Stern was collecting resumes on BMW's behalf to send to the company. I threw my resume on the pile, almost as a joke, just to see what would happen. A few days later, I received a phone call inviting me to interview.

What is your career history or prior work experience?

Prior to business school, I was the associate promotion producer for the ABC television morning show, *Good Morning America.* I created, wrote, and produced promos for the program for four years. I had been a journalism major as an undergraduate at New York University and worked for *Good Morning America* immediately out of college. When I decided to return to business school, I left to return to Stern full time.

How did your education impact your career?

My education has had a direct impact on may career. I never would have considered BMW and they probably would not have considered me had I not gone to business school. Earning my MBA not only enabled me to initiate a career change as I expected it would, but also helped me to think more broadly. I began to consider new career options. My MBA supplied me with knowledge and, more importantly, with the tools to use that knowledge. I learned to be more resourceful, to be a problem solver and to think more creatively.

My education was not exclusively what I learned from studying. It was important to me to be exposed to everything Stern had to offer. I was an advanced management communications teaching assistant for two semesters. I was co-editor-in-chief of the school newspaper. I was actively involved with student clubs and events, and was a representative on several committees. This involvement helped me form important relationships. It also taught me to prioritize, honor deadlines, deal with diverse personalities and stressful situations, and successfully juggle and complete several important projects at once. I have found that these skills are just as important for survival in the workplace as are knowledge and experience.

What are the key points in your answer to the question,"Why hire me for my ideal job?"

Never think that because you have not worked in a specific industry that it is off limits to you. I knew little about cars when I joined BMW, but had many other qualifications they were looking for. In interviews, I was always quick to point to my organizational skills and my experience in managing others. I talked about all of the places I had traveled to and about how those experiences changed my life. In many interviews, the interviewer is only looking for a certain title in job experience and it is up to you to explain why what you did is important and the right experience for the particular job you seek. Be proud of your accomplishments and explain how you grew and broadened your knowledge through them. Cite examples of times where you took a chance, thought of a creative solution, or motivated others to do the same.

Do you have any pearls of wisdom for people with similar aspirations?

Don't ever believe that you are not capable. I never would have guessed before business school that I could do any more than I was doing in the television industry. If I had limited my thinking to just that I would never have progressed. Be daring and seek out everything available to you.

During our semester break in my first year of business school, I was selected to represent Stern and travel to Asia on a four-week business study tour. One of our stops was Shanghai and on one of the weekends we visited an old village. There were gardens and temples and many people walking through the streets. I stopped next to a man who was painting fortunes on large pieces of parchment with ink and a large brush. He noticed me looking at him and he reached out and felt my hand. He lifted his brush and painted one large character on the parchment and gave it to me. I had to ask another student what the character meant because the man did not speak English. It said *perse-vere*. Many nights when I was studying or interviewing or preparing for a presentation, when I was stressed out about where I would be working, or when I had lost sight of why I had gone to business school in the first place, I would look over at this scroll. I think that man must have seen in me both my potential and my capacity for frustration. My ability to persevere despite disappointments has helped me continue to strive for success. I believe it is always important to persevere.

FINDING YOUR WAY IN THE NOT-FOR-PROFIT WORLD

The Not-for-Profit sector is special in ways that go beyond the absence of the profit mission. Typically, the nonprofits offer a culture of commitment, a pervasive dedication that goes beyond a professional interest to personal reasons for joining such organizations. These people care deeply about the work they are doing and its benefits for society. Often the structure is informal with flexible job responsibilities and a collegial atmosphere. There is usually a broad, rather than highly compartmentalized, exposure to various management functions such as strategy, marketing, and finance—with a strong emphasis on fund raising. The needs are always growing faster than the available resources. As these challenges have become more demanding, so more professional, better trained management is required, an opportunity for the MBA dedicated to work in the nonprofit sector. The profiles in this section cover unusual missions such as education in art history, conservation, and historical preservation; more effective delivery of healthcare; conservation projects to transform industries threatening the environment; operations management at a university hospital to improve health care services; community service training to prevent crime; community development management to improve quality of life; and management development in the nonprofit sector.

▶ Lisa Ackerman is Vice President at Samuel Kress Foundation. She received a BA in Italian and Art History from Middlebury College in 1982 and an MBA from New York University Stern School of Business in 1986.

What do you do on the job?

I have been at the Samuel H. Kress Foundation since 1982, and I have held a wide array of jobs during this time. The nonprofit world is an interesting arena in which to be employed. While the tangible rewards in this sector might not be as great as those of the for profit world, in general, you are surrounded by individuals who are passionately dedicated to the mission of an organization and who are willing to wear a variety of hats to accomplish that mission. During my years as Administrative Assistant, Programs Assistant, and so on, I was as likely to be fixing the postage meter, calling the plumber, or asking the carpenter to build new shelves as I was to be reviewing grant proposals, meeting with project directors or researching for the board a new area of potential support. For some this range in activities would be frustrating, for me it has always been exhilarating.

What are your favorite and least favorite aspects of this job?

Every job has its ups and downs. On balance, I adore my job. I look forward to coming to work each day. That, for me, is essential. There are moments when the workload seems overwhelming and I cannot imagine why I have to work so many hours, but then I receive a letter from one of our grant recipients expressing thanks for being able to complete a project because of our funding and I am reminded of how wonderful it is to facilitate the important work of others.

What steps led you to this opportunity?

After graduation from college and a brief employment as a research assistant, I interviewed for a job at the Kress Foundation as the assistant to the recently hired Executive Vice President.

The Foundation was entering a new era. The staff that had been in place for nearly 30 years retired and my boss was hired to help shape the Foundation's grant programs. The executive vice president had a doctorate in art history, but little office experience. I was interested in the Foundation's areas of support: art history, conservation, and architectural preservation. I also speak three languages fluently and could assist in communications with project directors coordinating projects in Europe. I found the areas supported by the Foundation and arriving at the Foundation during a time of evaluation, change, and growth combined for a good job opportunity.

The executive vice president had only been in place 10 months and was just beginning to "define" her job. I took the job thinking that it would be interesting to work at the Foundation for a while and then move on to something else. As it happens, the job grew and could not have been more tailored for my skills.

How did your education impact your career?

As an undergraduate at Middlebury College, I majored in Italian and art history and was not terribly worried about what job I might find. This is not to say that I didn't have to find a job upon graduation! Rather, I believed that the education you receive at a liberal arts college provides you with educational tools that you carry with you for life and that are not job specific. I believed that in studying languages, art history, and other related areas of interest, I was developing a mode of thinking that would be valuable in any context.

I discovered that after a number of years in the nonprofit field, many people know their area of concern quite well, but are at a loss as to the business side of their organization. After all, nonprofits are, in effect, businesses. Foundations have responsibilities for managing their money, maintaining proper records, paying bills, and, of course, reviewing the budgets included in grant applications. Grant recipients have the even greater challenge of utilizing scarce resources. In addition, grant seeking agencies must be terrific marketers of their causes. Thus, I entered the MBA program at Stern because I felt that my educational background had not prepared me for coping with the economic realities of the nonprofit world. As the competition for grant funds from the government and corporations increases, the need for nonprofit managers better versed in business will also increase. In a performing arts center, an artistic director is critical to the success of the operation, but a business or administrative director is just as necessary.

What do you see as the most challenging issues in your industry?

The field has changed as dramatically as all other sectors of our economy. One must know much about computers. And nonprofits are not likely to have an information systems department. Most people in this sector are forced to sort through the manuals and coax information out of friends. Since our grants are awarded to people in the academic world, it was essential that we get e-mail because university faculty are used to communicating in this manner. For many in the field, the greatest challenge in recent years has been to keep up with appropriate office equipment and communications systems.

What are the misconceptions people hold about this kind of work?

I would say that many people still think nonprofits are somehow not as serious as organizations in the for-profit sectors. However, most people do not realize how many organizations with which they deal regularly are nonprofits.

What do people need to know to get into this field? What are the most important skills to have?

The knowledge skills needed for most jobs in the field are some understanding of the issues, flexibility, creativity, and initiative. Nonprofits are notoriously understaffed and overworked and the needs serviced by such agencies are limitless.

How can someone get your job?

Many people have asked me how to get a job at a foundation and I always say that I am not sure I am qualified to answer. I did not plan to work for a philanthropic organization. I never even planned to stay here this long. However, I cannot imagine working elsewhere.

I have become well acquainted with the fields that we support and I truly care about the state of education in the history of art, conservation, and historical preservation. I see more and more that these areas need critical attention. A concern for the preservation of our built environments extends to a concern for the preservation of our natural environments. Similarly, the training of art historians, conservators, museum curators, art educators, preservationists and other such professionals extends to many related fields, such as urban planning, the creation of "greenways" corridors, and similar crafts fields. If anything, I feel that the world in which I function has become wider rather than narrower.

Thus, my advice to individuals interested in the nonprofit arena is to find an area that concerns them. Surely there must be at least one nonprofit area that interests each person. The nonprofit sector is much more a part of our lives than most of us realize. It extends to health care, environmental issues, legal issues, housing, employment training, education, community service agencies, and so on.

What is your favorite quote?

My favorite quote is from a trustee: "Grantmaking foundations are the venture capitalists of the academic world." He offered this comment to illustrate that it is important for foundations to encourage universities, research institutes, and other organizations to venture into new territory and that it is okay for some grants not to produce spectacular results. If nothing ever veered off course, what would we learn?

Where do you see yourself in 5 to 10 years?

I don't know. I suspect that I will not be at the Kress Foundation, although it is possible because there are always new challenges and new projects. If I am here, I know that I will continue to be proud of the work that we support and amazed that a $4 million per year program is administered by 5 people. If I am not here, I hope that I will be in a job as interesting and working with people as pleasant as those I have encountered during my years here. Further, I know that all I have learned here can be put to good use in other areas. One other hope would be to work just a few less weekends and to see what it would be like to leave the office at 5 P.M. People tell me it is still light out then.

▶ Don Irie is a Project Manager in Financial Analysis and Support Services with Kaiser Permanente Foundation Health Plan. He received his BS in City and Regional Planning from Cornell University in 1986 and his MPPM from Yale School of Management in 1991.

How would you summarize your experience following graduate school?

After graduation, I moved out to San Francisco with a job as an economic consultant at a small consulting firm. Suffering through three bad months, I left and moved to a public policy research firm as a Research Associate. Six months later, I joined the United Way. Initially, I was hired as an Assistant Vice President in Community Planning and Research. After two years, I was promoted to Vice President of Donor Services. Recently, I shifted into the health care field to my present position. During my time in the Bay area, I have also joined boards of directors of two community nonprofit organizations.

What was your career target at graduate school?

In entering graduate school and upon completing my degree, I wanted to focus on public service. I was looking to work for a cause and not just to develop a profession. I felt that these "cause-related" organizations would find a person with my skills and educational background to be valuable, especially in strategic planning, marketing and financial management.

Given your diverse employment experiences, what are your thoughts about identifying an ideal career?

You have to know your interests, skills, and optimal work styles. I feel that the most important aspect in considering these factors is to understand what is in your heart. It seems pointless to spend a lot of time and effort building your career without really enjoying what you are doing. Next, you need to recognize what strengths and weaknesses you bring to your work. I found that self-assessment tools and books such as *What Color Is Your Parachute* to be effective. Finally, you need to understand in what environments your skills are best applied. For me, experiencing different types of positions in various fields helped me to develop an understanding of what types of environments I enjoy working in. This type of exposure can be gained through experimenting with different jobs, doing contract work, volunteering, and by talking with people in different jobs.

What have you learned about the qualities needed to successfully pursue the ideal career?

Beyond being able to perform the job, the qualities I found most important to employers are a sincere interest in and commitment to the field and position you are interviewing for. This means going beyond demonstrating only a professional interest and indicating some personal reasons for wanting the position. In doing some hiring interviews myself, I have found this thinking to be a much looked for quality from a hirer's perspective.

How did you identify target organizations?

Oddly, personal contacts were never a big source of job leads for me. I found them to be more beneficial in learning about the industry and finding out what types of jobs are possible. Many of my job leads came from newspaper classified ads, the one place you are likely told not to look. Sometimes, I was not the best person for the job. However, since I was able to communicate my skills and interests in the field, my resume was passed on to other departments for consideration. This is how I got my current job. Ironically, the job I got was better than the one I initially applied for.

What are your ideas on communications to obtain employment interviews and preparations for such interviews?

Cover letters and resumes must be customized to each job. They should be short and to the point. You should be acquainted with the industry and the position for which you will be interviewing. Along with this understanding, you should know your resume inside and out. It is important to be able to talk through your background quickly and to provide relevant highlights in a concise yet comprehensive manner. Some questions I have usually heard during interviews are: (1) Why are you applying for this particular position?, (2) How would you briefly describe your background? and (3) Do you have any questions for us? Be sure to have your own good challenging questions ready.

What do you like best and least about your job?

Since I have been in my current position for only a short time, I will comment on my last position at the United Way. The best part of this job was to be able to apply and to experiment with many aspects of managing people and work processes. I was able to step into a new function, build a team, and work for optimal effectiveness. All this work was in the context of helping to build healthier communities through the promotion of workplace philanthropy. The worst part of this job was that there was so much to do without enough budget and in so little time. The work environment was changing so rapidly, one had to work very hard to be proactive. Another problem was compensating for the ineffectiveness of other managers.

What additional tips might you offer on career thinking?

First, you should always follow your heart and do what you really want to do. Try to consider prestige and money as secondary. Second, you should realize that the environment you will work in will significantly impact on your experience regardless of the type of work you are doing. My first job out of graduate school was a typical MBA type of position as a consultant. Although the work was not public service oriented, I was going to work for a few years, pay off my loans, move out to San Francisco, and then do the type of work I really wanted to do. During my short tenure, I found out that the work environment was horrible and I was not happy with my compromise. I got sick and needed to leave for my own well-being. This was a great lesson in, "A bad job is worse than any job!"

▶ Karin Kreider is Associate Director with Rainforest Alliance. She received her BFA from New York University in 1985 and her MBA from New York University Stern School of Business in 1996.

As background, what is your employment outline since graduation?

I have been with the Rainforest Alliance since 1987, and after graduating in December 1996, I continued to work for the Alliance. I did my MBA part-time while I continued at my job. While I was working on my MBA I had a title change from director of finance and administration to associate director.

How would you define your career target at the time you were completing your MBA?

Before I started my MBA, I knew that I wanted to continue to work in nonprofit management. I was interested in a graduate degree that would expand my ability to work for a range of organizations and on a range of issues. Many nonprofit managers have degrees related to the field in which they are working: science, international development, or social work, for example. Because I did not want to limit myself to a specific area and I had a particular interest in running a "business-like" nonprofit, the MBA was a logical choice.

I had no intention of leaving my current position when I finished my degree. The Rainforest Alliance has grown from two staff members to 40 in the 10 years that I have worked here, and it was important for me to develop my ability to manage a larger organization. I knew that the MBA would be useful in our conservation work as well as in general organizational management. In our conservation efforts we work to transform industries. This means understanding how corporations work and feeling comfortable working with them. I knew that an MBA, versus a public management degree, for example, would be very useful in this regard.

So I really defined my career targets before I started my MBA, rather than as I was finishing.

How did you identify your ideal career?

I found my job somewhat by accident, and the career part of it evolved over time as my job grew and developed. It took a few years in my job before I decided for sure that I wanted to make a career of nonprofit management. For me the "ideal" part also has a lot to do with organizational culture and values. It is important for me to work in an organization without too much bureaucracy, where people are committed to their work at every level of the organization. It is also great to be in a place full of smart people who enjoy learning new things. So the organization itself is as important as the specific position within it.

How did you decide what key qualities and competitive edges you needed to offer to employers for your ideal career?

Since I was already in an ideal position, I had a good sense of what I needed just by doing the job day-to-day. In upper levels of smaller nonprofits you often handle a wide range of functional areas, from human resources to accounting and MIS. So I knew from experience that I needed a broad management background. Many nonprofits recruit by sending job announcements to other nonprofits, so I get to scan a steady stream of information about the types of positions being filled and the employers' requirements.

What special tips do you have for writing cover letters?

If you are an MBA looking for a position with a nonprofit, it is essential that you understand the mission and culture of the organization. Read its web site and annual report. Stop by to pick up information. You can learn a lot about an organization's culture from a visit to its office. It is important to most nonprofits, especially smaller ones, that you really care about the work they are doing. Make sure you explain in your cover letter why you are interested in the organization and its work. If you have solely corporate experience, you should explain your interest in a move to the nonprofit sector. Try to get a sense of the salary ranges of the organization. Sending a cover letter with a salary requirement double that of the executive director will only draw laughs or groans.

What are the trends in your present career field and what are the key hiring requirements?

The environmental movement has followed some of the globalization trends of the world economy. Many environmental conservation projects are moving toward finding market-based alternatives to deforestation, which gives a business "spin" to many jobs. Many of these jobs would require a foreign language and international experience at a grassroots or small-business level. Nonprofits in general have also become more accountable and require experienced managers to run them. This provides openings to MBAs to work in a range of traditional jobs like financial management, human resources, marketing, or promotion. Fund-raising is also an area where MBAs could have an impact nonprofit sector.

What do you like best and least about your current work?

I really love working on something that I feel is important and meaningful. Working for a small organization, I enjoy being involved in the overall management and direction of the organization. Because the Rainforest Alliance has been growing steadily for 10 years, it is a constant challenge to develop new systems. My job evolves as the organization grows, so it never feels repetitive.

It is often frustrating to have great ideas for improving systems or procedures and not be able to follow through for lack of funds or staff. Things sometimes move slowly in nonprofit, so you have to be patient and wait until the time is right to implement changes. At the same time it is nice not to be in a big bureaucracy. Sometimes I can blame only myself for things not moving more quickly!

What spiritual beliefs or principles govern your career thinking?

I come from a family that was very involved in social issues. No one in my family works for a large corporation, so a nonprofit career and life style was very acceptable. Before working at the Alliance, I worked in film production, mainly on television. commercials. Although the day-to-day work was exciting, it felt hollow after awhile. I had just started looking informally for something more meaningful when I met one of the founders of the Rainforest Alliance and was able to start working there.

My approach to professional progression incorporates my love of learning and doing new things. I like to take on new challenges and responsibilities, which works well in a young, growing nonprofit. Going to business school was one way of making sure that my skills were keeping up with what was needed for a larger organization, and that I wasn't stagnating in my job.

Reflecting on all your work experience to date, what additional tips might you have?

Finding the right organization and position in the nonprofit sector will be a challenge, requiring a lot of networking and patience. Most organizations will not hire many MBAs, so positions may not open up regularly. If you have several target organizations that you would like to work for, try to develop a relationship so that you will know when a position becomes available.

▶ Peter S. Nyberg is the Assistant Chief Operating Officer at the Duke University Medical Center. He received his BA in History from Yale in 1986 and an MPPM from the Yale School of Management in 1992.

What is your employment history?

1986–1988   Teacher, Coach, Dormitory Master, Avon (Connecticut) Old Farms School

1988–1990   Commodities Arbitrage Futures Trader, Singer/Wenger Trading Company (New York, New York)

1992–1993   Administrative Fellow, Duke University Hospital (DUH)

1993–1994   Assistant Administrator, Special Projects and New Program Planning, DUH

1994–1995   Administrative Director, Surgical Services, DUH

1995–1996   Administrative Director, Corporate and International Programs, DUH

1996–   Assistant Chief Operating Officer, Duke University Medical Center

What was your career target when you were completing your graduate degree?

I wanted to explore the health care industry on the provider side (i.e., hospital/medical center) with an initial focus on understanding the operations of such complex organizations.

How did you identify the opportunities in your target career?

After my first year in graduate school, I obtained a summer position as an Administrative Intern in the Department of Regulatory Affairs at Memorial Hospital for Cancer and Allied Diseases in New York City. In addition, I drew on graduate course work specific to the health care industry and contacts with my graduate school alumni in the health care field.

How did you identify the key qualities and competitive edges you needed to pursue your ideal career?

I read professional journals specific to health care management. Also, I met with health care executives at Yale-New Haven Hospital, St. Raphael's Hospital (New Haven), and other provider organizations.

How did you identify target organizations for your ideal career?

I used a guide to post-graduate fellowships and residencies in health care management published annually by the American College of Health Care Executives.

Who was in your career search network?

My contacts included my graduate school alumni, career counselors, family, and friends.

What special tips do you have for writing resumes and cover letters?

Resumes need to quantify accomplishments, convey the capability to be both team leader and team player as needed, and demonstrate the ability to work with a variety of constituents, often simultaneously. Cover letters should be short and to the point, answering these reader questions: What do you have to offer? What do you want? What is the next step?

How do you suggest preparing for an employment interview?

Practice using a video camera so you can see and hear yourself in action. Minimize the use of the word "I." Instead, talk of "We" and "Team" accomplishments.

What do employers in your career field look for when they are hiring people?

Organizations in my health care management field look for business people with a clinical background (e.g., MD/MBA, RN/MSN, and MD/JD/MBA). They also seek the professional who is multiskilled, that is multifunctional (i.e., operations, finance, strategic planning, and the like). And finally, they want people who have good interpersonal and communication skills along with the right attitude and proven flexibility.

What do you like least and best about your current work?

I like best the diversity of projects, the dynamic nature of the industry, and the opportunities to be creative and innovative. This career is personally and professionally rewarding and fulfilling. I like least the bureaucracy of large organizations and inertia.

What principles govern your career thinking?

I want to contribute to my community and society. Working in the health care field enables me to accomplish personal and professional goals and objectives simultaneously. I have gained a high degree of satisfaction and fulfillment working to improve the health care delivery system.

What additional tips might you have for graduating MBAs?

You should get meaningful experience during graduate school via internships during the summer and also during the school year. Participate in the relevant student interest groups. Explore options, take the initiative. After all, it is your career and you are ultimately responsible for it.

▶ Laurie Richardson is a Training Manager of National Service Programs with the National Crime Prevention Council. She received her BSFS (Foreign Service) in Humanities in International Affairs from Georgetown University in 1979 and her MPPM from Yale School of Management in 1991.

What was your career before your present position?

For approximately four years, I was an independent consultant. Some of my clients and assignments included the University of Michigan Business School (managing a research project on corporate social responsibility), Coverdale International (writing case studies on resource management in developing countries), New York Cares, and the Council on Economic Priorities.

What was your initial career target and path?

I wanted to get into nonprofit community development, management training, and training program management. I started in consulting first (by necessity) and then after four years, joined a national nonprofit engaged in improving life, safety, and health in U.S. communities.

How did you settle on your ideal career?

Through a consulting assignment, I met a senior international management trainer and asked him to be my mentor. Two months later, he introduced me to the deputy executive director at my current employer. She was looking for a training manager for a major training program around the United States, an ideal opportunity because it was community service, manager training, and training management.

I had 10 years' work experience, a first career actually, before starting my master's degree, so I knew pretty well "what" I wanted to do and the "how" of it. Also, after doing some private sector interviews, I decided I wanted to stay in nonprofit or public and international or domestic development organizations. I think the best strategy is to read, network, attend meetings, volunteer, network, and network.

What is your advice on identifying target organizations?

I am a believer in personal networks. Perhaps for high-tech careers, the Internet is valuable, but in my field and in my experience, it is "who you know and personal relationships" that count. Find a mentor. Join local branches of professional associations. Go to meetings. Volunteer.

What are your tips on writing cover letters?

Most effective for me has been formatting my cover letters to indicate how my skills and experience fit the needs of the prospect and the qualifications sought by the prospect. Also, do your homework so the reader knows you know about the organization. Be up front about your skills. Be sure they are easy to see, specific and relevant.

What is key to preparing properly for an employment interview?

Be sure you can explain why the position interests you and how your experience is related to it and prepares you for it. For example, after four years as an independent consultant, working with a variety of clients, I was often asked in interviews to explain why I want to work for someone else.

What do you like best and least about your current work?

I like it all, but am thinking a bit about going back to consulting. I would try to do what I am doing now as a consultant without a full-time commitment, just because I am interested in doing other things (e.g., continuing education, travel, and volunteer work).

What special tips do you have for thinking about a career?

Find out what you love and find out how to do it. Then do it. Keep your skills and interests updated. Read, study, stay current. Find a mentor who is where you would like to be.

▶ Monica Roers is Vice President of Community Resources and Director for the Center for Effective Nonprofit Management with United Way of New Orleans. She received her BA in Sociology from College of St. Catherine in 1989 and her MPPM from Yale School of Management in 1993.

What has been your career history?

My career path has been fairly well defined since I was 17. At that age, I was fairly certain I wanted to be vice president of a nonprofit social service agency. However, I spent the next six years in a variety of organizations to confirm this decision. At 16 to 18, I worked in a day care center. At 19 to 20, I interned at a stock brokerage firm just to make sure I really did not belong in the business world. At 21 (the summer prior to my senior year in college), I did telemarketing and realized sales was not for me. At 22, I interned with a regional governmental organization the summer before moving to Washington, DC, to work at the Federal government for a year after college. By this time I knew I wanted to eventually work in the nonprofit sector and thought it was important to understand how the Federal government worked. Also, I wanted to see if I would like work in this sector. I hated the bureaucracy. Prior to graduate school, I spent another year, now age 23, in a national nonprofit organization in Washington. At 24 to 26, I was in graduate school and interned with the United Way in New Haven. My career objective was clearly nonprofit social service management. Since graduation, I was Director of Planning and Allocations for the United Way in Worcester, Massachusetts, for two years and in my present position for two years. Within the next few months, the Center for Effective Nonprofit Management will spin out of United Way and I will become the organization's Executive Director.

How did you identify your ideal career?

Through my participation in Junior Achievement in high school, I learned a lot about functional roles people played in the business world (i.e., marketing, accounting, human resources, and the like). I knew enough about my personal interests and aptitudes for working as a manager in the business organization world from high school classes, Junior Achievement, and aptitude tests taken in high school. When I got to college, I combined a business curriculum with sociology for a broader exposure to the cross-over between business and nonprofit management. I also learned a lot about my ideal career through internships, jobs, and informational interviews. I knew exactly what kind of career I wanted when I got to graduate school. Thus, after jobs and internships in all three major sectors (i.e., profit, public, and nonprofit), I had confirmed my initial intuition that I belonged in a management role in the nonprofit sector.

How did you identify target positions that would fit your path to an ideal career?

I had a great career counselor in undergraduate school who explained how people got jobs through personal contact, networking, and the like. I followed her advice and developed a large network of contacts through college alumni and other relationships. I talked to a lot of people early in my career in informational interviews and thereby learned about the positions available in nonprofit and government agencies.

How did you identify target organizations for your ideal career?

Given that the MBA schools, even Yale that attracted many students interested in nonprofit management, did not have a lot of resources and connections for students interested in social service management, I did a lot of research of my own. I read nonprofit publications such as the Chronicle of Philanthropy and Community Jobs. In addition, I made my own database on index cards I had started collecting when I was 21.

Who was in your career search network and what roles did they play?

I got great advice when I was in college from my career counselor and I took it. That is, I kept track on my index cards of all of the folks I talked to in my job search. I have gone back to those index cards each time I have looked for a job since I began collecting them in 1989. And, the pile of cards has grown. My career counselor was the biggest support in helping me develop a system for job searching,. In addition, my counselor helped me to realize that building a career is something you need to continually work at. I also benefited from several people who took an interest in me and opened doors for me, including the president of my college, alums, and previous supervisors.

What special tips do you have for writing resumes?

On resumes, use action verbs, be concise, explain the impact you made in each position you had. And above all, remember that a resume is a "work in progress." It is never really "final." You should always keep adding to it and tweaking it to the audience you are targeting. I have a good resume, but I have enough old drafts to wallpaper an entire house.

What special tips do you have for employment interviews?

Practice asking yourself questions, out loud, in front of a mirror before you interview. It is useful to hear your answers to tricky questions like "What are your weaknesses?" while you still have time to revise your responses, rather than having them stumble out of your mouth for the first time in an interview.

What are the trends and opportunities in your present career field?

The nonprofit management sector is becoming more professionalized. In the eight years since I graduated from college, there are more and more nonprofit management degree programs, undergraduate and graduate, cropping up across the country. In the nonprofit sector, the master's degree is becoming more essential. However, it is still more important to have proven leadership and fund-raising experience to get the top jobs in the sector.

What do you like the best and least about your current work?

I know I am in the sector and job that is the best fit so far for my skills and interests. I feel like I am making a contribution to something that is essential to the community. The least satisfying aspect of my job is that there is great demand for the services my organization provides and I do not have enough resources to meet the need.

What spiritual beliefs or principles have guided your career thinking?

I was raised in a strong lower middle class Catholic family in the populist state of Minnesota, where there is a great sense of community and a thriving nonprofit sector. This upbringing has influenced my career choice in many ways. "You cannot take it with you when you die," is what I reminded myself when I considered whether or not I should move to the corporate sector to get my loans paid off more quickly. My religious upbringing taught me that my whole life, including my work, should have a greater purpose than simply to pay the bills. I believe I am very lucky to be able to pay the bills and still add value to the community in which I live. I know I am one of the lucky ones to have found my calling at such an early age.

▸ Lori A. Roth is a Director with the Institute for Not-for-Profit Management at Columbia University Graduate School of Business. She received her BA in Art History from Brandeis University in 1983 and her MPPM from Yale School of Management in 1990.

What is your employment history since graduation?

I graduated from the Yale School of Organization and Management in 1990 and worked independently from 1991 to 1995 in the areas of research, executive education (teaching and coaching), and consulting. Research projects included a study of middle management practices in the pharmaceutical industry and also the development of a feedback instrument and guidebook to help organizations become more customer focused. I became involved in training and development, working in several subject areas, as a lecturer, facilitator, and coach. My primary client in that period was the Executive Education Department at Columbia University's Graduate School of Business, where I served on the faculty of several open-enrollment and customized programs. Other clients included consulting firms and nonprofit organizations. In the spring of 1995, Columbia identified the need for a director of its Institute for Not-for-Profit Management and recruited me for the position.

What was your initial career target?

At graduation, I was interested in both consulting and nonprofit management (specifically the arts), but was not clear as to how I might fuse the two. I was also interested in organizational development. I conducted my search in both the for-profit and nonprofit sectors, interviewing for internal and external consulting positions, and also for some positions in museum administration. I had held several jobs in museums and galleries prior to graduate school and found arts administration both interesting and compatible with my background. As for consulting, I was aware that it represented a major career change, one that might be difficult to achieve in the then current economic environment of the early 1990s.

How did you identify your ideal career?

My understanding of "ideal" for my career evolved over time with the accumulation of both work and life experiences. From my initial career in the arts, I learned that I enjoy fields in which employees are passionate about their work. From my experiences in the classroom as both instructor and coach, I learned that I had a natural gift for bringing organizational theory to life for my students and that our time together could have a significant impact on their lives. From my training in organizational behavior (largely experimental at graduate school) and my consultation to organizations in the midst of rapid change, I learned that I could engage others in discussions of interpersonal issues and how those issues affect business outcomes. I also learned that I could work effectively with people in authority. This training and consulting experience increased my effectiveness in facilitating organizational change efforts. In short, the first step in identifying "ideal" was to know myself and my talents.

To find out where these talents might fit into a single job, I tried to gain as much exposure as possible to the full range of career options in my fields of interest. I conducted many informational interviews, starting with my graduate school faculty, graduate school alumni (identified by referral and through directories), personal contacts, and their colleagues. Also, I joined a professional association (i.e., Organization Development Network) and attended its meetings and conferences. In addition, I attended meetings, conferences, and workshops of other organizations, such as the International Society for the Psychoanalytic Study of Organizations, Metro Association of Applied Psychologists, William Alanson White Institute, and A.K. Rice. And, I attended lectures and panel discussions sponsored by the alumni associations of both my undergraduate and graduate schools.

How did you decide what qualities to promote and which organizations to target?

I did not "decide" on key qualities. I simply offered potential employers everything I could. I think I oversold myself at first, appearing overqualified for some aspects of these jobs, underqualified for other aspects, and over-anxious. A prolonged search and unemployment were not easy to sustain emotionally. Approximately six months after graduation, I decided to search for projects and these came more easily. This approach gave organizations the opportunity to sample my skills, and this work led to more work. I enjoyed a fairly steady flow of independent projects, which were not only interesting, but also offered high visibility, variety, and little to no organizational politics. I also had time to lead a balanced life with time for hobbies and relationships. Indeed, independent consulting was an excellent phase in my evolving career.

Given my atypical interests, career books, organization communications, position advertisements, and job fairs were not helpful to me. I did not hire the services of a career counselor. Nor were campus recruitment and my graduate school career planning office services a fit for my special needs, as the consulting firms that recruited on campus were largely strategy firms with no focus on nonprofit organizations or organizational development. I had to create my own path through the contacts I mentioned earlier.

I identified target organizations through networking and database resources, selecting those that were engaged in work that I found interesting. I read the published articles and books of thought leaders in my field and met with two of them, and with members of their staffs. I found this research both exciting and informative.

Who was in your career search network and what were their roles?

My network, outlined below, was formed in an "organic" fashion. People who knew me and respected my capabilities referred me to individuals they respected. I asked for only moments of their time and behaved professionally throughout these contacts. I rarely found a contact unwilling to take my calls. Nearly all were generous with their advice and encouragement. Most offered names of additional people to contact.

Individuals	Roles
Graduate school faculty and alumni	Advice, contacts, and target information
Classmates	Referrals for project work, support
Colleagues (other consultants)	Professional support (i.e. technical advice), contacts, referrals
Selected clients	Contacts, referrals, advice
Search consultants and firms	No support or assistance at all

What are your tips on cover letters, resumes, and other written communications?

Be sure all correspondence is succinct and clear. It is permissible to be general about your desired career path, but you must be specific about the help you are seeking (e.g., advice, information, resources, or referrals), offering your contacts some details about your strengths and aspirations. Never send a resume without a cover letter that states, or reiterates these strengths and aspirations. Always behave graciously and thank in writing those who help you. The people who assist you are giving you a gift of their time, insights, and possibly contacts. Make helping you easy and express your appreciation.

What are the most important tips you have for students preparing for employment interviews?

Preparation is key! Know the organization and field you are exploring. Review recent media coverage and try to speak with insiders in advance so that you are aware of basic organizational values, practices, and challenges. Enter the interview prepared to discuss how your skills and preferences match the organization's needs. If you do not know the fit, be prepared to explore the subject during the interview. Learn from insiders about opportunities for growth. Where possible, follow up on all rejections to receive honest feedback. If interviewers understand that you wish to learn from the process, they might be willing to offer frank comments about your performance. This information can be very helpful as you explore other opportunities.

What do you like least and best about your current work?

I like best the intelligence, commitment and values of the clients I serve, the funders that support them, and my peers who provide them with technical support and training. Also, I enjoy the modest size of the field and thereby the ability to know the key providers of "technical assistance" and support in my geographic area and to collaborate and study with them. We are a close-knit network. Finally, I value the knowledge that we have a significant impact on the health of our communities through our work, and that I continue to learn and grow in my work.

I least like the current political and economic climate that has become hostile to the provision of services to the needy. Nonprofits are now asked to fill enormous gaps left by government, but with reduced resources and very narrow time frames. This situation makes it difficult for agencies to devote the time and resources they need to develop their management capacity, a catch-22. In addition, nonprofit work tends to require that we do more with less. My colleagues and clients often conduct professional activities on shoestring budgets. Columbia University is similarly constrained. The Institute for Not-for-Profit Management's faculty and staff accept this handicap in exchange for the meaning and pleasure we derive from the work, but at times this challenge can be difficult.

What philosophies and principles have guided your career search?

I have always pursued career choices based on my interests and passions. From my first museum internships and gallery jobs to my current work with nonprofits, I have directed my energies toward the most stimulating opportunities available to me. It is important to me to enjoy my work. It is also important to me to contribute in a tangible way to the personal and professional growth of others. In building the managerial capacity of nonprofit organizations, my colleagues and I increase the impact these organizations have on the people they serve. I derive much meaning from my work and am continually inspired by my clients. I have tried, through successive projects and positions, to increase my contributions to their effectiveness. I expect that my future choices will be driven by similar values and will reap similar rewards.

Looking at your extensive job search experience, what additional tips would you give to MBA students?

In recent years, I have encountered MBA candidates who appear obsessed with the job search. While I think that conducting a serious search is important, I imagine that many students sacrifice attention to their studies and to the exploration of new subjects and opportunities. My discovery of the subject of organizational behavior while at graduate school was a surprise to me. I gave it tremendous attention and stood out among my classmates for my talent and commitment. As a result, the faculty helped me in my professional endeavors. Years spent in school are often more precious than we realize at the time. And if we are fortunate to have generous faculty teaching us, we have opportunities for lasting relationships that will serve us well. MBA students would do well to learn early the value of a long-term perspective.

5

Resources to
Assist Your Search

There are many useful references for various aspects of the search for an ideal career. We have listed some books that present interesting, practical ideas for this job search process, some quite procedural and some quite philosophical. We suggest that in addition to scanning these books, you should make use of the appropriate databases (e.g., Kennedy's or Gale's directories of management consultants, *Hoover's Book of American Companies, The 100 Best Companies to Work for in America,* among others). Periodicals can also be a useful source of information (e.g., advertisements in business publications such as the *Wall Street Journal* and sector job guides such as Community Jobs). Some graduate schools (e.g., the Harvard Business School) publish annual profiles of major organizations recruiting MBAs, many available for purchase by students in other schools. Finally, there are numerous online job databases and organization databases. Typically, a discussion of your interests and needs with your research librarian will identify the best information sources for you out of the many that are available. What follows is not an exhaustive listing, but will provide enough resources to start you on your way in whatever industry you wish to pursue.

General Reference Materials

American Salaries and Wages Survey (Gale Research, 1999).

The Directory of Executive Recruiters (Kennedy Publications, 1999).

Peter F. Drucker, *The Effective Executive* (Harper Business, 1993).

Susan E. Edgar, *Companies and Their Brands, A Gale Trade Names Directory* (Gale Research, 1999).

Hoover's Handbook of American Business: Profiles of Major U.S. Companies (Hoover's Business Press, 1999).

Hoover's Handbook of Emerging Companies: Profiles of America's Most Exciting Growth Enterprises (Hoover's Business Press, 1999).

Joyce Lain Kennedy, *Hook Up, Get Hired! The Internet Job Search Revolution* (Wiley, 1995).

Robert Levering and Milton Moskowitz, *The 100 Best Companies to Work for in America* (Plume, 1993).

Mary Scott and Howard Rothman, *Companies with a Conscience: Intimate Portraits of Twelve Firms That Make a Difference* (Citadel Press, 1994).

John Sibbald, *The New Career Makers* (Random House Value, 1995).

Small Business Profiles: A Guide to Today's Top Opportunities for Entrepreneurs (Gale Research, 1998).

Morgan Hal and Kerry Tucker, *Companies That Care: The Most Family-Friendly Companies in America* (Simon & Schuster, 1991).

Job Search/Interviewing

Richard H. Beatty, *Job Search Networking: Learn How More than 68% of All Jobs Are Found* (Adams Media, 1994).

Richard H. Beatty, *The New Complete Job Search: The Best Guide to Matching Yourself with the Perfect Job* (Wiley, 1992).

Richard H. Beatty, *175 High-Impact Cover Letters* (Wiley, 1996).

Richard H. Beatty, *The Perfect Cover Letter* (Wiley, 1996).

Richard N. Bolles, *What Color Is Your Parachute?* (Ten Speed Press, 2000).

Julie Adaire King and Betsy Sheldon, *The Smart Woman's Guide to Resumes & Job Hunting* (Chelsea House Publications, 1996).

Carol Kleiman, *The Career Coach: Inside Tips to Getting and Keeping the Job You Want* (Berkley Publications, 1995).

Peterson's Hidden Job Market 1997: 2,000 Fast-Growing High-Technology Companies that Are Hiring Now (Peterson's Guides, 1996).

Stephen A. Stumpf, *Choosing a Career in Business* (Simon & Schuster, 1984).

Kate Wendleton, *Through the Brick Wall: How to Job Hunt in a Tight Market* (Random House, 1993).

Martin Yate, *Knock 'Em Dead 2000: The Ultimate Job Seeker's Handbook* (Adams Media, 1999).

International Job Search

Dun's Asia/Pacific Key Business Enterprises (Dun & Bradstreet, 1995).

Moira Forbes, *Jobs in Russia and the Newly Independent States* (Impact Publications, 1994).

Victoria Harlow and Edward W. Knappman, ed. *American Jobs Abroad* (Visible Ink Press, 1994).

Hoover's Handbook of World Business 1995–96: Profiles of Major European, Asian, Latin American, and Canadian Companies (Hoover's Business Press, 1995).

Ronald L. Krannich and Caryl Rae Krannich, *Almanac of International Jobs and Careers: A Guide to over 1001 Employers* (Impact Publications, 1994).

Regional Job Search

The Atlanta JobBank (Adams Media, 1999).

The Boston JobBank (Adams Media, 1998).

The Carolina JobBank (Adams Media, 1998).

The Houston JobBank (Adams Media, 1998).

The Washington D.C. JobBank (Adams Media, 1999).

The Minneapolis St. Paul JobBank (Adams Media, 1999).

The Phoenix JobBank (Adams Media, 1998).

The San Francisco JobBank (Adams Media, 1999).

The Seattle JobBank (Adams Media, 1999).

Robert Sanborn, *How to Get a Job in Southern California* (Surrey Books, 1999).

Robert Sanborn, *How to Get a Job in Chicago* (Surrey Books, 1997).

Environmental

Susan Cohn, *Green at Work: Finding a Business Career That Works for the Environment* (Island Press, 1996).

Finance

Harvard Business School Career Guide for Finance (Harvard Business School Press, 1998).

Nelsons Directory of Investment Managers 1998 (Nelson Information, 1998).

Nelsons Directory of Investment Research (Nelson Information, 1997).

Management Consulting

Consultants & Consulting Organizations Directory: Descriptive Listings (Gale Group, 1999).

Directory of Management Consultants (Kennedy Information, 1999).

D&B's Consultants Directory (Dun & Bradstreet, 1996).

Marketing

Harvard Business School Career Guide for Marketing (Harvard Business School Press, 1996).

Media

Maxine K. and Robert M. Reed, *Career Opportunities in Television, Cable, Video and Multimedia* (Facts on File, 1999).

Music Industry

Shelly Field, *Career Opportunities in the Music Industry* (Facts on File, 1999).

Sports

Shelly Field, *Career Opportunities in the Sports Industry: A Comprehensive Guide to the Exciting Careers Open to You in Sports or Sports-Related Fields* (Facts on File, 1998).

Richard A. Lipsey, ed., *Sports Market Place: Guide to over 10,000 Sports Organizations, Teams, Corporate Sponsors, Sports Agents, Marketing and Event Management Agencies, Media, Manufacturers and Retailers* (Sportsguide, 1996).

Non-Profit

Daniel Lauber, *Non-Profits' Job Finder: Details on over 1,001 Sources of Job, Internship, and Grant Opportunities in Education, Social Services, Environment, Religion, Research, Fundraising, and Dozens of Other Fields* (Planning/Communications, 1994).

National Directory of Non-Profit Organizations: Organizations with Annual Revenues of $25,000–$99,000 (Taft Group, 1998).

National Directory of Non-Profit Organizations: Organizations with Annual Revenues of $100,000 or More (Taft Group, 1998).

Other Directories

Associations Yellow Book: Who's Who at the Leading U.S. Trade and Professional Associations (Monitor Publishing Company, 1996).

The Biotechnology Directory (Stockton Press, 1995).

R.R. Bowker, *American Art Directory* (Bowker, 1999).

Corporate Yellow Book: Who's Who at the Leading U.S. Companies (Monitor Publishing Company, 1996).

CorpTech Directory of Technology Companies: Company Profile (CorpTech, 1995).

CorpTech Directory of Technology Companies: Indexes and Company Rankings (Corporate Technology Information Services, 1995).

D&B Europa (Dun & Bradstreet, 1996).

Directory of American Firms Operating in Foreign Countries (Uniworld Business Publications, 1999).

Directory of Corporate Affiliations: U.S. Private Companies "Who Owns Whom" (National Register Publishing, 1997).

Financial Yellow Book: Who's Who at the Leading U.S. Financial Institutions (Monitor Publishing Company, 1996).

Million Dollar Directory: America's Leading Public & Private Companies (Dun & Bradstreet, 1999).

NASDAQ Yellow Book: Who's Who at the Leading Younger Growth Companies in the U.S. (Monitor Publishing Company, 1999).

Peterson's Internships: Over 35,000 Opportunities to Get an Edge in Today's Competitive Job Market (Peterson's Guides, 1996).

Pharmaceuticals Industry Guide: Drug Companies, Biotech Firms, and CROs (Institute for Biotechnology Information, 1997).

Principal International Businesses: The World Marketing Directory (Dun & Bradstreet, 1996).

Standard Directory of Advertising Agencies (The Agency Red Book) (1999).

Uniworld's Directory of Foreign Firms Operating in the United States (Uniworld Business Publications, 1998).

U.S. Directory of Entertainment Employers (BEJ Publishing, 1998).

Ward's Business Directory of Finance, Insurance, and Real Estate U.S.A. (Gale Research, 1995).

Ward's Business Directory of U.S. Private and Public Companies (Gale Research, 1995).